This study sheds new light on the complex relationship between cognitive and linguistic categories. Challenging the view of cases as categories in cognitive space, Professor Schlesinger proposes a new understanding of the concept of case. Drawing on evidence from psycholinguistic research and English language data, he argues that case categories are in fact composed of more primitive cognitive notions: features and dimensions. These are registered in the lexical entries of individual verbs, thereby allowing certain metaphorical extensions. The features of a noun phrase may also be determined by its syntactic function. This new approach to case permits better descriptions of certain syntactic phenomena than have hitherto been possible, as Schlesinger illustrates through his analysis of the feature compositions of three cases.

STUDIES IN ENGLISH LANGUAGE

Executive Editor: Sidney Greenbaum
Advisory Editors: John Algeo, Rodney Huddleston, Magnus Ljung

Cognitive space and linguistic case

Studies in English Language

The aim of this series is to provide a framework for original studies of present-day English. All are based securely on empirical research, and represent theoretical and descriptive contributions to our knowledge of national varieties of English, both written and spoken. The series will cover a broad range of topics in English grammar, vocabulary, discourse, and pragmatics, and is aimed at an international readership.

Already published

Christian Mair *Infinitival complement clauses in English: A study of syntax in discourse*

Charles F. Meyer *Apposition in contemporary English*

Jan Firbas *Functional sentence perspective in written and spoken communication*

Forthcoming

John Algeo *A study of British–American grammatical differences*

Cognitive space and linguistic case

Semantic and syntactic categories in English

IZCHAK M. SCHLESINGER

Department of Psychology, The Hebrew University, Jerusalem

CAMBRIDGE
UNIVERSITY PRESS

Published by the Press Syndicate of the University of Cambridge
The Pitt Building, Trumpington Street, Cambridge CB2 1RP
40 West 20th Street, New York, NY 10011–4211, USA
10 Stamford Road, Oakleigh, Melbourne 3166, Australia

© Cambridge University Press 1995

First published 1995

Printed in Great Britain at the University Press, Cambridge

A catalogue record for this book is available from the British Library

Library of Congress cataloguing in publication data

Schlesinger, I. M.
    Cognitive space and linguistic case: semantic and syntactic
categories in English / Izchak M. Schlesinger.
        p.   cm. – (Studies in English language)
    Includes bibliographical references and index.
    ISBN 0 521 43436 X (hardback)
    1. English language – Grammatical categories.   2. English language –
Semantics.   3. English language – Syntax.   4. English language –
Case.   I. Title.   II. Series.
PE1199.S35   1995
    425 – dc20   95-12805
                                                                      CIP

ISBN 0 521 43436 X hardback

For Avigail,
who made it possible

Contents

Preface

During the past twelve years or so I have been carrying out several linguistic and psycholinguistic studies on the relationship between cognitive and linguistic categories. The impetus for summarizing this work in book form came from Sidney Greenbaum. I then had to embark on the task of spelling out and developing the theoretical approach underlying my previous research work.

In this venture I was supported by many people who gave me an opportunity to discuss my ideas with them. In particular I would like to mention Professor Greenbaum, who read the whole draft in instalments and saved me from at least the worst blunders, and Professor Richard Hudson and two of his doctoral students, And Rosta and Nik Gisborne, with whom I met regularly during several months on my sabbatical in 1992. Richard Hudson also read most of the chapters, and I owe much to his criticism and insightful suggestions. Much of what is good (I hope) in this book is due to them, and I cannot thank them enough for their interest and support.

The studies were conducted with the help of many research assistants. Some of them were not merely helping with the technical side but were acting more in the nature of collaborators, participating in planning and taking on responsibility for data collection and analysis: Neta Bargai, Laura Canetti, Alon Halter, Dalia Kelly, Neta Ofer, Liat Ozer, Ruth Pat-Horenczyck, Anat Rappoport-Moscovich, and Smadar Sapir. If these studies had been published in journals, my assistants would have figured there as co-authors.

Anat Ninio and Naomi Goldblum each read and commented on most of the chapters in draft form, and I am very much indebted to them for their labors. I also thank Moshe Anisfeld, Edit Doron, Eyal Gamliel, Ainat Guberman, Yonata Levy, Anita Mittwoch, Ruth Ostrin, Rita Watson, Vlad Zegarac, and Yael Ziv for their comments on various parts of the manuscript; and Benny Shanon and Samuel Shye for valuable suggestions.

I am grateful to Annie Cerasi, who made a large number of very helpful suggestions regarding presentation of the material and checked the entire manuscript for errors in cross-references and infelicities of style.

Some of the research reported in this volume was begun while I was a Fellow at the Institute for Advanced Studies, The Hebrew University.

Support for some of the research reported here was made available by the Basic Research Foundation of The Israel Academy of Sciences and Humanities and in part by the Human Development Center, The Hebrew University. My debt to these institutions is gratefully acknowledged.

My greatest debt is to my wife, who provided the ambience and physical conditions conducive to my work, often at the cost of considerable inconvenience to herself. To her this book is dedicated.

Introduction

This book deals with one aspect of the perennial problem of the relation between language and cognition. Language has rules stating how meanings are expressed by linguistic constructions; or, put differently, grammar describes the (often complex and indirect) mappings from cognitive space into syntactic structures. In formulating these mappings, linguists resort, *inter alia*, to a construct that goes by various names: case, semantic relation or role, thematic role, theta role. In this book I use the term case, which has the advantage of brevity.

These days, the usefulness of such a construct is being questioned (Dowty, 1988; Ravin, 1990: 112). My analysis of various phenomena of English syntax shows that cases can do a lot of explanatory work if they are conceived of in a different way, namely, not as categories in cognitive space, but rather as linguistic constructs that are defined partly in terms of cognitive concepts. There must be a level between the cognitive structure and the linguistic expression; one may call this level semantic, but I will usually avoid this term, which has come to mean several disparate things.

In developing this conception it became clear that not only are the choices of the speaker limited by the resources of language, but the resources of the language spoken may determine the way the message is conceived of by the hearer. Some readers might be put off by such a Whorfian heresy, and I therefore hasten to remark that, as will be shown in due course, this is only a communicative effect of language; it does not imply anything regarding the classic Whorfian thesis of a more wide-ranging effect of language structure on cognition that goes beyond the communicative situation.

The concern of this book is the analysis of noun phrases that are complements of the main verb. The proposals made are largely neutral vis-à-vis currently contending theories of grammar.

The motivation for the linguistic work reported in this book came mainly from my interest in the theory of native language acquisition. It is difficult, if not impossible, to explain how syntactic functions and their correspondences with semantic relations might be acquired, unless one assumes that the child gains a hold on the former via the latter (Schlesinger, 1982, 1988). On this assumption, language learning becomes simpler the larger the correspondence between cognitive categories in terms of which the child conceives of the world around her and the linguistic categories she has to master. The plausibility of such a theory would therefore be vastly increased if it could be shown that syntactic categories, like the subject, are semantically relatively homogeneous (just as Jakobson, 1936/1971, has shown that Russian cases have certain abstract core meanings). Some studies I conducted – both linguistic and psycholinguistic – suggested that this may indeed be so (see also the discussion in Pesetsky, 1990, on the issue of linguistic ontogenesis). In developing the case system presented here, the homogeneity of syntactic categories served as a working hypothesis.

Semantic homogeneity also makes sense when one considers the phylogeny of language. One might assume (naively, no doubt) that to facilitate the use of language, the syntactic–semantic mapping would be maximally simple and straightforward. Now, there are many factors, historical and otherwise, that preclude such a one-to-one mapping of semantic and syntactic categories, but a theory that provides for more semantic homogeneity than others has an advantage over them.

The issue of homogeneity has been broached here in order to explain why and how I went about developing the present approach; it is not adduced as support for this approach. In fact, in the course of my investigations it turned out that the homogeneity hypothesis is only partially true. The subject category, for instance, is shown in Chapter 2 to be much more homogeneous than is usually assumed (but see Chapter 6), whereas the direct object is much less so (Chapter 8).

Throughout the book I have attempted to illustrate and support the linguistic argumentation with psycholinguistic studies. Many of these involve judgments of native speakers. Linguists usually rest content with referring to their own intuitions, supplemented perhaps by those of a few other people within easy reach. It has been found, however, that native speakers' judgments may differ from those of linguists more than they differ among themselves (Spencer, 1973; see also the studies by Quirk and Svartvik, 1966, and Greenbaum, 1973). It is necessary therefore to corroborate linguists' observations by data obtained from a larger sample of native informants (Schlesinger, 1977: 210–11).

The first chapter explores the nature of categories in cognitive space. Its conclusions are a starting point for developing the concept of cases in Chapter 2, which is in some respects the central chapter of the book. It deals specifically with the Agent, or A-case, and its relation to the sentence subject, and Chapter 3 then applies the same approach to instrumentals and the Comitative. Chapter 4 is based on it and deals with the instrument in subject position. These two chapters are independent of the remaining chapters (and the reader who likes skipping can do so here). A new case category, which is not usually recognized as such by case grammarians, is introduced in Chapter 6, with Chapter 5 preparing the ground. This case is then resorted to in

Chapter 7 in dealing with the subjects of mental verbs. Chapter 8 is devoted to objects, and in particular to the direct object, which is shown not to be amenable to a treatment in terms of case categories. Chapter 9 deals with the prototypical structure of linguistic categories. In the final chapter, the results of the analyses in the various chapters are reviewed and some areas of further research discussed.

Finally, let me point out in what ways this work is limited. All the analyses are of English sentences, with only desultory remarks made about other languages. Further, the units of analysis in this book are almost exclusively simple clauses. One respect in which the current approach will have to be elaborated is that of extending the analyses to complex clauses and sentences in a discourse setting.

1   Cognitive space

> . . . the relations are numberless and no existing language is capable
> of doing justice to all their shades.
>
> William James (1892/1962: 176)

1. Semantic and cognitive categories

This book deals with cases (also called semantic relations or thematic roles) and their relationship with cognition. It is often assumed that cases are conceptual or cognitive categories. Thus Wilkins (1988: 191–92) states that thematic roles ". . . are components of the mental representations of objects and concepts." This view seems to be shared by, *inter alios*, Nilsen (1973), DeLancey (1982), and Jackendoff (1983).

It is important to be clear about what is being claimed here. On one interpretation, the equation of cases with cognitive categories means only that cases are anchored in cognition, which is tantamount to the truism that language maps meanings into sounds. This, however, is apparently not what Fillmore had in mind when he wrote: "The case notions comprise a set of universal, presumably innate, concepts which identify certain types of judgments human beings are capable of making about the events that are going on around them, judgments about such matters as who did it, who it happened to, and what got changed" (Fillmore, 1968: 24). Here the much more interesting claim is made that case categories exist in cognition independently of language, presumably also prior to language, and that the linguistic system then makes use of these independently existing categories. According to this view, there is a single cognitive–semantic level that is mapped somehow, directly or indirectly, into the level of formal syntactic constructions.

One alternative would be to distinguish between a semantic level and a cognitive or conceptual one. Grammar, on this view, consists in a mapping from the cognitive level to the formal syntactic one via the semantic level. Cases belong to the semantic level, and they are of course defined in terms of cognitive categories, but they are not primitive cognitive concepts, as the previous view has it.

How can a decision between these two rival conceptions be arrived at? It seems that a prerequisite for any intelligent debate about this issue is at least some general idea about the nature of categories in cognitive space. Some

4

studies will be reported in this chapter which may serve to throw some light on the question of how people conceive of such case-like categories as Instrument and Agent. The term **notions**, rather than cases, will be used here for these case-like categories, and the term cases will be reserved for linguistic constructs that function in the grammar. The question whether the latter are primitive, universal categories in cognitive space, and their relationship with notions will be taken up again in the final section of this chapter.

The studies reported in this chapter address the following questions:

(i) Are the notions in cognitive space well-defined, mutually exclusive categories?

(ii) Are they homogeneous categories, i.e., is membership all-or-none or is it graded?

(iii) Are they mutually exclusive categories?

2. Instrument and Accompaniment – rating studies

The notions dealt with in the studies reported in this section are Instrument and Accompaniment. Both can be expressed, in English, by the same prepositional phrase:

(1) He opened the crate with a crowbar. (Instrument)
He opened the crate with his friend. (Accompaniment)

What is the nature of these notions? Suppose, for the sake of the argument, that they are identical to the cases in a grammar. Then it would be convenient for stating linguistic regularities if notions turned out to form clearly delineated categories. But a few examples suffice to show that this is not so. The noun phrases in some *with*-phrases are not classifiable as either Instrument or Accompaniment, but lie somehow halfway between these two notions; for instance:

(2) The pantomimist gave a show with the clown.
The general captured the hill with the soldiers.
The prisoner won the appeal with a skilled lawyer.
The hoodlum broke the window with a stone.

In the first sentence, the noun in the *with*-phrase expresses Accompaniment, whereas in the last one it expresses the Instrument; the other two sentences, however, intuitively seem to lie in between these clear-cut examples.

Now, a linguist's intuitions ought to be backed up by psycholinguistic studies on the judgments of native speakers under controlled conditions (Schlesinger, 1977: 210–11). There is evidence that judgments are sensitive to contextual effects (Greenbaum, 1973), and that native speakers' judgments may differ from those of linguists more than they differ among themselves (Spencer, 1973). The above intuitions were therefore tested by obtaining judgments on sentences like (2) from a larger group of native speakers.[1] But first a clarification is in order. Let us assume for the moment that the foregoing characterization of (2) is indeed correct; then there are two possibilities of describing the relation between Accompaniment and Instrument. One is that these are graded categories with fuzzy boundaries, that is the two notions lie on a continuum with no clear dividing line between them. In recent years such fuzzy categories have become increasingly recognized in linguistic theory (see, e.g., Ross, 1972b; Keenan, 1976). The other possibility is that these categories are partially overlapping: Rather than lying on the boundary line between Accompaniment and Instrument, *the soldiers* may belong to both categories, and so may *a skilled lawyer*.

These alternatives require some elucidation, since they involve a distinction between three properties of categories: gradedness, fuzziness of boundaries, and partial overlap. While these properties often co-occur, they are logically independent of each other. Thus, a given category may have members varying in degree of membership – that is, the category is graded – whereas the boundaries of the category are sharp and clearly defined (for instance, the category "low income group" is graded but may be defined as "having a monthly income below a certain sum"). Again, the boundary between two categories may be fuzzy (e.g., hirsute and bald) without the categories overlapping even partially (no one can be both hairy and bald).

2.1   First rating study – procedures

In a study carried out in collaboration with Ruth Pat-Horenczyck, sentences like those in (2) were presented to a group of native speakers of English, who were asked to indicate to which extent the *with*-phrase in each sentence was an instance of the notions Accompaniment and Instrument. The sentences were those listed in Table 1.1, below. Two rating scales were prepared, one for the notion Accompaniment – the *A-scale* – and one for the notion Instrument – the *I-scale*.

Instructions for the A-scale were as follows:

> The following sentences each contain a *with*-phrase. *With* has several meanings. Among others it can mean ACCOMPANIMENT, as in "He went to the movies with his friend." Please read the following sentences carefully and check for each sentence to which extent *with* has the meaning ACCOMPANIMENT, using one of the eight spaces between "yes, definitely" and "no, definitely". Please make sure to make only one check mark for each sentence. Please do not turn over until asked to do so.

For the I-scale, "INSTRUMENT or MEANS" replaced "ACCOMPANIMENT" in these instructions, and the example given was: *He wrote the note with a pencil.*

Table 1.1. *Median ratings for Accompaniment and Instrument*

	Accompaniment	Instrument
1. The pantomimist gave a show with the clown.	1.33	7.18
2. The blind man crossed the street with his dog.	1.37	3.96
3. The engineer built the machine with an assistant.	2.11	5.75
4. The acrobat performed an act with an elephant.	2.75	4.69
5. The general captured the hill with a squad of paratroopers.	3.27	3.91
6. The officer caught the smuggler with a police dog.	5.46	2.10
7. The prisoner won the appeal with a highly paid lawyer.	5.67	2.78
8. The Nobel prize winner found the solution with a computer.	7.62	1.17
9. The sportsman hunted deer with a rifle.	7.63	1.10
10. The hoodlum broke the window with a stone.	7.81	1.08

Notes:
1 Yes, definitely
8 No, definitely

The two rating scales were presented each on a separate sheet, and on each sheet the ten sentences were presented in the same arbitrary sequence (different from their sequence in Table 1.1). To these we added the example sentence for the corresponding scale. The eleven sentences were rated on an eight-point scale, as explained in the instructions.

The rating scales were given to 101 university students. About half the respondents were given the A-scale before the I-scale, and the other half the I-scale before the A-scale.

To check on the possibility that any one of the respondents misunderstood the instructions, we looked at their responses to the example sentence in each scale. A response of "no, definitely" to that sentence was taken as an indication that the respondent had reversed the meaning of the rating categories or had otherwise misunderstood the instructions. Adopting this criterion, data for four of our respondents were omitted from the analysis.

2.2 First rating study – results

Medians of the ratings for each sentence are presented in Table 1.1. The sentences are arranged in this table according to the degree they were judged as expressing Accompaniment (from low to high).

To assess the inter-respondent reliability of our results, Kendall's coefficients of concordance were computed. The W-value for the A-scale was 0.575 and that for the I-scale was 0.567 (both significant, at the 0.001 level), which indicates that our results are fairly reliable.

Table 1.1 shows that sentences differ in the degree to which they express the notions Instrument and Accompaniment. This was true also for individual respondents: respondents used several of the rating categories and there were hardly any who confined themselves to a dichotomy. These notions, then, are graded. Some noun phrases, such as those in sentences 1 and 2 of Table 1.1, are prototypical instances of the Accompaniment and some – for instance, sentences 6 and 7 – are poor specimens; but the latter, too, express Accompaniment to some extent according to the respondents' intuitions. Similarly, sentences 8–10 are prototypical Instruments, while sentences 3 and 4 express this notion only to some degree.

In general, the higher a sentence was rated on the A-scale, the lower it was rated on the I-scale. The Spearman rank-order correlation between the two scales was negative and very high: -0.95. The two notions are not only graded but the boundary between them is fuzzy; Instrument and Accompaniment blend into each other. The present study replicates a previous one, in which respondents ranked the same ten sentences from those in which *with* had the meaning "together with" to those where it had the meaning "by means of" (Schlesinger, 1979). The sentences were ranked rather consistently, and the rank order was largely the same as in the present study, in which they were rated rather than ranked. The Spearman rank-order correlation between the rankings obtained in the two studies was 0.95.

Further, the table shows that these two notions partially overlap. Thus, sentences 2 and 5 were rated as fairly high on both scales, and other sentences, too, were not judged as expressing exclusively one single notion. This result was obtained in spite of the within-subjects design adopted in this study, which required each subject to rate the sentences for both notions (with sequence of ratings counterbalanced; see Section 2.1). In the previous study, in which one group of subjects ranked the sentences as falling between the two poles Accompaniment and Instrument, it was obviously impossible to identify sentences expressing both notions.

2.3 Second study: Rating in context – procedures

In the preceding study, respondents were presented with sentences without any extra-sentential context. It seemed of interest to examine (i) whether similar results would be obtained with sentences embedded in a short paragraph; and (ii) whether respondents' ratings of Accompaniment and Instrument could be affected by manipulating the context.

Alon Halter conducted a study in which each of the sentences was embedded in a paragraph designed to suggest to the reader that the *with*-phrase should be construed as expressing the notion of Accompaniment and in another paragraph in which it would tend to be interpreted as closer to the notion of Instrument.

The sentences used in the previous studies were translated into Hebrew. The last two sentences in Table 1.1 obviously can be construed only in the instrumental sense, and it seemed unlikely that any manipulation of context might affect their interpretation in the direction of the notion of Accompaniment. For these two sentences, two short paragraphs were composed in which they could plausibly occur. For the remaining sentences (sentences 1–8 in Table 1.1) two kinds of contexts were constructed: *Context A*, designed to elicit judgments of Accompaniment and *Context I*, designed to elicit Instrument judgments. The following procedure was adopted for the generation of these contexts.

Two rating forms were prepared. In one form, *together with* was substituted for *with* in each of the sentences, and in the other form *use* was substituted for *with*. For instance, (3)a below (sentence 5 of Table 1.1) was reformulated as (3)b–c:

(3) a. The general captured the hill with a squad of paratroopers.
   b. The general captured the hill together with a squad of paratroopers.
   c. The general used a squad of paratroopers to capture the hill.

Each of these new sentences was then given to two respondents, who were instructed to compose a very short story in which the sentence was embedded. (Each of our respondents was asked to do this for four of the sentences in one of the forms.)

The resulting two sets of Context-A and Context-I stories were given to four independent judges, who were asked to rate each story on a five-point scale for plausibility. Those stories that received less than half the possible points were then discarded.

The respondents in our study were asked to rate the original sentences with *with* as in (3)a (and not the paraphrases in (3)b–c); let us call these the target sentences. As a further step in selection, the remaining stories were then presented to an additional group of judges. Each judge was given a pair of stories for the same target sentence, one Context-A and one Context-I story, and was asked to indicate for each story in the pair to what extent it was coherent. On the basis of these ratings we then chose for each target sentence the two stories which best expressed the two notions, Accompaniment and Instrument.

The following are examples of Context-A and Context-I paragraphs (translated from Hebrew) that were chosen for the same target sentence (sentence 5 in Table 1.1):

Context A:

> It has been repeatedly written about the officers of the Indonesian army that they send their soldiers into battle and stay behind themselves to give orders. But in the latest battle on the hill, despite what is customary in the Indonesian army, the general captured the hill together with a squad of paratroopers.

Context I:

> In the afternoon it was boring. The general did not know what to do with his free time. The general used a squad of paratroopers to capture the hill.

This pair of stories is the one that, on the face of it, appeared to differentiate most clearly between the two meanings of *with*. For the other sentences our respondents seemed to have been much less successful in this respect.

The stories generated in the above manner were used in the study proper, in which respondents rated the sentences in context for the two notions. For the purpose of asking respondents to generate stories appropriate for each of the two notions, we had to use paraphrases of the sentences in Table 1.1 with *together with* and *use* (instead of *with*). In the rating study, however, the original sentences, containing *with*-phrases, were embedded in the stories.

Two eight-point scales were prepared, as in the first study: an A-scale and an I-scale. For each scale two parallel forms were prepared. In the Context-A form, each of the sentences 1–8 (see Table 1.1) was embedded in a paragraph designed to elicit judgments of Accompaniment and in the Context-I form they appeared in paragraphs designed to elicit Instrument judgments. For the two last sentences, 9 and 10, the paragraphs in the two forms were identical (for reasons stated above).

Each of the two forms was given to thirty Hebrew-speaking students at The Hebrew University, who were asked to rate the target sentences on both the A-scale and the I-scale. Half the respondents were given the A-scale first and the other half the I-scale first. Instructions were similar to those for the previous rating study (Section 2.1) and stressed that the sentences were to be rated within the context of the respective paragraphs.

2.4   Second study: Rating in context – results

For each form, in each of the scales, the median ratings lay on continua similar to those obtained in the previous study; see Table 1.1. The Spearman rank-order correlations between the ratings in that study and those in the present one were uniformly high. In the Context-A form we obtained $r_S = 0.90$ for the A-scale and $r_S = 0.90$ for the I-scale, and in the Context-I form, $r_S = 0.92$ for the A-scale and $r_S = 0.94$ for the I-scale.

No consistent effect of context was evident in the ratings. The largest effect of context was found for sentence 5 of Table 1.1, where the median ratings on the I-scale were 4.00 on the Context-I form and 6.50 on the Context-A form (ratings were from 1, definitely expresses the notion, to 8, definitely does not). The remaining differences between the two forms, both on the I-scale and the A-scale, were small, and they were in the expected direction for only about half the sentences.

When the data were collapsed over the two forms, ratings on the two scales (each for sixty respondents) again formed a continuum. Spearman rank-order correlations with the results of the previous study (see Table 1.1) were $r_S = 0.88$ for the A-scale and $r_S = 0.95$ for the I-scale. The A-scale correlated negatively with the I-scale: $r_S = -0.97$.

As in the previous study, there were sentences expressing both the notion of Accompaniment and that of Instrument, according to respondents' ratings. The Hebrew translation equivalent of sentence 2 of Table 1.1 obtained a median rating of 2.33 on the A-scale and of 2.41 on the I-scale, and that of sentence 6 obtained a median rating of 3.93 on the A-scale and of 2.41 on the I-scale.

This study, then, replicates the results of the rating study with sentences in another language, Hebrew. This provides some evidence for the generality of our results. Contrary to expectation, embedding the sentences in contexts appropriate to *together with* and *use* paraphrases did not affect their interpretation consistently in the direction of these paraphrases. We have no way of telling whether this was due merely to the lack of inventiveness in the respondents constructing the context stories or whether judgments like these are relatively unaffected by context.

2.5 An objection considered

We have interpreted our findings as showing that in the native speakers' judgment notions need not be mutually exclusive and membership in a given notional category admits of differing degrees. We now have to deal with a possible objection to this interpretation.

Conceivably, one might argue, the studies involving ratings and paraphrasability judgments do not tap respondents' intuitions about the meanings of the sentences; instead, they pertain to language use. The respondent, on this interpretation, considers various situations in which the judged sentence might apply and may conclude that it could express the Instrument in one context and Accompaniment in another. In responding, he or she therefore strikes a sort of compromise and indicates that it expresses a certain notion only to a certain degree. According to this alternative explanation, then, our findings reflect the respondents' way of resolving the conflict between two meanings that a given sentence may have in different situations. They are compatible with the claim that notions form mutually exclusive categories.

This alternative explanation failed to be supported by an additional study, in which the findings of the first study were replicated. In the replication, respondents were instructed to think of only a single situation in judging a given sentence. Furthermore, the conflict hypothesis does not mesh well with the results of the above rating study, where embedding sentences in contexts appropriate to paraphrases with *together with* and *use* did not affect ratings. Presumably this was due to the fact that the original sentences (with *with*-phrases) were unequivocal in the first place and did not admit of such interpretations, contrary to the conflict hypothesis. But suppose, for the sake of the argument, that a target sentence does have an Accompaniment interpretation alongside an Instrument interpretation. To take both of these into account, as the conflict hypothesis has it, readers would have had to supply contexts appropriate to these two interpretations, and considering that the target sentence was already embedded in such a context, it seems quite unlikely that they exercised such inventiveness. Their ratings therefore cannot plausibly be construed as resulting from compromises between alternative readings.

To rule out the possibility that ambiguity was the only factor responsible for the obtained rating patterns, we presented students of a training course for translators with the sentences in Table 1.1 and asked them to state whether the meaning of the *with*-phrase – i.e., whether it denoted Instrument or Accompaniment – depended on the context. In fact, many affirmative responses were given. Before presenting more details on the responses it should be pointed out that the effect of the task posed to these students was to draw attention to the possibility of such an ambiguity. Suppose now that in response to this question such an ambiguity is detected by the person questioned; then this does not mean that he or she would have noticed any ambiguity on encountering the same sentence in other circumstances where attention is not drawn to it.

Consider now what patterns of ambiguity judgments would emerge if ambiguity were to account for the pattern of results. If this were the case, it should be expected that sentences expressing both Accompaniment and Instrument – notably sentences 3–7 of Table 1.1 – would be those judged as most ambiguous. Actually, however, the pattern of ambiguity judgments was quite different. Sentences 1–6 were considered ambiguous by many of the students in the study, whereas sentences 7–10 were each judged to be ambiguous much less often. In the former set, sentences 3–6, which in the rating study showed overlap of the notions Accompaniment and Instrument, did not receive more ambiguity judgments than sentence 1, which was found to express only Accompaniment.

It is still conceivable, though, that the intermediate ratings result from summing the results over respondents: Some of them may have rated a given sentence as expressing one of the notions to a large extent, whereas others may have judged it as expressing the other notion to an equally large extent. However, the study to be reported in the next section argues against this possibility, because it deployed sentences that appear to be quite unequivocal, so that it is extremely unlikely that respondents might conceivably have had two interpretations in mind. Finally, evidence discrediting the alternative explanation was obtained in the interviews to be reported in Section 4.4.

3. Ratings of Instrument, Accompaniment, and Manner

In an experiment carried out in collaboration with Ruth Pat-Horenczyck, the notion Manner was studied alongside Accompaniment and Instrument. Sentences like the following were deployed:

(4) a. He cooked the meat with care.
   b. He cooked the meat with a pressure cooker.
   c. He cooked the meat with potatoes.
   d. He cooked the meat with pepper.

In (4)a the *with*-phrase expresses Manner, in (4)b the Instrument. Sentence (4)c might be paraphrased by replacing *with* by *together with*. However, they involve deep structures that differ from those in the sentences rated in the previous studies. It is not the sentence subject with which the object of *with* can be conjoined or interchanged (**He and the potatoes cooked the meat*, **The potatoes cooked the meat with him*). Sentence (4)d, again, expresses a somewhat different relation: it is not "together with" pepper that the meat is cooked, but, rather, the pepper is an ingredient of the stew.

3.1 Procedures

The sentences included in this study were those listed in Table 1.2. Their sequence was arbitrarily determined and did not correspond to that in Table 1.2. Respondents were asked to rate these sentences on three rating scales: an *A-scale*, an *I-scale*, and an *M-scale*. Instructions were the same as those in the rating study in Section 2.1, namely, to rate the sentences for "Accompaniment" and for "Instrument or means," respectively, and in the M-scale for "Manner." The example sentences for this study were *He cooked the meat with his friend* (for the A-scale), *He cooked the meat with a new contraption* (for the I-scale), and *He cooked the meat with ease* (for the M-scale).

The three scales were printed each on a separate sheet. Each scale contained twelve sentences: the nine experimental sentences given in Table 1.2, and the three example sentences. The experimental sentences appeared in the same arbitrary sequence (different from that in the table) in each of the three scales, and the three example sentences appeared at the end of each scale; the sentence that served as example for the particular scale was the last of the three.

There were 107 university students participating in this study. Each respondent was given all three of the rating scales, but the sequence differed, all six permutations (A-I-M, A-M-I, I-A-M, etc.) being represented about equally often. Where it was evident from the responses to the relevant example sentence that the respondent had misunderstood the instructions (see procedures in Section 2.1), the data were discarded (nine A-scales, four I-scales, and three M-scales).

3.2 Results

The median ratings on sentences appear in Table 1.2. As in Table 1.1, the sentences are arranged according to the degree to which they express Accompaniment.

Table 1.2. *Median ratings of Accompaniment, Instrument, and Manner*

	Accompaniment	Instrument	Manner
1. He cooked the meat with potatoes.	3.44	7.80	6.96
2. He cooked the meat with wine.	3.82	7.69	5.67
3. He cooked the meat with the bones.	4.11	7.76	6.18
4. He cooked the meat with pepper.	4.12	7.67	5.75
5. He cooked the meat with enthusiasm.	7.52	7.56	1.18
6. He cooked the meat with care.	7.66	7.56	1.14
7. He cooked the meat with intelligence.	7.68	6.48	1.29
8. He cooked the meat with a pressure cooker.	7.70	1.08	6.06
9. He cooked the meat with his left hand.	7.72	2.78	2.92

Notes:
1 Yes, definitely
8 No, definitely

Inter-respondent reliability was determined by computing Kendall's coefficients of concordance. The W-value for the A-scale was 0.418, that for the I-scale was 0.514, and that for the M-scale, 0.431. Our results are thus fairly reliable.

The nine sentences seem to fall into three groups, with some discontinuities in the values obtained.[2] (i) Sentences 1–4 do not have very high ratings on any one of the scales (suggesting that additional notions are expressed in them), but the ratings on the A-scale are higher than on any of the other scales; (ii) sentences 5–7 are high only on the M-scale; (iii) sentences 8 and 9 are highest on the I-scale. However, sentences 1–4, which most clearly express Accompaniment, were also judged to express Manner to some degree; sentences 7–8 express both Manner and Instrument to varying degrees; and sentence 9 received about equal median ratings on these two notions. Clearly, then, the notions studied here are graded, fuzzy, and partially overlapping.

This study thus generalizes the findings obtained in the studies in Section 2 to an additional notion – Manner. The sentences deployed here were rather unequivocal, and as stated in Section 2.5, this is further evidence that the conflict hypothesis does not provide a plausible alternative explanation of our results.

4. Notions expressed by *with* – a qualitative study

The sentences in the foregoing studies were formulated by the investigator, and the question may be raised whether the findings hold up with other sentences as well. The purpose of this additional study, carried out in collaboration with Neta Ofer and Anat Rappoport-Moscovich, was (i) to replicate the findings of the foregoing studies regarding overlap of notions, and (ii) to provide a more fine-grained analysis of the tendency, revealed in the previous studies, to assign more than one notion to a given sentence.

Such a study should be based on ratings of each sentence on several notions, but such a design implies that only a very limited number of sentences can be tested at a single setting. As a first step we therefore conducted a preliminary study, adopting a different design, in order to find out which sentences were likely to be rated as expressing several notions. These could then be deployed in the main study.

4.1 Preliminary study

For this study we first sampled sentences collated by Hill (1968) under the heading *with*. The objective of Hill's monograph is to classify the various uses of English prepositions for teaching purposes. In his classification, Hill uses terms such as Accompaniment, Instrument, Manner, etc., and it seems reasonable to expect that the examples in his book would tend to be biased, if at all, toward clear-cut illustrations of these notions rather than toward peripheral ones and those that illustrate overlapping categories.

The sentences we deployed in this study were selected from Hill's examples of sentences with *with*-phrases under the heading "Elementary." We included sentences where (i) the *with*-phrase pertained to an active verb (e.g., not *was cursed with*, which is passive, and not *are at war with each other*), and (ii) the subject of the verb was not abstract (e.g., not *What he just said conflicts with* . . .). Some of Hill's example sentences were included in a somewhat abbreviated form, and questions were turned into declarative sentences. At this stage we wound up with thirty-five sentences.

Sentences were rated on the following six notions: Instrument, Opposition, Accompaniment, Manner, Cause, and Material. These were briefly defined for the respondent and illustrated by means of examples. Thus, for the notion Instrument the definition given was: "the instrument by means of which the action or event occurs." The examples given for each of the six notions were:

(5) Instrument
    He cut the rope with his knife.
    He covered her with a blanket.
Opposition
    What he just said conflicts with what you told us.
    France went to war with Germany.
Accompaniment
    John came back with the newspapers.
    He went to the movies with his wife.
Manner
    She left with a laugh.
    They stood with their hats off.

Cause
>
>She was charmed with the film.
>
>He was paralyzed with fright.

Material
>
>He cooked the potatoes with pepper.
>
>He built the wall with bricks.

It will be noted that for each of these notions two rather different examples were given. These examples thus suggested to the respondents that the terms Instrument, Opposition, etc., should each be understood as applying to a rather broad category.

Presenting the respondent with a lengthy list of sentences, few of which contained the notion of, say, Instrument, might induce him or her to rate more sentences as exhibiting that notion than he might have done in other circumstances. To avoid such a bias, the instructions stressed that in many sentences *with* did not have the meaning indicated.

To avoid misunderstandings, the following paragraph was included in the instructions (for Instrument, and similar ones for the other notions):

> Please be very careful: The question is *not* whether there is an instrument in the sentence, but whether the expression after *with* indicates the instrument by means of which the action or event occurs. Take, for instance, the sentence, "He put the knives with the forks." Knives and forks are obviously instruments, but *with the forks* does not describe the instrument by means of which the action – *put* – is performed.

A separate questionnaire was prepared for each of the six notions. Respondents were asked to rate each sentence on a scale from 0 ("not at all") to 4 ("very much"), in respect to the extent to which the notion was expressed in it.

As stated, this was just a preliminary study designed to locate sentences with high "loadings" on more than one notion, which would then be used in our main study. The results will therefore not be reported here at length. Suffice it to point out that (i) quite a few sentences exhibited several notions, and (ii) in spite of the caution taken in phrasing the instructions, the labels Opposition and Material were not properly understood by a large proportion of the respondents; in the main study these two notions were therefore not included.

4.2 Main study – procedures

From the materials used in the preliminary study we chose sentences that were found to exhibit the following four notions: Instrument, Accompaniment, Manner, and Cause. On the basis of the results, we chose two kinds of sentences:

Table 1.3. *Sentences from the preliminary study used in the main study*

	Main notion expressed
(i)	
1. We cook with gas only.	Instrument
2. She was shivering with cold.	Cause
3. The picture fell with a crash.	Manner
4. They threatened him with instant death.	Instrument
5. Our balloons all burst with the heat.	Cause
6. They began work with sleeves rolled up.	Manner
7. You can remove spots with this powder.	Instrument
8. John was roaring with pain.	Cause
9. Mix this red paint with yellow paint.	Manner
(ii)	
10. John has run away with Mrs. Cummings.	Accompaniment
11. She still lives with her parents.	Accompaniment
12. I went to the cinema with my mother.	Accompaniment

(i) Sentences whose mean score over the different meanings was greater than 1.00 (where a score of 0 indicated that the meaning in question did not apply to the sentence), and which had more than one meaning (i.e., had a score greater than 1.00 for more than one meaning). Of the twelve sentences that met this criterion, nine were selected whose score profile made it most likely that they would elicit more than one notion.

(ii) Sentences which, in the preliminary study, had been accorded predominantly a single meaning: Accompaniment.

Table 1.3 lists the twelve sentences included in the main study and the main notion expressed by each sentence according to the data collected in the preliminary study.

Three questionnaire forms were constructed: The Form-A questionnaire contained sentences 1–3 of Table 1.3, Form B contained sentences 4–6, and Form C sentences 7–9. In addition, each of the three forms contained two of the three sentences expressing Accompaniment (with sentences 10, 11, and 12 each appearing in two forms).

Instead of responding to a separate questionnaire for each notion, as in the preliminary study, each sentence had to be rated on the four notions – Instrument, Accompaniment, Manner, and Cause – consecutively. Instructions were similar to those given in the preliminary study. The respondent was asked to indicate on a four-point scale (from 0, "not at all," to 4, "very much") the extent to which *with* in the sentence expressed each notion. The sequence of sentences within a given form was randomly determined.

Each form was given to twelve native speakers of English. Six of these were interviewed after completing the questionnaire. The findings will be presented in two parts: Section 4.3 reports the data from the rating scales and Section 4.4 some interviews with the respondents.

Table 1.4. *Judgments of 1, 2, 3, and 4 notions per sentence for the sentences in Table 1.3*

	Number of judgments	Percent of judgments
Sentences 1–9		
1 notion	77	71.3
2 notions	26	24.1
3 notions	5	4.6
4 notions	0	0.0
Total	108	100.0
Sentences 10–12		
1 notion	48	66.7
2 notions	18	25.0
3 notions	5	6.9
4 notions	1	1.4
Total	72	100.0

4.3 Main study – findings

Before presenting the results for individual sentences, a short quantitative analysis of the number of notions ascribed to a sentence will be given.

There appeared to be a strong tendency to assign more than one meaning to experimental sentences. Contrary to our expectations, this tendency was just as strong for the sentences that obtained relatively few ratings of more than one notion on the preliminary study (i.e., sentences 10–12) as for the others. Table 1.4 presents the number and percentage of judgments involving one or more notions. As stated, for sentences 1–9 each set of three sentences was responded to by twelve respondents. Hence there was a total of 108 (12 × 9) judgments for these sentences. Each of the last three sentences in Table 1.3 appeared in two of the three forms, and each form was responded to by twelve respondents; hence, 72 (12 × 2 × 3) judgments were made on sentences 10–12.

Another way of looking at the data for sentences 1–9 is in terms of the number of sentences – out of the three judged by each respondent – judged as exhibiting more than one notion. More than one notion per sentence was given for all three sentences by eight respondents, for two of the three sentences by ten respondents, and for one of the three sentences by ten respondents.

Examination of the responses showed that respondents frequently interpreted the labels for the notions as applying to a much wider concept than the one intended. Thus the notion Accompaniment was frequently judged to be expressed in sentences 2 and 3, the notion Instrument was judged by some to be expressed in sentences 5 and 9 (recall that in the instructions the term "means" was used alongside "instrument"; see Section 4.1), and the notion

Cause was thought by four of the twelve respondents to be one of the notions expressed in sentence 1.

Let us turn now to a more detailed discussion of the responses to sentences 1–9. If we disregard here response patterns obtained from only one respondent each (which is reasonable, considering that these may have been based on some misunderstanding), these sentences fall into three groups:

Group 1

This is the largest group, comprising six of the nine sentences. These were each accorded predominantly one notion; but one or more notions were given as additional meanings or even as the only ones by some respondents. This group includes sentences 1, 3, 4, 5, 7, and 9.

Sentence 1: *We cook with gas only.* The notion predominantly accorded to this sentence was Instrument. Four respondents (out of twelve) gave this as the only meaning, and seven others as the highest rated meaning. An additional notion given by five of the respondents for this sentence was Manner, but only one respondent gave this as the only meaning; the remaining four gave this as a subsidiary meaning to Instrument. Another subsidiary meaning of this sentence was Cause, given by four respondents (who apparently took the label Cause as applying to a wider concept).

Sentence 3: *The picture fell with a crash.* The main meaning here was Manner, but three respondents gave Accompaniment as an additional meaning, and one gave Accompaniment as the only meaning.

Sentence 4: *They threatened him with instant death.* Most respondents judged this sentence to be highest on Instrument. Two additional notions given were Manner and Cause (three and two respondents respectively).

Sentence 5: *Our balloons all burst with the heat.* This sentence was judged to express Cause, but two respondents gave Instrument as an additional meaning.

Sentence 7: *You can remove spots with this powder.* This sentence was judged to express Instrument, but two respondents gave Manner as an additional meaning.

Sentence 9: *Mix this red paint with yellow paint.* For almost all respondents the main meaning of this sentence was Accompaniment (remember that Ingredient was not among the options given), but some respondents gave Instrument as a subsidiary meaning and two judged Manner to be one of the meanings or the only one.

Group 2

In regard to two sentences there was a difference of opinion as to the meaning or meanings expressed. For each of these sentences, some respondents thought that they exhibited the notion Cause, others that they expressed Manner, and still others thought that they expressed both Cause and Manner.

Sentence 2: *She was shivering with cold.* Three respondents (out of twelve) indicated that *with* in this sentence denoted both Cause and Manner.

Sentence 8: *John was roaring with pain.* Four respondents (out of twelve) indicated that *with* in this sentence denoted both Cause and Manner.

Group 3

Only one sentence was accorded a single notion, Manner, by almost all respondents (only one respondent gave Cause and Accompaniment as subsidiary meanings):

Sentence 6: *They began work with sleeves rolled up.*

4.4 Interviews of respondents

Six of the respondents – two for each form – were interviewed after they had filled out the questionnaire.

In Section 2.5 we considered an alternative explanation for our experimental findings, according to which respondents considered more than one situation for a given experimental sentence. One of the questions asked in the interviews was to what extent the respondents had different situations in mind when rating the sentences. None of the respondents stated that they had thought of different situations. In discussing their ratings of the sentences, respondents expressly stated in several instances that they had had only one situation in mind. Thus one respondent observed in regard to sentence 12 (*I went to the cinema with my mother*): "The sentence describes a situation in which both meanings are present"; and in regard to sentence 9 (*... with yellow paint*): "... both of the meanings are coexisting in the same situation."

There were also comments to the effect that there were different aspects to the situation referred to by a given sentence, and that therefore different notions were discernible in it. One respondent commented on sentence 2 (*She was shivering with cold*) that this was a situation "with a clear meaning, which contained several aspects" (she had rated the sentence as having to some extent Manner and Accompaniment, in addition to Cause). Another respondent's comment on sentence 7 (*You can remove spots with this powder*) was: "I also put down Manner, because I also think about the process. The rating Instrument was obvious from the sentence itself, and you arrive at Manner after imaging the situation." The same respondent rated sentence 11 (*She still lives with her parents*) as having the notion Manner to some extent, because, as she explained, "... the sentence also says something about the style of living. The word *still* is significant here in giving it a qualitative tone, which justifies the rating Manner."

Respondents occasionally made observations regarding the importance of context. Concerning sentence 12 (*I went to the cinema with my mother*), one respondent said that the rating Instrument is not applicable in a "normal situation," but would be appropriate in one where a little boy speaks about his mother taking him to the movies. This comment suggests that to the extent that more than one situation is taken into account, more than one notion may be accorded to a given sentence. But it is worth repeating here that none of the comments showed that the respondent had in fact had two different situations in mind. This is important in interpreting the results of the studies in Section 2.

In Chapter 3 the semantics of *with*-phrases will be taken up again. In the next section we turn to other notions.

5. Agent and Experiencer

In this section a small study is described that extends the findings obtained with Accompaniment, Instrument, and Manner to additional case-like notions.

Sentences with activity verbs usually have subjects that are classified as Agents. The subjects of verbs describing mental experiences, by contrast, are not called "Agents" but "Experiencers" (or, by some writers, "Datives" or "Themes"). It appears, however, that Agent and Experiencer are not two clearly delimited notional categories; rather, there seems to be a gradient, much like that found in the foregoing for Accompaniment and Instrument.

Consider, for instance, the following set of sentences:

(6) a. She figured out the answer.
    b. She computed the answer.
    c. She guessed the answer.
    d. She knew the answer.

The subject of (6)a is definitely an Agent, that of (6)d definitely an Experiencer. But how about (6)b–c? These subjects appear to partake of both these notions.

To substantiate this analysis we have to resort again to the judgment of native speakers. Now, unlike words like *accompaniment*, *instrument*, and *manner*, used in the previous studies, the words *agent* and *experiencer* are not used in everyday parlance and have no single generally accepted sense. One therefore cannot ask to what extent a given sentence expresses the Agent or the Experiencer; instead, the notion of agency has to be tapped indirectly. To do so, we deployed a property that is typical of the Agent, namely activity.

5.1 Procedures

Native English speakers were presented with sentences and asked to indicate to what extent each sentence involved activity.[3] The set of verbs in these sentences is given in the left-hand column in Table 1.5. Instructions included the following text:

> Some sentences describe situations in which there is much activity; for instance: *The police hunted down the burglar*. In others there is much less activity.
>
> Please indicate for each of the following sentences the degree of activity described by circling one of the digits from 1, for "very much activity," to 7, for "very little activity."

Two sets of sentences were employed. Set A included sentences with the verbs *remember*, *guess*, and *know* – cf. (6) – which refer to cognitive experiences. The sentences in Set B included also some verbs referring to mental experiences that are more emotionally colored. The form of the sentences in Set B was: *The little boy ... his father*, with a present-tense verb in place of the blank. The complete list of verbs in the two sets is given in Table 1.5. The sentences in each set were presented in a randomly determined sequence.

The two sets of sentences were given to two different groups of respondents, all native speakers of English. There were fifteen respondents for Set A, but in checking through the filled-out questionnaires it was found that one of them did not differentiate between the sentences at all, that is, he gave the same response (namely, "2") to all of them, which suggested that this respondent either did not understand the task or did not apply himself seriously to it. After discarding the data for this respondent from the analysis, we were left with fourteen respondents for Set A, and fourteen different respondents for Set B.

5.2 Results

Mean Activity ratings for the two sets of sentences are given in Table 1.5. To assess inter-judge reliabilities of the ratings, Kendall's W was computed. The value of W for Set A was 0.248 and that for Set B 0.253; both values, though rather low, are significant at the 0.01 level.

The table shows that Activity ratings form a gradient. This suggests that there is an Agent–Experiencer continuum, exemplified by each of the two sets of sentences in this study.

Consider now the possibility that the results obtained were due to pooling across respondents, and that each individual respondent distinguished clearly between Agent and Experiencer. The data in Table 1.6 show that this was not the case: Only two of the twenty-eight respondents used a dichotomy; all the rest used three or more categories.

The notion of Experiencer will be taken up again in our chapter on mental verbs (Chapter 7). In the following we will discuss the lessons to be learned from our studies.

Table 1.5. *Mean Activity ratings for sentences with two sets of verbs*

Set A	Mean Activity Rating	Set B	Mean Activity Rating
figure out	2.79	hug	2.47
write down	3.00	smile at	4.13
outline	3.21	love	4.13
compute	3.79	miss	4.20
remember	4.64	admire	4.33
guess	4.86	see	4.47
know	5.50	recognize	5.29

Notes:
1 very much Activity
7 very little Activity

Table 1.6. *Number of rating categories used by respondents*

	Number of Respondents	
Number of Categories	Set A	Set B
2	0	2
3	3	3
4	5	4
5	6	5
	14	14
Mean number of categories per respondent	4.21	3.86

6. Cognitive space and grammar

Our explorations into cognitive space have taught us something about the structure of case-like notions entertained by people. Let us now ask ourselves what we can learn from this about the nature of cases in a grammar.

6.1 Are notions cognitive primitives?

At the beginning of this chapter we discussed the Fillmorian conception of cases as "universal, presumably innate" cognitive primitives. The studies reported in the preceding sections suggest that linguistically unsophisticated speakers of English and Hebrew have intuitions about case-like cognitive categories we have called notions. People differ among themselves, however, regarding the notions they assign to noun phrases (Section 4), and this fact is already sufficient to show that notions cannot be equated with cases.

That speakers of a language have intuitions about case-like categories does not imply that the latter are cognitive primitives. Recall that in the studies reported in Sections 2–4 our respondents were supplied with verbal labels, each of which of course represents a concept. The latter may have been acquired in the course of learning the meaning of the verbal label. Not every word stands for a cognitive primitive. The words *tool*, *means*, and *instrument*, for instance, have closely related but by no means identical meanings.[4] Other languages may have similar terms but are likely to carve up this semantic field somewhat differently. Which, if any, of the many concepts relating to instruments and tools for which there are words in the languages of the world are cognitive primitives? All of them? Only those represented in English?

People's responses will not furnish us with an answer. Some relevant information may be obtained, however, from developmental studies, which have shown that preverbal infants have some idea of causality, and that they understand the principle that tools may assist in achieving certain results. It is plausible to assume therefore that these particular notions are cognitive primitives. Whether the same is true of other notions will have to be decided in each instance.

6.2 Language-specific cases

Let us turn now to case-like categories for which there is no commonly used word in everyday speech. The word *agent*, for instance, may express different concepts for a linguist and a non-linguist, which is why we did not ask (in the study reported in Section 5) for ratings of agency but, instead, for one of the properties associated with this linguistic concept: activity. That sentences can be judged on this property proves no more than that the concept of activity is accessible to people, not that it is a cognitive primitive. At any rate, activity seems to be a plausible candidate for a cognitive primitive: infants may be credited with some intuitive grasp of this notion from early on. The same goes for other concepts used to define agents, namely, volition, intention, and animacy.

Several concepts that figure in current case theories, like Agent, Benefactive, Patient, and Theme, may be definable in terms of cognitive primitives, but it is highly unlikely that they are themselves cognitive primitives. In fact, their definitions often vary from one theorist to another. For some (e.g., Chafe, 1970), animacy is a defining property of the Agent, for others (e.g., Fillmore, 1968), Agents need not be animate; some writers prescribe that an Agent must act intentionally, while others put up with unintentional agency.

I propose therefore that cases be viewed as linguistic constructs, which are not necessarily represented in the cognitive space, although they can be defined in terms of concepts in cognitive space. In practice it may be exceedingly difficult to formulate such definitions,[5] but in principle they have to be at least definable in terms that can themselves be defined by cognitive primitives.

This view of cases differs from Fillmore's conception of cases as universal concepts. The innate structure of cognitive space is presumably the same in all human beings and if cases are cognitive primitives they must be universals. Not so in our view that cases are semantic but not necessarily cognitive constructs.[6] This leaves open the possibility that cases are language-specific.[7] For one language, a given case may be best defined in one way, whereas for some other language a different definition may render a more economical and perspicuous statement of linguistic regularities. For instance, for accusative languages the Agent should presumably be defined so that it includes the subjects of intransitive verbs, whereas in ergative languages its definition should perhaps exclude these.[8]

6.3 The Principle of Linguistic Relevance

How should one go about determining the set of cases in a language? Suppose we take our lead from the labels of semantic relations that we have called notions. If, as proposed in the foregoing, we do not require cases to be universal, we might regard Accompaniment, Instrument, Manner, Agent, and Experiencer as cases. A moment's reflection shows, however, that this will not do, for there are a multitude of terms that would have to be considered, and the problem of deciding which of these designate cases would remain. Why should Instrument be a case and not Implement, Device, Tool, Apparatus, Contrivance, or Appliance? Or, taking a cue from the sentences in Table 1.2, why should not Ingredient, Component, and Material be cases? These terms are not completely synonymous, and each applies to sentences like those in Table 1.2 to a different degree. But no purpose seems to be served by encumbering the grammar with such a plethora of cases. Grammatical regularities that can be stated for Instrument will not differ from those statable for Implement, and so on. What we need is a criterion for selecting case categories among the many possibilities that suggest themselves.

In fact, no theorist has adopted such a vocabulary-centered procedure. What many linguists have done instead is to take sentences of a language and examine which semantic relations are exhibited in them. Applying a sort of common-sense ontology, they have each proposed a set of cases. But this approach, too, does not offer a principled solution to the question of how to identify cases. As a consequence, the literature is replete with diverging views on the boundaries between cases and the fragmentation of certain notions; also, more and more candidates for the status of case keep appearing in the literature (see Dowty, 1991, for an extended discussion).

My proposal that cases be viewed as primarily linguistic constructs points the way to a criterion for identification of cases. A conceptual distinction is to be admitted as a case if and only if it subserves the statement of some linguistic regularity. Thus, if it turns out that there is no linguistic construction distinguishing between Accompaniment and Ingredient, or between Instrument and Contrivance, there will be no motivation for positing these as distinct cases. A case is what makes a difference, linguistically. This criterion is akin in spirit to Dowty's (1991: 562) proposal for the identification of cases, or thematic roles. Let us call this the **Principle of Linguistic Relevance**.

Attempts at giving a full account of conceptual distinctions (see, e.g., Jackendoff, 1990) might appear to be diametrically opposed to the present approach. It should be realized, however, that these are two different enterprises and have different objectives. Cognitive theory might benefit from the alternative research program; a linguistic theory, I submit, should subscribe to the Principle of Linguistic Relevance.

Linguistic relevance is language-specific. A linguistically relevant distinction in one language may be devoid of any effect on syntactic rules in another language. This dovetails with the conclusion arrived at in Section 6.2 that cases are language-specific. In the chapters that follow an attempt is made to apply the Principle of Linguistic Relevance to English grammar. Some cases will be identified, and it will be shown how they figure in grammatical rules. Some of the notions dealt with in the foregoing studies will be seen to be linguistically relevant and hence represented at the semantic level – either as cases, or as features that define cases – and some will have to be redefined in terms of more primitive cognitive concepts or will not be of any use in a linguistic theory.

6.4 Gradedness, fuzzy boundaries, and overlap

While the studies reported in this chapter have tapped only a few notional categories and some of the findings may be open to alternative interpretations, they suggest that categories in cognitive space, and specifically the case-like categories we have called notions, are fuzzy categories having a graded structure (i.e., admitting of various degrees of membership) and no clearly delineated boundaries, and they tend to overlap, that is a given noun phrase may be an instance of two different notions. That much is true for notions, but what does this entail for the nature of cases?

The Principle of Linguistic Relevance has implications for this issue, too. Take the notion Instrument and suppose that there is a corresponding case in terms of which syntactic regularities can be stated. That the notion Instrument has been found in our studies to have a graded structure does not mean that the Instrumental – if there is such a case – must be graded as well. The case will have to be regarded as graded if and only if it can be shown that the degree of instrumentality makes a linguistic difference, i.e., that it is involved in some syntactic rule. Even where a case corresponds to a cognitive notion, then, it may be differently structured. In Chapter 2, Section 4.1, it will be shown that certain linguistic regularities can be stated in terms of graded categories.

Similar observations apply to overlapping membership. Some case grammarians admit partially overlapping case categories and would assign to a given noun phrase more than one case (e.g., Nilsen, 1973: 52, 79, 93, 162; Culicover and Wilkins, 1986; and Broadwell, 1988). According to the Principle of Linguistic Relevance, this is justified wherever noun phrases belonging to two cases are subject to syntactic rules applying to both. The finding of our study that the two notions Experiencer and Agent overlap (Section 5) does not imply that there are two corresponding cases with overlapping membership, unless it can be shown that there are noun phrases that may behave both like those in one case and like those in the other; in fact, it even does not imply that there are two corresponding cases (see Chapter 7 on this issue). In the following chapters it will be argued that case categories do in fact overlap (see especially Chapter 6, Section 4.1).

To conclude, intuitive judgments give us a clue to the nature of cognitive categories, but they should not dictate the way the system of cases is set up. Cases are linguistic constructs, and their formulation should be informed by syntactic phenomena. Their semantic nature is due to their being definable in terms of cognitive categories.

2   Agent and subject

> I never know how people are able to pick out thematic relations with such security, I can't.
>
> Chomsky (1982: 89)

1. The semantics of the subject

It is generally held that the syntactic category of subject is semantically heterogeneous. While most subjects express the Agent of the action, there are those that express the Experiencer, the Instrument, the Patient or the Theme, to name only some of the cases that have been associated with the subject.

Now, the rationale for introducing cases in the grammar is that they enable us to state certain semantic–syntactic correspondences. As pointed out by Dowty (1988, 1991), the most important generalizations that can be stated in terms of cases pertain to what he calls argument selection, as for instance in the selection of the sentence subject. Having observed that the subject is semantically heterogeneous, some linguists have gone on to propose subject selection hierarchies. Case categories are ordered in respect to the subject. First in line stands the Agent. If the sentence includes an Agent, the latter becomes subject; if not, the subject is the noun phrase in the case next in line.

There has been little agreement among linguists as to the precise sequence of cases in the hierarchy (compare for instance the hierarchies proposed by Fillmore, 1968; Givón, 1984a: 151; Broadwell, 1988: 117; and Jackendoff, 1990: 258). Moreover, there is an element of arbitrariness in all the hierarchies that have been proposed. Why, for instance, should the Instrument precede the Theme in the subject selection hierarchy rather than the other way round? The hierarchies proposed do not seem to have any rationale. Furthermore, there seem to be some obstacles in principle to constructing a subject selection hierarchy. This can be shown by the following examples, which apparently defy any description in terms of a hierarchy.

First example:

(1) a. This key will open the door.
    b. The door will open with this key.

If the Instrument precedes the Patient in the hierarchy, only (1)a, and not

(1)b, will be grammatical; and vice versa if the place of these two cases in the hierarchy is reversed.

Second example – Causal phrases:

(2) a. Our neighbor died from pneumonia.
    b. Pneumonia killed our neighbor.

The two sentences refer to the same state of affairs. *Pneumonia* should therefore be either higher in the hierarchy than *our neighbor* or lower; it cannot be both.

Third example – Converse verbs:

(3) a. Mary sold a book to John for five dollars.
    b. John bought a book from Mary for five dollars.

Mary has the same case role, on the current conception of cases, in (3)a and in (3)b (and the same goes for *John*), and there thus seems to be no hierarchy which might determine which becomes subject.

Fourth example:

(4) a. The meteor collided with the moon.
    b. *The moon collided with the meteor.

The meteor and the moon are equally "responsible" for the collision. So why is (4)a much better than (4)b? An explanation in terms of a selection hierarchy does not seem to be in sight.

These problems should make us stop and rethink the question of the semantic composition of the subject. In this chapter, evidence will be presented to show that the subject comprises far fewer semantic categories than has been held previously. The reason why this has not been recognized earlier is that the current conception of cases rests on the implicit assumption that it is possible to categorize relations that are "out there." When two sentences differing in syntactic structure have the same truth value (e.g., an active sentence and its passive counterpart), the corresponding noun phrases are necessarily assigned the same case. In this manner, classifications of relations into cases were arrived at that are essentially common-sense ontologies, and these are just as naive and can lay as little claim to validity as previous proposals, outside of linguistics, for taxonomies of real-life events and situations. In fact, classifications into cases abound in the literature and there have been proposals comprising as few as three (Anderson, 1971) up to an estimated forty to fifty categories (Dixon, 1991: 10). Dissatisfaction with the current state of affairs is becoming widespread. As Rappaport and Levin (1988: 8) observe: "The definitions given for θ-roles are typically vague, and as a result they either cannot be applied easily outside the core classes of verbs which have been used to motivate the θ-roles or are extended in unprincipled ways to new cases."

The approach taken in this book is based on the Principle of Linguistic

Relevance, which accords the status of case to a notion only when it makes a linguistic difference (Chapter 1, Section 6.3); that is, a category that does not figure in the formulation of a syntactic regularity is not to be considered a case. A taxonomy of cases must take into account not only the situation and the way it is perceived, but also the formal system by means of which these are linguistically realized. The rule of case grammar mentioned in the foregoing that identical situations require identical case assignments is therefore abandoned; *This key* in (1)a need not be assigned the same case as *this key* in (1)b, and similarly for (2)–(4). The ideal would be to have cases stand in a one-to-one relationship with syntactic categories, but of course this is an unattainable goal. Still, an attempt should be made to define cases in such a way that syntactic categories turn out to be maximally homogeneous in terms of the case categories they express. Additional reasons for pursuing this course were discussed in the introductory chapter.

In this chapter, the Agent is defined in a way that differs from the common-sense notion that goes by this name, and as a result many of the subjects that have previously been accorded various case categories turn out to be Agents. The Agent is regarded as a cluster concept defined in terms of more primitive features, none of which is a necessary condition for agency. The fruitfulness of this view will depend on the types of linguistic regularities that it permits us to state. It will be shown that the proposed conception of the Agent category enables us to account, among others, for the problems raised by the foregoing examples (1)–(4).

The plan of this chapter is as follows. First, the features that are characteristic of the Agent are discussed (Sections 2 and 3). Then it is shown how the Agent concept may be defined in terms of these features (Section 4), and linking rules for the Agent are stated (Section 5). While the Agent is practically always expressed as subject, there are subjects that are not Agents (Section 6). The phenomenon of converse verbs is discussed in Section 7, and the final section sums up the lessons learned.

2. Features of the Agent

In defining the Agent, the heuristic adopted was to start from the fact that the typical subject is an Agent, and then to examine a large variety of subjects with a view to finding out what they had in common with Agents. This required breaking up the concept of an Agent into more primitive **features**, which are cognitively anchored. Features correspond to what have been called notions in the previous chapter. But clearly, not every conceivable notion is a feature; rather, any feature that figures in the linguistic system will be chosen from the indefinitely large number of notions that can be formed in cognitive space and defined in accordance with the demands of the system.

The definition of the Agent in terms of features is liable to vary from language to language. Cases are conceived of as linguistic constructs, mediating between cognitive space and linguistic expression (cf. Chapter 1, Section 6.2).

The present proposal is very much in the spirit of Starosta (1988), who proposes that cases be defined on the basis of syntactic criteria, on the one hand, but assumes that "there are some semantic characteristics that [cases] are found to have in common" (123), on the other. But Starosta's requirement is too strong: rather than having semantic characteristics "in common," there may be a set of characteristics such that each instance of a case has some of this set. The conclusion arrived at by an examination of the syntactic category of subject and the semantic one of Agent is that the latter is best conceived of as a cluster concept. At the center of this concept are Agents having all of the agentive features, and at the periphery those having only one of them. This is in line with the approaches of Cruse (1973) and of DeLancey (1984). Similarities between the present approach and that of Dowty (1991) will be readily apparent, and so will the differences.

2.1 Three agentive features

The following sentences have subjects that are what one might regard as typical Agents:

(5) a. The little boy threw the ball.
    b. They pushed the chair to the table.
    c. The girl drank her coffee.

The subject in each of these sentences refers to an entity that is in motion, causes the activity and controls it; it has the features CHANGE, CAUSE, and CONTROL. These features characterize the Agent case. A prototypical Agent will have all three features, and is expressed by the sentence subject.

This much is generally agreed upon. Now, there are many subjects that do not exhibit all three features. For example:

(6) a. The butter melted in the sun.
    b. My little dog remained indoors all day long.
    c. The guard is standing near the entrance.

Such subjects usually have only one or two of the characteristic agentive features, and it is proposed that these are also in the Agent case. Such a concept of Agent presents a departure from the way the term is commonly used. To allay the feeling of discomfort some may feel at such a stretching of the term, I will often use the term **A-case**, instead of Agent.

A noun phrase that has any one of the three features CAUSE, CONTROL, and CHANGE is a candidate for being assigned the A-case, and hence for becoming subject. It is only a candidate, though, because there may be additional noun phrases in the clause that have one or more of these agentive features. How such competition between noun phrases is resolved will be discussed in a later section.

CAUSE, CONTROL, and CHANGE appear to be very good candidates for the status of primitive cognitive concepts.[1] One of the earliest cognitive achievements of the infant is the ability to notice change. Leslie and Keeble (1987) have recently shown that six-month-old infants already have the notion of cause, and have speculated that their understanding is based on a perceptual mechanism. The notion of control is, intuitively, more complex than those of cause and change, and it may be expected therefore that CONTROL begins to function as a feature in the child's language somewhat later than CAUSE and CHANGE; but there are no data bearing on this, to my knowledge. Presumably, the above three features are universal; the Agent and other case categories defined in terms of such features, by contrast, may be language dependent.

A caveat is in order here. It is not claimed that Agents have the above three characteristics only, but merely that the latter are needed for the delimitation of the Agent concept. Dowty (1991: 572) includes "sentience" (and/or perception) among the "contributing properties to the Agent Proto-Role," but I do not find that the delimitation of the A-case stands to gain from the introduction of this feature. (Dowty's properties "causing," "volitional," and "movement" seem to correspond roughly to CAUSE, CONTROL, and CHANGE, respectively.)

Customarily, features are regarded as binary, being either present in a noun phrase or not. This, of course, is a simplifying convention which does not do justice to the way things are in reality; a moving train, for instance, moves faster than a bicycle, that is it exhibits more CHANGE. Recall that in our rating studies in the previous chapter, respondents judged notions to be present in various degrees. This is a fact about cognitive space, and does not imply that features, which are constructs at the semantic level, have to be graded as well. But the degree to which a feature is present is linguistically relevant, because it may affect case assignment (Section 4.1). We will therefore speak of the **strength** of a feature in a given noun phrase.

2.2 Definitions of features

2.2.1 CAUSE and CONTROL
The feature CAUSE is taken here as encompassing any source of an activity, event, or situation. This feature is assigned not only to noun phrases referring to entities affecting other entities – that is, not only to subjects of transitive verbs like (7)a (below) – but also to those of intransitive verbs like (7)b.

(7) a. John kicked the ball.
    b. John jumped up.

That the use of this term for such "internal" causes is somewhat problematic (see Thalberg, 1972) need not deter us, because no claim is implied here about the nature of causation; we merely propose a cognitive notion that enables us to state linguistic regularities, and it is of little importance which label is chosen for it.

When a noun phrase refers to a human being, the features CAUSE and CONTROL typically co-occur, as they do, for instance, in (5) and (7). Conceptually, however, these two features differ. CAUSE may be assigned to a noun phrase when the entity referred to by the latter makes something happen. Once an event has been caused, there may be an entity that is in CONTROL of the event: it steers the activity in the event and may be able to terminate or obviate it.

The notion of CONTROL bears some affinities with those of intention and volition, but CONTROL may also be a feature of a computer or a robot, as long as purposefulness is involved. CAUSE, by contrast, does not imply volition, intention, or purposefulness. Nor does it imply awareness, and it can therefore be a feature of inanimate entities, which do not have CONTROL; see (8).

(8) a. Mirrors reflect light.
    b. Salt increases blood pressure.
    c. The Gulf War strained the economy.
    d. Experimental findings invalidate this claim.

A rough-and-ready test for CAUSE is provided by adding *deliberately* to the sentence or reformulating the verb phrase with *try to*. This test, however, applies only to humans, and not, for example, to the subjects of (8). A test for CONTROL is to try fitting the verb phrase into the slot *You should not* ..., or *Don't* .... Thus, instead of (5)a, one can say

(9) a. The little boy threw the ball deliberately.
    b. The little boy tried to throw the ball.
    c. You shouldn't/don't throw the ball.

Human subjects usually have both CAUSE and CONTROL, and this is true not only where the predicate refers to an overt activity, as in (5), but often also where there is no such activity. Take sentences with *remain*, *stay*, and *ignore*. These verbs refer to refraining from an activity (unlike most verbs, that refer to the execution of an activity). Now, when one refrains from doing something, one is the cause of refraining from it, and refraining is under one's control. Thus, in (10), the subject may be credited with both causing the situation referred to in the sentence and controlling it, as shown by the above tests:

(10) a. She remained in the room.
            She remained in the room deliberately.
            Don't remain in the room.
     b. Our visitor stayed for dinner.

Our visitor tried to stay for dinner (but we made him leave).
You shouldn't stay for dinner.
c. He ignored the warning.
He tried to ignore the warning.
You shouldn't ignore the warning.

The subjects of verbs like *stand* and *lie* have traditionally not been analyzed as Agents. Our test for CONTROL, however, shows that these have the agentive feature CONTROL, and they are therefore regarded here as candidates for the Agent case.

(11) a. Carla stood on the pedestal.
You shouldn't stand on the pedestal.
b. Dan was lying on the operating table.
Don't lie on the operating table.
c. Ervin sat on the piano.
Don't you dare sit on the piano.

Conversely, the test for CONTROL may be failed by a noun phrase that obviously does have this feature. Thus, one can normally avoid owning something – one can give it away, etc. – and yet (12)b sounds strange.

(12) a.   Beatrice owns a country house.
b.   ??Don't own this house.
c.   ?You shouldn't own a house when you don't have enough to eat.

This is due to pragmatic factors. One would expect more specific advice: what should be done with the house (should it be sold, donated to charity, or what else)? But (12)c sounds better than (12)b. A useful discussion of CONTROL is to be found in Siewierska (1991: 47–49).

In assigning the features CAUSE and CONTROL one has to take into consideration that an event may have a chain of causes. Suppose John steps carelessly off a sidewalk and is run over by a car. Who caused the incident – the car or its victim? In (13) it is the car that is assigned the feature CAUSE, because it is the *immediate* cause, whereas John is only the distant cause (and in principle there will always be an indefinitely long chain of previous causes: John was careless because he didn't sleep well, because he had quarreled with his wife, because he forgot her birthday, because . . .).

(13) The car ran over poor John.

Similar considerations apply to the feature CONTROL. When the teacher asks the pupil a question and the latter answers him, the teacher is in some sense both the cause of answering and in control of the situation. However, in (14) the feature CONTROL is assigned to *the pupil*, since it is he who is most immediately in control of the action of answering. Likewise, *the pupil* is assigned CAUSE, because he is the immediate cause of the action of answering.

(14) The pupil answered the teacher.

In some instances, though, there may be some doubt as to which noun phrase is to be assigned the features CAUSE and CONTROL. Suppose someone solves a problem by means of a computer: Who causes the problem to be solved? And who is in control? Such borderline instances do not detract from the importance of the distinction between immediate and distant cause and control.

2.2.2 CHANGE

This feature may co-occur with CAUSE and CONTROL; cf. (5). It can also appear in a noun phrase to the exclusion of the two other agentive features. The feature CHANGE is assigned when motion is involved, as in (15)a–c, or when there is a change of state, as in (15)d–f:

(15) a. The plumber fell from the roof.
  b. The arrow disappeared.
  c. The ball reached the white line.
  d. The frog turned into a prince.
  e. The old janitor died.
  f. John grew up.

Noun phrases like the above are usually regarded as Themes (or Patients). As will be shown in Chapter 8, there is no need for a separate case category Theme in the present framework. It is proposed, therefore, that CHANGE, like the other two agentive features, is sufficient for making a noun phrase a candidate for the A-case. Dowty (1991: 573), too, regards noun phrases that have only "movement" as Proto-Agents.

The decision to view the subjects in (15) as A-case is also in line with studies concerning the way noun phrases with CHANGE are conceived of by children. Braine and Wells (1978) found that, when presented with sentences like *The train runs on the track*, preschool children regarded the vehicles as "actors" (but see Section 3.3.1, below).

The subjects of the verbs in (16) are customarily regarded as Patients or Themes.

(16) a. The mine blew up.
  b. The door opened.
  c. The vase broke.
  d. The pansies are growing fast.
  e. The ice is melting.

In fact, the sentences in (16) describe the same situation as sentences with transitively used verbs (like *Somebody blew up the mine/opened the door*, etc.), where the noun phrases of (16) are undergoers, that is, Patients or Themes according to most current analyses. On the present approach, however, identical situations do not necessarily have to be analyzed in terms of identical cases (Section 1). Cases are linguistic constructs and are determined by the way a given language structures the situation. It is proposed to analyze (16) like (15). The subjects in (16), like those in (15), have the feature CHANGE and are accordingly assigned to the A-case.

In the light of this analysis we can now explain why the acceptability of this construction depends not only on the verb but also on the nature of the subject noun phrase, as illustrated by (17). Levin and Rappaport Hovav (1992: 103–107), to whom these examples are due, point out that peeling an orange requires an animate agent and so does clearing a table. By contrast, paint may peel due to natural causes without intervention of a human agent, and similarly, the sky may clear all by itself; and it is only such events, they claim, that can be referred to by unaccusative constructions like (16). The reason is, I propose, that in (17)c–d the activity (of peeling or clearing) is felt to be under the control of an unmentioned agent. This interferes with the construal of the noun phrases as A-case, and hence they cannot become subjects. (But Levin and Rappaport Hovav regard the subjects of (16) and (17)a–b as underlying objects.)

(17) a.   The paint peeled.
     b.   The sky cleared.
     c.   *The orange peeled.
     d.   *The table cleared.

A similar explanation applies to (18)c. Compare (18)a with the corresponding passive sentence, (18)b. The latter implies that there is some agent responsible for blowing up the mine, whereas in (18)a it may have blown up all by itself; there need be no other agent (cf. Siewierska, 1988: 268). What (18)c shows is that, since (18)a already has an Agent – namely *the mine* – no prepositional phrase referring to an agent can be added to it. In this (18)a is unlike the passive, which can include a *by*-phrase; see (18)d.

As for (18)e, Katz (1972: 35) observes that sentences like this are "inconsistent," whereas (18)f is not. The reason is that passive sentences like (18)b may readily be completed with a *by*-phrase – as in (18)d – and in (18)b and (18)e we therefore sense another agent lurking in the background.

(18) a.   The mine blew up. (= (16)a)
     b.   The mine was blown up.
     c.   *The mine blew up by the engineer.
     d.   The mine was blown up by the engineer.
     e.   *The mine was blown up, but without anyone doing it.
     f.   The mine blew up, but without anyone doing it.

Finally, the sentences in (16) sound odd (at least out of context) when *deliberately, inadvertently, reluctantly, on purpose,* or (Anita Mittwoch, personal communication, 1993) a phrase starting with *in order to* (or the like) is added. Passives, by contrast, permit such addition; see (19).

(19) a. ?The mine blew up deliberately.
     b. The mine was blown up deliberately.
     c. *The mine blew up in order to clear a passage.
     d. The mine was blown up in order to clear a passage.

2.3 Dimensions of CAUSE

The feature CAUSE is hierarchically organized, in the sense that it has second-order features. Each of these has a gradient, which is why they are called **dimensions** here.

One dimension is **activity** (act). A noun phrase having CAUSE may refer to an entity that engages in an activity, like the subjects in (20), or else it may refer to one that does not "do" anything, like the inanimate subjects in (8), above.

(20) a. Jack ground the coffee.
     b. Jill walked the dog.
     c. Joe is painting in his study.
     d. Jean writes for *The Times*.
     e. The bat hit the ball.
     f. The axe cut the wood.

The subjects of (20)e–f are customarily assigned to the Instrument case. However, the bat is the cause of the ball's motion and the axe causes the block of wood to be severed. Since they have the feature CAUSE, these noun phrases are in the A-case (see Chapter 4, Section 1, for further discussion).[2]

An additional distinction is that between extrinsic and intrinsic causation. In (20), the entity referred to by the first noun phrase is the cause of something that happens to some other entity: the coffee gets ground, the dog has an outing, a painting is created, *The Times* is enriched by Jean's contribution, etc. Alternatively, an entity may effect a change only in itself, like those referred to by the noun phrases in

(21) a. John runs five miles.
     b. Jane turns a somersault.
     c. Jessie ran to the next block.
     d. Jeff looked at the painting.
     e. Jerry works for pleasure.
     f. The sirens are howling.

Let us call this dimension **affecting** (aff).

The distinction between +act and −act – i.e., between activity and its absence – is presumably a cognitive primitive and is available to children from early on. The same seems to be true of the distinction between + aff and – aff. In early child language, "morphological and syntactic choices based on a transitive/intransitive distinction are acquired without error in the ergative languages Greenlandic Eskimo, K'iche', and Warlpiri (as they are in Kaluli)" (Slobin, 1992). It is important to note, however, that the dimension of affecting pertains to semantic, not syntactic, transitivity. As shown in (21)a–b, the presence of a direct object does not imply that the subject noun phrase is CAUSE + aff; nor does the absence of a direct object imply that the subject is CAUSE – aff, as may be seen in (20)c–d.

Distinctions are also possible within the feature CHANGE. CHANGE may be overt, as when an entity is in motion – see for example the subjects in (21)a–c, above – or covert, as in the subjects of (16)c–e, which undergo a change of state. These are cognitive distinctions which, as far as I am aware, do not have any linguistic effect. Therefore no dimension of overtness needs to be introduced for the feature of CHANGE. We may, however, state that a noun phrase in motion (overt CHANGE) normally has greater strength of CHANGE (Section 2.1) than one that only undergoes a change of state.

Returning to the dimensions of CAUSE, we note that, theoretically, there is an indefinitely large number of values on the dimension of activity (as we saw in the study reported in Chapter 1, Section 5) and likewise on that of affecting. But in actual practice it will usually be feasible only (and sufficient for most purposes) to limit oneself to just two values, + and –. The two dimensions thus permit a classification of noun phrases that have the feature CAUSE:

CAUSE + act + aff, as exemplified by the subjects in (20)
CAUSE + act – aff, as exemplified by the subjects in (21)
CAUSE – act + aff, as exemplified by the subjects in (8)

The combination CAUSE – act – aff will be discussed in the following section.

2.4 Middle verbs

Consider

(22) a. The woolens wash well.
b. Mary scares easily.
c. The cookies sold fast.
d. This wine drinks like water.
e. Our new car drives effortlessly.
f. This poem does not translate well into English.

Such middle constructions occur with quite a few verbs (in addition to the above – with *clean, bribe, ride, pull*, etc.; Antonopoulou, 1991: 156). In (22)a the fact that the woolens wash well is due to some property of the fabric; if it were due to the skill of the person who washes them, the passive construction (*The woolens are being washed well*) would have been preferred (Dixon, 1991: 325). Similar observations apply to the other examples in (22). Discussing the subjects of middle verbs, Lakoff (1977: 248–49) states that these have "primary responsibility"; in the present terminology they are CAUSE −act −aff. As evidence, Lakoff cites sentences like (23)a: The tent has no characteristics that make it put-upable in backyards; see also Van Oosten (1977). For the same reason (23)b–c are inadmissible.

(23) a. *The tent puts up in my backyard.
     b. *The wall touches easily.
     c. *The cookies sold last week.

Contrary to the way most current case theorists might analyze them, then, it is proposed that subjects in (22) have CAUSE and hence are in the A-case. Support for this analysis comes from the fact that (unlike the passive) no agentive phrase can be added to them; see (24)a–b (Antonopoulou, 1991). Also, as shown in (24)c, these sentences do not take prepositional phrases referring to purpose (Booij, 1992); it is not the cookies that sell fast which have a purpose but rather the seller, who is not referred to explicitly in the sentence.

(24) a. *The woolens wash well by Mary.
     b. *Mary scares easily by thugs.
     c. *The cookies sold fast to raise some money.

The subjects of (25) should be analyzed in the same way as middle verbs.

(25) a. This room sleeps two.
     b. The town hall seats 500 people.

It is a characteristic of the room in (25)a that makes it possible and sufficiently convenient for two people to sleep in it. In (25)b the size of the hall is a factor determining its seating capacity. The values of the subjects in (25) on the dimension of CAUSE are −act and −aff. In (25)a, the fact that the room sleeps two need not affect anyone (there may never be anyone sleeping in it);[3] and similarly for the seating capacity of the hall in (25)b. Like (22), these sentences accept neither agentive phrases nor prepositional phrases of purpose:

(26) a. *This room sleeps two by the landlord.
     b. *The town hall seats 500 people to earn more money from the sale of tickets.

3. Feature assignment

In assigning the features discussed in the preceding section, certain principles have to be followed, as will now be explained.

3.1   The first principle of feature assignment

Our first principle may be formulated as follows: Features are assigned to a noun phrase relative to the event that is referred to by the predicate.

For instance, a noun phrase is assigned CHANGE if and only if the change is brought about by the event in the predicate. The italicized noun phrases in (27) are not assigned CHANGE, although they undergo a change of position or a change of state:

> (27) a. He jumped on the *moving bus*.
>   b. The car drove over the *melting ice*.
>   c. The *speeding train* was tooting.

The sentences do not say that the bus moved because someone jumped on it, that the ice melted as a consequence of the car driving over it, or that the train speeded because of its tooting. In other words, the change in the entity referred to by the noun phrase does not result from what is stated by the predicate verb. To assign the feature CHANGE to the italicized noun phrases would be an instance of confusing categorial with relational notions, which Fillmore (1971: 65) has warned against (see also Dowty, 1991: 572, note 16).

Likewise, in (28), the italicized phrases are not assigned CAUSE − act.

> (28) a. The police arrested *the suspect*.
>   b. The governor expelled *all refugees*.
>   c. The judge reprimanded *the criminal*.
>   d. The thug approached the *intimidating policeman*.

The suspect, the refugees, and the criminal in (28)a–c have characteristics that make them susceptible to arrest, expulsion, and reprimand; in a sense, then, they are causes of the events referred to in the predicates. This information, however, is not contained in the sentence: It is only by virtue of our knowledge of the world that we believe them to have led to the event. Consider that in (28)d one would normally not regard the policeman as a contributory cause of the thug's approaching; our knowledge of the world does not suggest this interpretation. The italicized noun phrases in the structurally similar sentences (28)a–c should also not be analyzed as CAUSE, because only contingent information would warrant such a construal. There is nothing inherent in the events described by the predicates *arrested*, *expelled*, and *reprimanded* that decrees that the italicized phrases refer to their causes.[4] See also Chapter 8, Section 1.3, note 3.

The subjects of all these sentences, by contrast, will be assigned CAUSE.

They are causes of the events described by the verb and must be viewed as such even without any information beyond that stated explicitly in the sentence.

The first principle also determines feature assignment of:

(29) John's ball reached the white line.

In (29), John may be the cause of the motion of the ball. But the argument of the predicate *reach* is *John's ball* and not *John*. The subject noun phrase therefore has CHANGE, but not CAUSE. (Furthermore, the sentence says no more than that the ball somehow "belongs" to John and not necessarily that John threw it.)

Before presenting the second principle of feature assignment, some remarks are in order regarding lexical entries of verbs, since it is these which will be seen to contain the information regarding features.

3.2 *Lexical entries of verbs*

In the previous subsection we saw that assignment of features is determined by the event referred to in the predicate verb. Here the further claim is made that the lexical entry for a verb plays a central role in the proposed system and contains the information for assigning features to the noun phrases in the sentence.

The lexical entry for a verb describes the **role** of each of the verb's arguments. The lexical entry for *jump*, for instance, contains information specific to the "jumper" argument, i.e., it refers to an entity engaged in up-and-down movement (which typically occurs when someone jumps). The entry for *hit* describes the roles of two arguments: one pertaining to the entity having an impact on something or somebody, and the other to the entity undergoing this impact.

The features of each of the arguments fall out of these roles. The role in the entry for *jump* specifies that its argument has features CAUSE +act −aff, CONTROL, and CHANGE, which are typically present when up-and-down movements are engaged in. In the entry of the verb *hit*, the argument having the role pertaining to the "hitter" has the features CAUSE +act +aff, CONTROL, and CHANGE − because one typically has control of hitting and the "hitter" is engaged in a movement − and the other argument of this verb, pertaining to the thing that is hit, has none of these features.

While the features of each verb are specified in the lexicon, the strength of a feature (Section 2.1) will be determined by the particular sentence the verb appears in. The entry for the verb *move*, for instance, will include an argument with the feature CHANGE, but the amount of motion, hence the strength of CHANGE, will depend on whether the sentence refers to a moving bus or a moving snail.

The arguments referred to in the foregoing are what will be called here

core arguments; that is, they are those arguments the roles of which are essential to the meaning of the verbs. There may also be other arguments that are not essential to the activity referred to by the verb, that is, arguments that are not part of our mental definition of the verb. Thus, the verb *jump* may have arguments pertaining to the purpose and the beneficiary of the action (*jump for fun, jump for Barbara*); but it is also possible to think of jumping without any purpose and not for the sake of anyone. A core argument, by contrast, pertains to the role that is inherently implicated in the event or state expressed by the verb; that is, for the event or state to occur it is necessary that there be a participant having such a role. The verb *jump* has only one core argument, corresponding to the subject of this verb: It is inconceivable for jumping to take place without the one who jumps. The verb *hit* has not only the "hitter" as core argument but also the object that is hit, because one cannot think of hitting without something that is hit; both these roles belong to our implicit mental definition of *hit*.[5] The importance of the distinction between core arguments and other arguments will become clear further on.

The concept of core argument, then, is a semantic one; it refers to the meaning of the verb. There is an obvious relationship between this semantic concept and the syntactic concept of an obligatory argument: core arguments are typically obligatory, whereas others are optional. The overlap between these two constructs is not complete, however, because of the possibility of ellipsis. One of the core arguments of *eat*, for instance, involves substance taken into the mouth and swallowed (one cannot think of eating without something being eaten); but it is perfectly normal to say *he has eaten* without mentioning what is consumed.

To summarize, the lexical entry of a verb contains, *inter alia*, the role of each argument and its features; furthermore, it specifies which of its arguments are core arguments. As will be seen further on, the semantic features in the lexical entries make it possible to predict syntactic information, such as which noun phrase is the subject. Specification of this syntactic information in the lexical entry would thus be redundant. By contrast, syntactic information by itself does not suffice for the statement of semantic–syntactic correspondences.

The lexical entry of the predicate verb plays a central role in the assignment of features, as will be seen in the following sections.

3.3   The second principle of feature assignment

3.3.1   Contracted features

The second principle places the burden of feature assignment on the lexical entry of the predicate verb. The rationale for this will become clear on considering the following pair of sentences:

(30) a. Gregory lay on the floor.
      b. Gregory lay unconscious on the floor.

If features were assigned on the basis of the situation described in each particular sentence, *Gregory* would be assigned CONTROL in (30)a but not in (30)b. This would have the untoward consequence that only in (30)a would *Gregory* be A-case, and not in (30)b, where the relation between *Gregory* and *lay* is the same. The analysis of the sentence would be completely changed by the addition of a single adverb.

We therefore introduce a principle which is central to our conception of features and cases. Assignment of features, we stipulate, is determined by the verb and its lexical entry. The verb *lie* is such that its core argument has CONTROL (cf. (11)b, Section 2.2.1). Consequently, *Gregory* in (30)b is assigned CONTROL, and the addition of *unconscious* does not affect feature assignment.

It is proposed, then, that features and the cases that are defined in terms of them are not determined exclusively by the objective situation; instead, a crucial factor is the way our perception of the environment has been crystallized in the lexicon. This is stated by our second principle, which reads as follows:

> The features listed for the arguments in the lexical entry of a verb are assigned to the respective noun phrases expressing them.

It is not proposed, however, to go so far as to consign the whole task of assigning features and cases to the lexicon. The strength of a feature, for instance, is determined by the situation referred to and not by the lexical entry; see also Section 3.3.2, below.

As another illustration of this principle, take (31). Judging by the situation described, *the arrow* in (31)a has no agentive features (and, by the way, it is far from clear what case might be assigned to *the arrow* in current theories of case). That *point* came to be used for an arrow must have been due to the similarity between a pointing person and the function of an arrow. Now, pointing typically involves CAUSE, CONTROL, and CHANGE (motion of the hand), and the lexical entry for *point* will include these features in one of the arguments. In (31)a this argument is expressed by *the arrow*, and this noun phrase therefore will have CAUSE, CONTROL, and CHANGE. Due to the similarity perceived between a pointing arrow and the pointing of a person, the meaning of *point* has been extended and the agentive features are assigned to the arrow. Speakers, then, agree to accord the arrow features which, from an "objective" point of view, it does not have. This is the nature of metaphor.

(31) a. The arrow is pointing to the entrance.
      b. The guard is pointing to the entrance.

We will say that agentive features are **contracted** by *the arrow*, and will call a feature that is assigned only by virtue of a lexical entry a **contracted feature**.

The second principle applies to various kinds of metaphorical extension.

In (32), the human subjects have only CONTROL, and this feature is contracted by the inanimate noun phrases in the corresponding sentences.

(32) a. The boy stands in the marketplace.
     a'. The statue stands in the marketplace.
     b. The boy lies in bed.
     b'. The city lies on the river estuary.

In (33) the animate subjects of the first sentence in each pair have CAUSE and CONTROL. These features are registered in the lexical entries of the relevant verbs, and consequently the inanimate subjects in the corresponding sentences have the same features assigned to them. Here, again, the use of the verb has been extended by dint of similarity.

(33) a. Soldiers surrounded the palace.
     a'. A moat surrounds the palace.
     b. Hannibal crossed the Alps.
     b'. The road crosses the Alps.
     c. The Smiths occupy most of the top floor.
     c'. The hall occupies most of the top floor.
     d. The librarian is holding a dozen books (in his hands).
     d'. The shelf holds a dozen books.

The inanimate subjects of (33) are usually viewed as Themes. Having contracted agentive features, they are analyzed here as A-case.

3.3.2 Subentries
In applying the second principle, account must be taken of the fact that the lexical entry of a verb may have more than one subentry, reflecting the fact that the arguments may have different roles. Thus, verbs like *melt* have one subentry with two core arguments (for the one who engages in melting some substance and for the object melted), and one with only one core argument (for the object that melts).

It is important to note that contraction does not operate across subentries. The verb *hang* can be used both transitively and intransitively – see (34) – and therefore has two subentries.

(34) a. The boy hangs the lamp on the ceiling.
     b. The lamp hangs from the ceiling.

For the transitive use of *hang* the subentry has:

one argument with CAUSE and CONTROL (*the boy* in (34)a)
one argument with CHANGE (*the lamp* in (34)a)

For the intransitive use of *hang* the subentry has:

one argument (with the role "the thing that is suspended"), which does not have any one of these features.

According to the rule that a noun phrase in a sentence with a verb having one subentry cannot contract any feature from the other subentry of this verb, the features CAUSE and CONTROL will not be contracted by *the lamp* in (34)b. Likewise, although *the lamp* in (34)a has CHANGE, this feature is not contracted by *the lamp* in (34)b. As a consequence, the subject of (34)b is not in the A-case. (Non-agentive subjects will be discussed in a later section.)

Verbs that permit middle constructions – e.g., *wash*, *scare*, and *sell* – also have two subentries each: one for the transitive use of these verbs and one for their use in middle constructions like those in (22). The latter subentries do not specify that there is an argument having the feature CAUSE − act − aff. Rather, the situation described in (22) is such that the subjects of these sentences have this feature. This is an instance of a feature that is not determined by the lexical entry of the verb. In (23), by contrast, the situation does not warrant assigning this feature to *the tent*, *the wall*, and *the cookies*, and these are therefore not in the A-case and hence should not be subjects.

3.3.3 Negation and modals

A corollary of the second principle is that negation and modals never cancel a feature. For instance, the lexical entry for *catch* has the features CAUSE + act + aff and CONTROL in one of the arguments. Therefore these features are assigned to the subject, *Barbara*, not only in (35)a – where this seems to accord with the situation referred to – but also to the subjects of (35)b–d, although there is no event actually going on over which Barbara might exercise CONTROL or the CAUSE of which she might be.[6]

(35) a. Barbara catches the ball.
     b. Barbara does not catch the ball.
     c. Barbara can catch the ball.
     d. Barbara might catch the ball.
     e. Barbara would catch the ball (if she could).

4. Case assignment

When a noun phrase has any one of the three agentive features, CAUSE, CONTROL, and CHANGE, it is a candidate for the A-case. The A-case, or Agent, then, is conceived of here as a cluster concept which does not have necessary and jointly sufficient conditions, but ties together related notions in such a way that two members of the concept do not necessarily have anything in common.[7]

In a given sentence there may be more than one noun phrase having one of the agentive features, and the question then arises which one is to be assigned the A-case.

It is proposed that assignment to the A-case is determined by three factors: (i) the relative strength of features; (ii) their number; and (iii) their differential weights. The principles involving these factors, discussed in the following sections, have been formulated with a view to achieving the greatest possible overlap between the A–case and the subject category.

4.1 Relative strength of features

A feature in a given noun phrase will have a certain strength. We now stipulate that, other things being equal, the noun phrase having the greater strength on an agentive feature will be assigned to the A–case.

This rule cannot be stated when features are treated as binary. In Dowty's (1991: 572–73) system, the notion of relative strength is implied by including "movement (relative to another participant)" as one of the "contributing properties" to the Agent proto-role. The example given by Dowty (1991: 585) is *the truck collides with the lamppost*: the truck is in motion, whereas the lamppost is not. However, there are sentences describing two entities in collision, where both are in motion, as in example (4), repeated here as (36):

> (36) a. The meteor collided with the moon.
>   b. *The moon collided with the meteor.

Here both "participants" are in motion. Which is to be in the A–case? The rule for noun phrases of varying strength of features provides a possible answer. The meteor moves faster than the moon, that is, it has a larger strength of CHANGE. Hence *the meteor*, and not *the moon*, is A–case (and therefore the subject).

The subject in (37) is assigned the A–case because of greater relative strength of CAUSE and CONTROL.

> (37) The sergeant marched the soldiers across the square.

The predicate *marched* refers to an activity caused by another participant. It is implied by (37), of course, that the soldiers marched, but attention is focused on what the sergeant did, not how the soldiers reacted to this (consider that when the sergeant tried to march the soldiers, the latter might have refused to obey). *The soldiers* therefore have only very weak CAUSE, which is outweighed by the stronger CAUSE accorded to the sergeant. Moreover, the sergeant has more CONTROL over the activity than the soldiers.[8]

That strength is a determinant of the subject has also been found in psycholinguistic experiments. Osgood (1971) reports that when shown a scene with two moving objects, people tend to encode as sentence subject the one that is moving faster. Conversely, Kasof and Lee (1993) found that when given sentences like *Car A collides head-on with Car B*, people judged the speed of Car A to have been greater than that of Car B.

4.2 Number of features

In each of the sentences in (38), below, there are two noun phrases having the feature CHANGE. The noun phrases do not seem to differ in strength, and therefore an account in terms of the relative strength principle does not explain why one of them is selected as subject. However, one of the noun phrases (the subject) has the additional feature CAUSE, and this is why it is assigned to the A-case.

> (38) a. The cook stirred the soup.
>   b. Jack is hanging the washing on the line.

In (39), the features of the Prepositional Phrase are a proper subset of the features of the subject. The subjects have CAUSE and CONTROL, whereas the oblique objects have only CAUSE. Hence the subjects are in the A-case.

> (39) a. John wrote the letter with a pencil.
>   b. John sent the letter by mail.
>   c. John opened the door with his left hand.
>   d. He shouted for joy.
>   e. He roared with pain.

As will become clear in Section 4.4, there is an additional principle due to which the subject noun phrases in (39) are A-case.

4.3 Differential weight of features

A mere count of features does not suffice for case assignment, unless the relative weights of features are known. Only if the features of one noun phrase are a proper subset of those of the other can the assignment be made; when one noun phrase has the features X and Y and the other has only the feature Z, the latter may nevertheless be in the A-case due to the greater weight of Z.

This brings us to the next factor in assignment. In assigning cases, differential weights of the various features must be taken into consideration.

CAUSE has more weight than CHANGE when these two features compete. (This is in line with the pre-theoretical notion of the Agent, which brings to mind primarily the feature CAUSE; see also Dowty, 1991: 574.) For instance,

> (40) a. The match ignited the gas flame.
>   b. The remote control sent the toy car rolling.

The subjects in these sentences have the feature CAUSE, and the other noun phrases have the feature CHANGE. CAUSE carries more weight than CHANGE, and the former are therefore A-case.[9]

The heuristic principle that has guided us in defining the A-case has been to aim for maximal correspondence between this case and the syntactic category subject. The three principles of case assignment formulated in the foregoing ensure that the noun phrase in the A-case becomes the subject of the sentence.

There are sentences, however, where our principles do not prefer one noun phrase over the other; for instance:

(41) The snow melted with the ice.

Here both *the snow* and *the ice* have neither CAUSE nor CONTROL but only CHANGE, and there is no difference between these noun phrases in respect to the strength of this feature. Example (41) thus has two noun phrases in the A-case (and further on we will see what determines subject selection in such sentences).

4.4 *The Core Argument Principle*

Consider now an apparent exception to the rules of case assignment discussed in the foregoing.

(42) a. The king died from poison.
     b. He choked from the gas.
     c. The baby burped because of the violent motion.
     d. He shivers with cold.
     e. He started with fright.
     f. He died of cold.
     g. The balloon burst with the heat.
     h. He arrived with a/by plane.

Here it is the oblique noun phrase that is CAUSE, whereas the subject noun phrase has only the feature CHANGE. The rule stated in Section 4.3 that CAUSE has more weight than CHANGE implies that only the oblique noun phrase is in the A-case.[10] If this were so, it would subvert our aim of having the subject correspond as closely as possible with the A-case.

We note in passing that examples like these also pose a difficulty for the traditional approach which resorts to a subject selection hierarchy. This becomes clear by comparing (42)a–b with two sentences having the same meanings, and consequently – on the traditional account – identical case assignments for the corresponding noun phrases:

(43) a. Poison killed the king.
     b. The gas choked him.

Suppose the case assigned to *the king* in (42)a is X and the case assigned to *the king* in (43)a is Y. Then X would have to precede Y in the subject selection hierarchy in order to account for (42); but Y would have to precede X to account for (43). See also the discussion of (2), above.

To deal with the difficulty posed by (42), it is necessary to introduce an additional principle. The **Core Argument Principle** states that the A-case is to be assigned to a core argument (as defined in Section 3.2). Thus, the lexical entry for *die* contains only one core argument ("the organism that ceases living"), which has the feature CHANGE and is expressed by *the king*. People may die of indiscernible causes; our mental definition of *die* does not contain the cause of dying, and the latter is not a core argument.[11] Because of the feature CHANGE, *the king* is assigned to the A-case. By contrast, the lexical entry for *kill* has two arguments (for the one who kills and for his victim). In (43)a these are expressed by *poison*, which has the feature CAUSE, and *the king*, which has the feature CHANGE. According to the rule of differential weighting of features discussed above, CAUSE outweighs CHANGE, and hence *poison*, and not *the king*, will be assigned to the A-case.

The Core Argument Principle also suggests a solution to the problem posed in (1), repeated here for convenience:

> (1) a.   This key will open the door.
>   b.   The door will open with this key.

Note, first, that the lexical entry for *open* must have two subentries, one for the transitive sense of the verb, as in (1)a, and one for the intransitive sense, as in (1)b:

> *open₁*: one core argument with role of "opener";
>   features: CAUSE and CONTROL;
>   one core argument with role of "thing that is opened";
>   feature: CHANGE.
> *open₂*: a single core argument with role of "thing that opens";
>   feature: CHANGE.
>   *The door will open* can be understood although no instrument is mentioned. The mental definition of *open₂* does not include the instrument, and this notion is not a core argument.

Open₁ is implicated in (1)a: *the key* expresses the "opener" core argument and *the door* the other core argument. *The key* is in the A-case because it has CAUSE and CONTROL, whereas *the door* has only CHANGE. Support for this analysis will be presented in Chapter 4, Section 1.

Open₂ appears in (1)b, where *the door* expresses the only core argument. The instrument in (1)b – *the key* – is thus barred from being A-case by dint of the Core Argument Principle. *The door* has the feature CHANGE, and in the absence of a competing core argument this makes it A-case, hence subject.[12]

5. Linking

So far we have discussed the assignment of features and the assignment of the A-case on the basis of these features. In this section we examine the question of how the A-case may be linked to syntactic constructions in simple clauses.

It will be seen that, as far as the A-case is concerned, the most common linking rule may be stated in terms of the case category, whereas other linking rules have to be formulated in terms of features that define this category.

5.1 Linking to the subject

In the preceding sections it has been shown that noun phrases in the A-case can be the subject. (The reverse is not always true; as will be seen in Section 6, there are subjects that are not A-case.) The A-case encompasses a larger number of roles than has customarily been included in the Agent category.[13] When the subject is what is customarily called the Instrument, it is analyzed as A-case (Section 2.3). To account for instrumental subjects like (20)e–f, it is therefore no longer necessary to resort to the stipulation that in the absence of an Agent the Instrument becomes subject. Similarly, the Theme is customarily held to be eligible for subject position in the absence of any other case preceding it in the subject selection hierarchy. As shown for (15), (32), and (33), we analyze such "Themes" as A-case. On the present approach, then, there is no need for a subject selection hierarchy, and the problems attending subject selection hierarchies (Section 1) do not arise if we let selection of the subject be governed by the feature composition of noun phrases in the sentence.

In some instances, more than one noun phrase in a simple clause may be in the A-case. In (41), repeated here, both *the snow* and *the ice* are in the A-case, because both have the feature CHANGE and no other agentive feature.

(41) The snow melted with the ice.

These noun phrases thus compete for subject position. In such sentences, the subject will be selected on the basis of pragmatic factors: what is given and what is new information, which noun phrase is focused on, etc. Euphony, too, may at times have a role to play, and finally, the choice of subject may at times be haphazard.

5.2 Linking to the noun phrase in a by-*phrase*

The A-case may also be linked to a *by*-phrase of a passive sentence,[14] as in

(44) The region has been devastated by locusts.

There are various pragmatic determinants of the choice between the active and passive voice (see Anisfeld and Klenbort, 1973; Ertel, 1977; Osgood and Bock, 1977).

Not all A-case noun phrases may appear in *by*-phrases, however. The determinant here is the feature composition of the noun phrase. The rule is as follows:

A noun phrase may be in a *by*-phrase of a passive sentence if and only if it has either CONTROL, CAUSE + act, or CAUSE + aff.[15]

A noun phrase having CONTROL in *by*-phrases is, for example, that in (45)[16] (on *own* see (12), Section 2.2.1).

(45) The apartments are owned by landlords who live in London.

Noun phrases with CAUSE + act or CAUSE + aff can also appear in *by*-phrases.

(46) a. The window was smashed by the falling brick.
 b. The data are stored by the computer.
 c. The first two miles were run by Fred in five minutes.
 d. She was healed by medicinal herbs.

The falling brick in (46)a has CAUSE + act + aff. CAUSE + act or CAUSE + aff is each sufficient by itself for licensing the *by*-phrase (see also Chapter 4, Section 5.2); this is shown by (46)b, where *the computer* is CAUSE + act − aff, and (46)d, where *medicinal herbs* is CAUSE − act + aff. *Fred* in (46)c is also CAUSE + act − aff, but has CONTROL in addition.

The above rule may also be stated negatively: a noun phrase may *not* appear in a *by*-phrase of a passive sentence when it has only the feature CHANGE or the feature CAUSE − act − aff. For example,

(47) a. *Ten feet were fallen from the roof by John.
 b. *The hill was rolled down by the barrel.
 c. *Vapor was turned into by water.
 d. *Four people are slept by this room.
 e. *Five hundred people are seated by this hall.

In (47)a–b the noun phrase in the *by*-phrase has only the feature CHANGE; in (47)c–e it has only CAUSE − act − aff.

We have already had occasion to remark that CHANGE is a very "weak" indicator of agency: in the assignment of the A-case, CAUSE takes precedence over it (Section 4.3). Here we see that CHANGE does not suffice to license a *by*-phrase: the latter requires a more prototypical Agent.

An additional constraint on passivization is discussed in Chapter 6, Section 4.2. Section 4.1 of that chapter deals with the case that is assigned to the surface subject of passive sentences.

The linking rules discussed in this section involve the features CHANGE, CONTROL, and CAUSE, and the dimensions activity and affecting. All these are thus linguistically relevant.

5.3 *Implications for sentence production*

The foregoing discussion of feature assignment, case assignment, and linking has certain implications for a model of production. The following comments go only as far as the A-case and the noun phrases linked to it are concerned.

In deciding on a sentence to describe a given situation or event, the speaker will, *inter alia*, go through the following steps (not necessarily always in the same order, but possibly working in both directions, making loops, etc.):

1. Decide what is to be the predicate of the sentence and what are to be its arguments. This is a purely semantic decision.

2. Select a verb for the predicate and noun phrases for the arguments.

3. Consult the lexical entry for the verb chosen for the predicate, and proceed as follows for each argument:

   (i) Find the noun phrase that fits the role specified in the entry for this argument;
   (ii) Assign to this noun phrase the features associated with this role (Section 3.3.1).

4. Assign the A-case according to the feature composition of the various core arguments, following the rules regarding relative strength of features, their number, and relative weights.

5. Link the A-case to the sentence subject or, when the feature composition licenses this, to the noun phrase in the *by*-phrase. When both options are open, the choice between them is to be made on the basis of pragmatic considerations. When more than one noun phrase is in the A-case, the subject is chosen on the basis of pragmatic considerations (Section 5.1).

The lexical entry for the verb, then, determines the feature compositions of the noun phrases in a clause, and the latter determine which syntactic functions these noun phrases may fulfill.

6. Non-agentive subjects

In the preceding it has been shown that subjects that are traditionally viewed as Themes or as Instruments are analyzed in the present framework as Agents by dint of their having agentive features, either due to the situation referred to, as in examples (15) and (20)e–f, or through contraction, as in examples (32) and (33). Subjects of converse verbs (like *buy* and *sell*) are discussed in the following section, and those of mental verbs ("Experiencers") will be dealt with in Chapter 7. The present proposal thus differs from previous ones in viewing the subject as semantically much more homogeneous.

Not all subjects are in the A-case, however. The subjects of copular verbs –
be, can, have, etc. – and those of several other verbs – see, for instance, (48) –
do not have any of the agentive features and therefore are not in the A-case.

(48) a. John deserves a promotion.
　　b. Two and two equal four.
　　c. John resembles his uncle.
　　d. The car lacks a hand brake.
　　e. John needs a new suit.
　　f. He weighs 100 pounds.
　　g. The blue dress becomes her.
　　h. The lamp hangs from the ceiling. (= (34)b)
　　i. The lamp glimmers/shines.
　　j. The rotting plants smelled/reeked/stank.

Likewise, *comprise, suit, relate to,* and *belong to* take subjects that are not
Agents.

What all these verbs have in common with copular verbs is that, unlike the
examples in the preceding sections, they refer to states rather than to events.
The verbs in (48)a–g also have in common that they carry little information
content without their complements.[17] In Chapter 6 a proposal will be made
concerning the case of the subjects of these sentences.

There are only a handful of verbs the subjects of which have no agentive
features and also do not have the above two characteristics, for instance:

(49) a. The landowners benefit from the new law.
　　b. She came into an inheritance.
　　c. Jennifer sustained an injury.
　　d. Joe inherited a large estate.

Now, some of the verbs in (49) have other uses where their subjects have
agentive features; cf.

(50) a. The law benefits the landowners.
　　b. She came into the room.
　　c. They sustained the destitute.

The subject of (50)a has the feature CAUSE, and those of (50)b–c have CAUSE,
CONTROL, and CHANGE. It might be argued therefore that these features are
contracted by the subjects of (49)a–d. However, this would mean stretching
the notion of contraction too much. The different uses of the same verb –
such as the intransitive and transitive uses of *benefit* in (49)a and (50)a –
should be regarded as belonging to different subentries. As argued in Section
3.3.2, contraction operates only within a subentry.

To uphold the claim that the subjects of (49) are in the A-case, one might
resort to the history of the individual verbs. There may have been stages
when a verb took a truly agentive subject. Thus, *inherit* originally meant "to

make (someone) heir." Features, as we have observed before (Section 3.3.1), reflect experience as crystallized in the lexicon. In the original meaning of *inherit* one of the verb's arguments had agentive features, and these remained with the verb even after its meaning had changed. This is a diachronic version of the foregoing feature contraction account. It may apply even to cases where we have no information about a different meaning of the verb that would justify an A-case subject, since conceivably such a meaning may have existed at a historically remote period that is no longer accessible to us.

Be that as it may, the merit of the present proposal does not depend on such speculations, because no brief is held for a complete correspondence between the A-case and the subject (or of case categories and syntactic categories, in general). The subjects of (49), then, need not be assigned the A-case.

But if so, what case should be assigned to these non-agentive subjects? While it would be easy to supply some cognitive, case-like notion for each of the subjects, it is not clear what purpose would be served by such an exercise. As argued in Chapter 1, Section 6, cases should not be identified with cognitive notions. It is obvious to everyone what notions are expressed by the subjects of (49), but endowing these notions with a case label does not give us any extra mileage. Cases thus introduced will not have any merit unless they subserve the formulation of linguistic regularities. The assumption made in previous writings on case theory that there must be a case for every noun phrase should therefore be abandoned. Cases should be introduced only where there is some linguistic regularity to be stated.

In (49) the lexical entry does not specify for any one of its arguments that it has agentive features, nor does it specify any other features that would lead one to assign these noun phrases to another case. In instances like these, subject selection must be guided directly by the lexical entry for the verb. Unlike lexical entries for the vast majority of verbs, which indicate features for the various core arguments, the lexical entries for the verbs in (49) must specify directly which of each verb's arguments is to be the subject.

7. Converse verbs

7.1 Differences between converse verbs

Converse verbs, it has been argued in Section 1, jeopardize any attempt to formulate a subject selection hierarchy. For instance, in (3), repeated here as (51), Mary has the same role in both sentences, and so has John. If this is so, it becomes impossible to formulate a hierarchy of cases that determines which noun phrase is to become the sentence subject.

> (51) a. Mary sold a book to John for five dollars.
>   b. John bought a book from Mary for five dollars.

Fillmore (1977) has suggested that these sentences differ in the relative saliency of the entities involved; see also Dixon (1991: 86), who refers to the factor of saliency. Dowty (1988: 23; 1991: 579–80) holds that *John* and *Mary* in these sentences have an equal number of agentive features, and that both noun phrases are therefore equally eligible for subject position (see Section 5.1, where a similar balance leads to according two noun phrases to the A-case). Due to this tie, alternative lexicalizations are possible (and the choice between them will presumably be made by other factors, such as topicality).

These proposals do not solve the problem of case assignment. Once a given verb is chosen from a pair of converse verbs, what are the rules that lead to the assignment of the A-case to one noun phrase rather than to another? The two sentences in (52), for instance, may be used to describe the same event. It might therefore be argued that whatever case is accorded to *the officer* in (52)a should also be accorded to *the officer* in (52)b.

(52) a. The officer is leading the band.
     b. The band is following the officer.

Or should it not? Perhaps the fact that the verb *lead* was chosen in the first sentence to describe the situation was due to the officer's role being perceived in a somewhat different way from the way it is perceived in the second sentence? A good case can be made for this conjecture. Features and cases should not be determined solely by the situation described; the crucial factor is, rather, the way this situation is encoded by the syntactic structure of the sentence.

Consider the lexical entry for *lead*. This comprises two arguments, each containing a role (Section 3.2) and its relevant features. For one argument the entry will specify (roughly) "going in front" and the features CHANGE (since the entity referred to in this argument is in motion) and CAUSE. For the other argument it will specify "going behind" and the single feature CHANGE (not CAUSE). In other words, the lexical entry will take account of the fact that the one who goes in front – the officer in (52)a – is causing the action of leading (i.e., is the immediate cause; see Section 2.2.1). While both the officer and the band may be causing the event as a whole, only one of them is the CAUSE of *lead*, viz. the officer. Hence *the officer* is in the A-case in (52)a. The entry for *follow*, by contrast, specifies that the one who is "going behind" has the feature CAUSE. In (52)b, then, it is *the band* and not *the officer* which is in the A-case. By referring to the lexical entry – which indicates for a particular verb which argument (if any) has the feature CAUSE – the problem of converse verbs receives a straightforward solution.

An observation that lends some support to this explanation pertains to possible differences in the use of sentences with converse verbs, as illustrated by (53) (after an example suggested by Anita Mittwoch, personal communication, 1993).

(53) a. We came in for a surprise.
      b. David bought a used car from Brian.
      c. Brian sold a used car to David.

Clearly, it makes quite a difference whether (53)b or (53)c is chosen to follow (53)a. It all depends what we are surprised at. If Brian is a shady character and David knows this, (53)b will be preferred; that Brian sold the car doesn't come as a surprise. Although the two sentences refer to the same situation, they do not mean the same (in some sense of "mean"). Sentence (53)b says something about David being the Agent of *bought* (the CAUSE), whereas (53)c pertains to Brian as the Agent of *sold*.

The solution to our problem, then, may lie in the feature composition of the noun phrases in question. For pairs of converse verbs, like *lead* and *follow*, there may be a difference in respect to assignment of the feature CAUSE by the lexical entry. The feature CONTROL may also contribute to the explanation, but here matters are much less clear. The entities referred to by the two arguments in (52) are very much dependent on each other, neither being able to begin, steer, terminate, or otherwise control the action referred to – whether by *lead* or by *follow* – without the other. Van Valin and Foley (1980: 335) nevertheless state that sentences like (52) differ in respect to who is the "initiating and controlling" participant.

To find out more about CONTROL in converse verbs, we conducted a study in which native speakers of English were asked to rate the degree of Control[18] of the two noun phrases in sentences like (51) and (52). It should be appreciated that speakers' ratings reflect the feature CONTROL only indirectly; what such ratings tap directly is a cognitive notion (which is why only the first letter of "Control" is capitalized here).

7.2 Ratings of Control in converse verbs

The hypothesis that the subject noun phrase would be accorded more Control than the other noun phrases in the sentence was tested for nine pairs of converse verbs. Each of the eighteen verbs was embedded in a sentence with two noun phrases, one of which was the subject noun phrase and the other the direct object, as in (52), or a prepositional object, as in (48) (e.g., *A buys something from B*, or *A leads B*). Respondents rated the degree of Control exercised by each of the two human participants on a nine-point scale. The study is described in full in Schlesinger (1992), and only the gist of the results is presented here.

Table 2.1 presents the mean differences between rated Control of the two human participants – the subject and the object noun phrases. A positive number indicates that the subject was rated as higher in Control, and a negative one that the object was rated as having more Control.

In Table 2.1, three sets of verbs can be distinguished:

Table 2.1. *Differences between ratings of subjects and objects of converse verbs*

trouble	3.0	worry about	2.3
lead	2.1	follow	2.7
sell to	2.2	buy from	1.7
lend to	1.2	borrow from	0.9
chase	4.6	flee from	−0.2
teach to	4.5	learn from	−0.1
please	2.0	like	−0.1
frighten	6.2	fear	−3.3
give to	3.0	receive from	−6.0

(i) For the majority of verbs the subject was accorded more Control than the object. It may be suggested, then, that in sentences with these verbs the factor of CONTROL reinforces that of CAUSE in the assignment of a noun phrase to the A-case. For most of these verbs the object noun phrase was also accorded some measure of Control, but less so than the subject noun phrase. Following our case assignment rules, whichever noun phrase has the relevant feature to a greater degree is in the A-case.

(ii) For three verbs – *flee*, *learn*, and *like* – the subject and the object did not differ much in the degree of Control accorded to them and the difference was not statistically significant.

(iii) For only two of the eighteen verbs was there a significant difference in the opposite direction: the subjects of *fear* and *receive* were accorded less Control than their objects.

Of the verbs mentioned in (ii) and (iii), *like* and *fear* are mental verbs, and the subjects of these verbs are discussed in Chapter 7. This leaves us with *flee*, *learn*, and *receive*. CONTROL does not explain how the subject of these verbs is determined. Presumably, the noun phrase that ends up as sentence subject of *flee* and *learn* is assigned the A-case due to the feature CAUSE, as has been argued in connection with (52), above. As far as I can see, this explanation will not fit *receive*, and it appears that this verb is one of the few that take non-agentive subjects (see Section 6).

8. Conclusions

Let us take stock now of what has been accomplished in this chapter. The concept Agent has been redefined in a way that permits analyzing as Agents those subjects that have previously been accorded to other cases, e.g., the Instrumental or the Patient. Subsuming various cases under one comprehensive Agent case might seem to be a mere terminological change, but this would be true only of a subsumption decreed by fiat. Our procedure was, instead, to break down the notion of an Agent (in the sense of "notion" set out in Chapter 1, Section 1) into components, called features. Subjects that have previously been regarded as Themes (or Patients) share the feature CHANGE with the prototypical Agent (Section 2.2.2), and those that have been analyzed as Instrument share with it the feature CAUSE (Section 2.3). Not all subjects are Agents, though. In Chapter 6 an additional case, the Attributee, will be introduced, which is assigned to many kinds of subjects.

Our features, and the second-order features we have called dimensions, are rooted in cognitive space, but are determined by the lexical entry of the verb rather than for each sentence separately (Section 3.3.1). Cases are not conceived of as cognitive primitives (Chapter 1, Section 6) but as theoretical constructs, which may be language-specific. Features are mapped into syntactic structures via cases. The latter serve as theoretical constructs which enable us to state some regularities more conveniently.

The present approach thus differs radically from traditional theories of case grammar. The latter are based on the assumption that in two sentences referring to the same situation the noun phrases must be assigned the same cases. This assumption has been rejected here. In assigning cases, one has to take into account not only what the sentence refers to but also the linguistic form deployed in referring to it. Thus, although the sentences *The king died from poison* and *Poison killed the king* have the same truth value, the A-case is assigned to *the king* in one and to *poison* in the other (Section 4.4); see also the discussion of converse verbs in Section 7.

The merits of our approach depend on the parsimony and perspicuity of the linguistic descriptions it engenders. It has been shown (Sections 4.1, 4.4, and 7) that some problems concerning semantic–syntactic correspondences (examples (1)–(4) in Section 1) receive a simple explanation within the present framework, and in subsequent chapters solutions will be proposed for problems raised by other linguistic phenomena.

An additional advantage of the present proposal lies in that it provides an account, in principle, of the way language is acquired by the child. Researchers of child language have noted that in the first stages of language acquisition the child appears to map certain notions – Agent, Location, and so on – into sentence positions or into inflections. This raises the question of how these mappings can serve as a basis for further grammatical development, given the lack of semantic homogeneity of syntactic categories such as the subject. If the child is assumed to perceive the situations referred to by language in terms of cognitively rooted features – such as CAUSE and CHANGE – rather than in terms of more global cases, this problem can be solved. These features may form the nucleus for developing the Agent concept which functions in the mature linguistic system and which largely coincides with the subject. It is beyond the scope of this work to discuss this proposal in detail; for an earlier presentation of an essentially similar solution the reader is referred to Schlesinger (1982, 1988).

The case for our approach will be strengthened if it can be shown to be applicable to other case categories as well. In the next chapter the procedures deployed in the present one will be applied in investigating another syntactic construction, the *with*-phrase, and an additional case category, the Comitative, will be introduced. Yet another case, the Attributee, is dealt with in Chapter 6.

3   The Comitative

In this chapter a new case category will be introduced: the Comitative. This is the case typically expressed by *with*-phrases, which have been dealt with in Chapter 1.

1. *With*-phrases

The English preposition *with* has many senses; the Oxford English Dictionary lists about forty. Only noun phrases that are arguments of the verb concern us here, because it is these that are assigned cases. The following *with*-phrases are not arguments of the predicate verb (arguably, they are not arguments at all but modifiers of arguments), and they are therefore beyond the scope of our analysis:

> (1) a. The man with the funny umbrella came to visit us.
> b. She poked fun at the lady with the green hat.
> c. He is a man with strong feelings.

In these sentences *with* has the sense of "having" (Quirk, Greenbaum, Leech, and Svartvik, 1985, Section 9.29). Compare (1)a to

> (2) The man came to visit us with the funny umbrella.

In (2), but not in (1)a, *with the funny umbrella* is an argument of the predicate *came to visit us*. In this chapter we will be concerned with phrases where the object of *with* is an argument of the predicate, like (2), and not with those like (1).

What case is to be assigned to *with*-phrases? The various suggestions in the literature are typically based on an analysis of reality, paying relatively little attention to the linguistic realization. This, we have claimed (Chapter 2, Section 1), is not a promising approach. We will proceed, instead, along the lines followed in our treatment of the A-case and try to discover the features that characterize most, if not all, objects of *with* and which can then be used in the definition of a case category. Our working assumption will be (as in the treatment of the A-case) that the syntactic structure in question, namely the *with*-phrase, has a semantic core that can be defined by features.

2. Features of noun phrases in *with*-phrases

2.1 Features

In Chapter 1 we studied several notions expressed by *with*-phrases. Three of these notions figure as features in our system: **Instrument, Accompaniment,** and **Manner**. These appear to be more complex than the agentive features introduced in Chapter 2; in the studies reported in Chapter 1, however, respondents appeared to have an intuitive understanding of these notions. These features are illustrated in (3) and will be symbolized here as INSTR, ACCOMP, and MANN. In Section 4 it will be shown that linking rules can be formulated in terms of these features, and they thus satisfy the requirement of the Principle of Linguistic Relevance (Chapter 1, Section 6.3).

> (3) a. They tried to eat spaghetti with a spoon.
> b. Linda ate spaghetti with Burt.
> c. They ate up all the spaghetti with great effort.

Let us now define these features.

> *Instrument* An argument referring to what assists another argument[1] in the clause, enabling it to perform the action referred to by the predicate, is said to have the feature Instrument, or INSTR.
> *Accompaniment* An argument that is associated with another argument in the clause in respect to the event or situation referred to by the predicate, other than by way of assisting it in the above manner, is said to have the feature Accompaniment, or ACCOMP.
> *Manner* An argument that describes the manner in which the event or situation referred to by the predicate is performed or occurs is said to have the feature Manner, or MANN.

INSTR differs from ACCOMP in that it pertains to some sort of assistance ("enabling it to perform the action") in respect to the activity referred to by the predicate, which ACCOMP does not.

ACCOMP also differs from INSTR in that it is symmetrical. In (3)b it is not only *Burt* but also *Linda* that is assigned ACCOMP. ACCOMP, then, is a three-way relation involving two noun phrases and the predicate.

MANN appears at the first blush to be quite different from the other two features, but it might be looked on as a metaphorical extension of ACCOMP: in (3)c, the effort in a way accompanies the activity of eating.

A clarification regarding ACCOMP is in order here. It appears that this feature is different from all the features introduced so far in that it is always assigned to two arguments in a sentence. One might object that this complicates matters – particularly since the fact that the subject (e.g., *Linda* in (3)b) is regarded as having ACCOMP does not have any linguistic effect, as far as is known – and that ACCOMP should be assigned only to that noun phrase that does not become subject. What this objection ignores is, first, that assignment of features has to precede linking to the subject and, even more importantly, that the notion of Accompaniment intrinsically requires at least two entities. A feature ACCOMP that relates the argument only to the predicate verb and to no other argument just does not make any sense. The reason why one of the arguments with ACCOMP is linked with the subject will become clear further on (Section 3.4).

INSTR and ACCOMP also have much in common. Unlike the agentive features discussed in the previous chapter, which relate only to the predicate, both INSTR and ACCOMP relate to another noun phrase as well. For INSTR this is invariably the noun phrase that is assigned the A-case, as far as I can tell. For ACCOMP this is not always so:

(4) a. *Shirley* cooks the meal with *her friend.*
   b. Barbara served *the coffee* with *milk.*
   c. The dress fits her with *the white sash.*
   d. The house belongs to her with *the garden.*
   e. Shirley entertained Barbara with *her friends.*
   f. *Shirley* served *the coffee* with *milk* with *Barbara.*
   g. He put the spoon in the drawer with *the knives.*

In (4)a, both italicized noun phrases have the feature ACCOMP: Shirley's friend does the cooking alongside her, and both are assigned ACCOMP. Here the oblique noun phrase is associated with the subject, *Shirley.* In (4)b, by contrast, the milk does not do the serving with Barbara; instead, *milk* accompanies *the coffee,* both of which have the feature ACCOMP. Again, in (4)c–d the oblique noun phrase is associated with the subject. Where necessary, these two types of ACCOMP will be indexed by subscripts: $ACCOMP_s$ for the noun phrases in (4)a, c, and d, and $ACCOMP_o$ for those in (4)b and g. Syntactic categories are assigned on the basis of features like ACCOMP (not vice versa), and the subscripts s (for subject) and o (for object) are indices to other arguments that eventually become realized as subject – whether these are agents as in (4)a or non-agentive subjects as in (4)c–d – and object. Note that, unlike dimensions, s and o are not graded. The ambiguity of (4)e can be described by referring to these two subscripts: either both *Shirley* and *her friends* are $ACCOMP_s$, or else both *Barbara* and *her friends* are $ACCOMP_o$.

In (4)f, we have a three-way relation between *Shirley* and *Barbara* – having $ACCOMP_s$ – and the predicate, and another three-way relationship between *the coffee* and *milk,* which have $ACCOMP_o$, and the predicate.

In (4)g, *the knives* may be an argument of the verb, and then the phrase has $ACCOMP_o$, or else it may be a modifier (of *the drawer*), as the oblique noun phrases in (1) are (Richard Hudson, personal communication, 1992). To disambiguate such sentences context will be needed.

Locative phrases cannot be joined by *with* (Richard Hudson, personal communication, 1992). Sentence (5)a can only mean that the teacher came in with the boys, not that he came in after them. Sentence (5)b has no plausible interpretation, at least not without context; it cannot be construed as stating that the door opened behind the boys and the girls.

(5) a.   The teacher came in *after the girls* with the boys.
  b. *The door opened *behind the girls* with the boys.

A feature, as this concept has been introduced in the previous chapter (Section 2.1), can have varying strengths, that is, it can be present in a given noun phrase to a greater or lesser degree. This goes some way toward explaining the results of the experiments in Chapter 1, where respondents rated some *with*-phrases as expressing two or three notions, each to a different degree; see Section 2.5, below, for further discussion.

A comment is in order here regarding the way the features introduced in the foregoing are represented. Some verbs require an Instrument in their mental definition. The lexical entry of the verb *cut* has three core arguments (Chapter 2, Section 3.2): one for the one who cuts, one relating to the object that is cut, and one relating to the instrument with which the cutting is performed – there is no cutting without an instrument. There are verbs for which there seems to be no need for core arguments relating to instruments: one can eat without a spoon, fork or knife, walk without a walking stick, and so on.

One possibility is to stipulate that lexical entries, like those of *eat* and *walk*, include an optional argument relating to an instrument (of eating, walking, etc.), and the feature INSTR will then be associated with this argument. If this approach is taken, optional arguments relating to MANN and ACCOMP, and to many other features, will also have to be included in the lexical entries of most verbs. Perhaps, however, it is unwise to burden lexical entries with too many arguments – those pertaining to locations, purposes, manner of activity, and so on – and only core arguments ought to be included in the entries. If so, the features INSTR, ACCOMP, and MANN differ from those introduced in the previous chapter in that they are not necessarily associated with lexical entries. Nothing of what is said in this chapter rests on a decision on this point, and I do not intend to examine this issue further here.

2.2 *Varieties of instruments*

Our definition of INSTR as an entity that assists in carrying out an action is a very broad one and admits a large variety of instruments. The following is a brief and not exhaustive list.

(i) *Tool* Knives one cuts with, sticks one hits with, and computers one performs various tasks with may be called tools. Nilsen (1973) regards "tool" as a subcategory of Instrument.

(6) a.   Jack cut the cake with a knife.
  b. She hit the horse with a stick.
  c. He retrieved the information with a computer.

(ii) *Means of transport* Under certain conditions (Section 4.6), these may be expressed by *by*-phrases:

> (7) a. She came home by plane.
>   b. She went to town by car.

(iii) *Proper part* The Instrument with which an action is performed can be a part of one's body, as in (8)a, or more generally, a proper part of the actor, as in (8)b (the case of the subject in (8)b is discussed in the next chapter). According to Nilsen (1973) "body part" is a subcategory of the Instrument case.

> (8) a. He peeled the apple with his left hand.
>   b. The car scraped the tree with its fender.

(iv) *Abstract instrument* Abstract entities may be instrumental in the performance of an activity:

> (9) a. You ought to persuade him with kind words.
>   b. Bob solved the jigsaw puzzle with patience.

(v) *Material* A substance may be instrumental in performing an activity without serving as a tool. Nilsen (1973) regards this as a subcategory of Instrument.

> (10) a. We washed the dishes with soap.
>   b. We covered the wood with varnish.

(vi) *Means of communication* These, too, may appear in *by*-phrases:

> (11) a. We informed him of the accident by phone.
>   b. They sent the message by satellite.
>   c. He was summoned by airmail.

In the above types, there is an Agent who acts on an Instrument, which "takes over" from the Agent and, in some of the instances, acts on another entity (the "undergoer"). There are Instruments of other types that assist the Agent but are not involved in the activity in its entirety; instead, the Agent performs at least part of the activity directly, without the Instrument as an intermediary. Here we can distinguish two types, (vii) and (viii):

(vii) *Secondary tool* There are tools that do not perform the activity in its entirety. Spoons assist in eating – they carry food to the mouth – but do not themselves eat; they do not make swallowing movements and do not ingest. Likewise, straws do not drink and glasses do not read.

> (12) a. Burt ate spaghetti with a spoon.
>   b. The boy drank the juice with a straw.
>   c. My brother reads only with glasses.

(viii) *Ingredient* A substance may enable the creation of some object by becoming – unlike Material in (v), above – an ingredient of that object.

(13) a. They built the house with bricks.
     b. The farmer baked bread with white flour.

(ix) *Ancillary instrument* By this term I refer to instruments which, unlike those belonging to the other types, do not have interactive contact with the Undergoer at all; they enable the activity to be performed, however.

(14) a. I changed the light bulb with a ladder.
     b. He fought the flames with a fireproof vest.

Finally, there are sentences where the Instrument is itself the Undergoer of the activity:

(x) *Instrument–undergoer* In (15), the entities denoted by the oblique noun phrases are essential in performing an activity and are themselves the objects of this activity.

(15) a. The little girl is playing with her dolls.
     b. The biologist experimented with some rabbits.

The actions are directed at the dolls and the rabbits, and these do not assist in acting on other things; yet they are essential for the activity.

The foregoing classification is based on an analysis of situations.[2] In Sections 4.4–4.6 we will see which of them have linguistic relevance.

Can we characterize the foregoing ten types in a more principled way? In part, at least, this is possible. Note, first, that the first group, (i)–(vi), comprises Instruments that have the feature CAUSE; the noun phrase preceded by *with* refers to a link in the causal chain of event or activity referred to by the predicate verb. Of course, it does not cause it in the sense that the Agent does; instead, it forms a chain, with the Agent as primary and the Instrument as secondary CAUSE.[3]

The Instruments in the other two groups are not causes of the activity. In (12a), a spoon is not the cause of eating, but only of bringing food to the mouth. Bricks are not the cause of building, although in the situation described by (13)a they enable the activity to be performed. And, of course, ladders do not change bulbs, and dolls and rabbits do not cause the activities of those who play or experiment with them.

Returning to the first group of causal Instruments, we observe that Tools, Means of transport, and Proper parts are usually active in the course of performing the activity, whereas Abstract instruments and Materials are not; the former are CAUSE + act and the latter, CAUSE − act. Means of communication and some Tools, like a computer − (6)c − occupy an intermediate position. As complex mechanisms we may ascribe to them some activity; remember that "activity" is not a binary property, but, as its name implies, a dimension; there is a gradient from + act to − act. But, in (11)c, *airmail* is more like Abstract instrument in being CAUSE − act.

The types of Instrument are summarized in Table 3.1. In the table, no distinction is made between different degrees of activity, "weak" activity being registered as CAUSE + act.

Table 3.1. *Types of Instruments*

Type	Examples	Feature
(i) Tool	cut with a knife retrieve with a computer	CAUSE +act
(ii) Means of transport	come by plane go by car	CAUSE +act
(iii) Proper part	peel with the left hand scrape with its fender	CAUSE +act
(iv) Abstract instrument	persuade with kind words solve with patience	CAUSE −act
(v) Material	wash with soap cover with varnish	CAUSE −act
(vi) Means of communication	inform by phone summon by airmail	CAUSE +act CAUSE −act
(vii) Secondary tool	eat with a spoon read with glasses	(not CAUSE)
(viii) Ingredient	build with bricks bake with flour	(not CAUSE)
(ix) Ancillary instrument	change a bulb with a ladder fight with a fireproof vest	(not CAUSE)
(x) Instrument–undergoer	play with dolls experiment with rabbits	(not CAUSE)

As we see in the table, the feature CAUSE and the activity dimension capture some of the distinctions we have made between varieties of Instruments, but not all of them. To distinguish between, say, Tool and Means of transport, or between Ingredient and Ancillary instrument, it would be necessary to add dimensions to INSTR or to break it down into more primitive features (or both), or else we would have to resort to more complex conceptual structures like those of Jackendoff (1990), for instance. But such a move would be necessary only if it turned out that the varieties of instruments discussed here do not merely represent cognitive notions, but have some linguistic effect. Whether this is so is a question we will return to in our discussion of linking (Sections 4.4–4.6).

2.3 A dimension of ACCOMP

The dimension **distributive** is posited for ACCOMP. It refers to the extent to which each of the two noun phrases having the feature ACCOMP can be said to engage by itself in the predicated event or situation. Consider:

(16) a.   Linda ate spaghetti with Burt.
      a'.   Linda ate spaghetti and Burt ate spaghetti.
      b.   Barbara served the coffee with milk.
      b'.   Barbara served the coffee and Barbara served milk.

(17) a.   Leopold came to the party with his threadbare jacket.
  a'. *Leopold came to the party and his threadbare jacket came to the party.
  b.   Lisa shopped with the baby yesterday.
  b'. *Lisa shopped yesterday and the baby shopped yesterday.

Sentences (16)a–b implicate (16)a'–b';[4] but (17)a'–b' do not follow from (17)a–b. Accordingly, *Linda* and *Burt* in (16)a and *the coffee* and *milk* in (16)b are ACCOMP + distr, whereas the noun phrases in (17)a–b are ACCOMP − distr.

Some verbs take an argument with ACCOMP − distr. It lies in the nature of wrestling and discussing that they require a partner. A contest between Lionel and the thug will therefore be described by (18)a; (18)a' will be construed as each of the two wrestling with someone else. Similarly, (18)b' will be construed as the two girls discussing the matter each with a different person, and (18)c' as Len and his uncle each corresponding with a third party. The noun phrases in these *with*-phrases, then, are ACCOMP − distr.

(18) a.   Lionel wrestled with the thug.
  a'. Lionel wrestled and the thug wrestled.
  b.   Louise discussed the matter with Laura.
  b'. Louise discussed the matter and Laura discussed the matter.
  c.   Len corresponds with his uncle.
  c'. Len corresponds and his uncle corresponds.

By contrast, there is nothing in the nature of coming to a party, and shopping, in (17)a–b, that requires an accompanying partner. Instead, it is the specific event described that makes these noun phrases ACCOMP − distr, and this is reflected by our rough-and-ready test of sentence conjunction.

Some verbs admit both ACCOMP + distr and ACCOMP − distr noun phrases, and the sentence context serves to disambiguate the *with*-phrase.[5]

(19) a.   Bob fought bitterly with Paul.
  b.   Bob fought with Paul at the Arnhem front in World War II.

Some verbs, like those in (18), which are always − distr, have lexical entries that register this fact. For most verbs, though, ACCOMP can be either + distr or − distr and the value of this dimension thus is not specified in the lexical entry.

Like all dimensions, distributivity is a matter of degree (unlike the distinction between ACCOMP$_s$ and ACCOMP$_o$). Consider:

(20) a.   The general captured the hill with a squad of paratroopers.
  b.   The general captured the hill.
  c.   A squad of paratroopers captured the hill.

In (20)b *captured* is not used in quite the same sense as in (20)c: the general does not take part in the actual fighting, but as commander of the fighting men he is credited with capturing the hill. In (20)a the feature ACCOMP is therefore less distributive than, e.g., that in (16)a, where *ate* applies to Burt in the same way as it does to Linda, and more distributive than, for instance, *wrestle*, *discuss*, and *correspond* in (18)a–c. On (20)a see also Section 2.5.1, below.

2.4 Feature assignment in Passives

Assignment of features and their dimensions to the objects of *with* is not affected by passivization.

(21) a.   The fire brigade put out the fire with the inhabitants.
　　 a'. The fire was put out with the inhabitants.
　　 b.   Barbara served the coffee with milk.
　　 b'. The coffee was served with milk.
　　 c.   They ate spaghetti with a spoon.
　　 c'. The spaghetti was eaten with a spoon.
　　 d.   They built the house with bricks.
　　 d'. The house was built with bricks.
　　 e.   They ate up all the spaghetti with great effort.
　　 e'. The spaghetti was eaten up with great effort.

ACCOMP, we have noted, is symmetric, and usually there will be at least two noun phrases having this feature. In a passive sentence without a *by*-phrase, though, there may be a single noun phrase with ACCOMP. The conjunction test illustrated for (16)–(17) is inapplicable to passive sentences like (21)a'. A passive sentence has the same value on the dimension distributive as that in the corresponding active one. The noun phrase in the *with*-phrase is ACCOMP + distr in (21)a; and so are the oblique noun phrases in (21)b'. Further, *the inhabitants* in (21)a' is ACCOMP$_s$, just as in (21)a.

Sentence (21)b' is an example of a passive sentence with two noun phrases having ACCOMP$_o$ – *the coffee* and *milk*.

The definition of INSTR (Section 2.1) refers to "another argument in the clause." In a passive sentence with a *with*-phrase, INSTR is assigned to the noun phrase that has this feature in the corresponding active one. *A spoon* and *bricks* have INSTR in (21)c'–d' as well as in (21)c–d, and the oblique noun phrase in both (21)e and (21)e' is MANN. Passive sentences with *by*-phrases will be dealt with in the next chapter (Section 5.1).

2.5 Multiple features

In the foregoing we have seen that many noun phrases with INSTR have CAUSE. Here we observe that the three features INSTR, ACCOMP, and MANN frequently co-occur.

2.5.1   ACCOMP and INSTR

Noun phrases in *with*-phrases may have more than one feature. In Chapter 1, Section 2, we observed that the notions of Accompaniment and Instrument overlap: Respondents judged that both these notions are expressed in each of the *with*-phrases in (22)a–c. The oblique noun phrases in these sentences will be assigned both ACCOMP and INSTR.

(22) a. The officer caught the smuggler with a police dog.
      b. The general captured the hill with a squad of paratroopers.
      c. The blind man crossed the street with his dog.

The police dog, the paratroopers, and the blind man's dog are, metaphorically speaking, tools by means of which the action in the predicate is performed, and they have the feature INSTR. Moreover, they are ACCOMP, because they accompany the officer, the general, and the blind man in the activity referred to in the predicate.[6]

2.5.2   INSTR and MANN

In Chapter 1, Sections 3–4, we encountered sentences that were judged to express the notions Manner and Instrument. Examples of noun phrases having both INSTR and MANN are:

(23) a. He peeled the apple with his left hand.
      b. The car scraped the tree with its fender.
      c. He was summoned by airmail.
      d. You ought to persuade him with kind words.
      e. Bob solved the jigsaw puzzle with patience.

In (23)a–b the *with*-phrases refer to Proper parts, in (23)c to Means of communication, and in (23)d–e to Abstract instruments (see Section 2.2). In addition, the *with*-phrases in these sentences describe the manner in which the event occurred. It may be argued, in fact, that whenever a noun phrase refers to an instrument of any type, it also describes the manner in which the action was carried out; the two concepts are closely allied.[7] (And conversely, some instances of MANN – as that on a sign warning: "Use care!" – may be viewed as INSTR.)

2.5.3   ACCOMP and MANN

Many noun phrases with ACCOMP − distr also have MANN. The notions Accompaniment and Manner also tended to occur together in our rating study in Chapter 1, Section 3.

(24) a. Barbara served the coffee with milk.
      b. Leopold came to the party with his threadbare jacket.
      c. Lisa shopped with the baby yesterday.

    d. Leo ran after her with cries of derision.

    e. The storm broke with loud peals of thunder.

2.5.4   *The ubiquitous* ACCOMP

MANN is very widespread in *with*-phrases; ACCOMP is probably always present. Whenever an instrument of any type is deployed it accompanies the agent of the activity (or its object – see (4)b), and the manner of carrying out an activity in some sense accompanies it. In our study (Chapter 1, Section 4.3), (25), below, was judged to express the notion of Accompaniment, and by some of the respondents, also Manner.

    (25) The picture fell with a crash.

3. The Comitative

3.1   *The C-case defined*

The three features, ACCOMP, MANN, and INSTR are felt to have something in common: they apply where entities referred to by noun phrases are functioning together in the occurrence referred to by the verb. This affinity in meaning leads to the frequent co-occurrence of these features in *with*-phrases that has been noted in the foregoing. It is proposed therefore to view these features as defining a single case, which we will call the **Comitative**. Each of the three features is a sufficient condition for a noun phrase to be assigned to the Comitative. Like the term Agent, Comitative describes the prototype of a much wider category to which it does not apply literally. To avoid connotations the term Comitative might have, I will occasionally use the term **C-case**.

Case categories are introduced to permit the statement of regularities. The A-case, as we have seen, may always be expressed as subject, and the C-case may always be expressed by a *with*-phrase (even where the preferred preposition is *by*, as in (7) and (11)). The reverse is not true, however: not all subjects are in the A-case, and as will be shown in Section 3.2, not all *with*-phrases have the C-case.

ACCOMP is a symmetrical feature: it is assigned to the noun phrase in the *with*-phrase and to the noun phrase associated with it. Thus, in (3)b, repeated here, both the noun phrases in italic type are ACCOMP. Both are therefore in the C-case.

    (3) b. *Linda* ate spaghetti with *Burt*.

It follows that one noun phrase may have two cases assigned to it: *Linda* is both C-case and A-case.[8] We will return to this point in Section 3.3.

It might be argued that here the C-case should be assigned only to the noun phrase in the prepositional phrase and not to the subject. What this argument ignores is that assignment of features and of cases precedes linking: the features of *Linda* and *Burt* are assigned on the basis of the speaker's intention in describing the event, and the decision as to which of these noun phrases is to be subject depends on this assignment.

3.2 Non-comitative with-phrases

In the course of its long history the word *with* has developed many senses. Not all of these can be expected to express a single case. The situation here parallels that of the A-case: not all subjects are in the A-case. In addition to *with*-phrases that are not arguments – see (1) at the beginning of this chapter – there are several kinds of non-comitative uses of *with*:

(i) Cause:

(26) a. He shivers with cold.
b. He started with fright.

Sentences like these are discussed in Chapter 2, Section 4.4.

(ii) Location and Time:

(27) a. I left the keys with my wallet.
b. She stays with her sister.
c. He took the letter with him.
d. The burden of proof lies with the accused.
e. They rose with the first cock's crow.
f. He has mellowed with age.

Example (27)d is a metaphorical extension of the locative use. Sentences (27)e–f are temporal.[9]

(iii) Specification of the action:

This category contains various uses of *with* having the sense of, roughly, *in respect to*:

(28) a. I will help with the nets.
b. He went on with his work.
c. He confused him with his brother.
d. This street forms a right angle with the main street.
e. They supply us with rations.

(iv) Obligatory *with*-phrases:

Omission of the *with*-phrase in (29) would result in unacceptable sentences:

(29) a. The garden swarms with bees.
b. He dealt with the matter.
c. Get through with it!
d. The river teems with fish.

(v) Miscellaneous:

(30) a. All's right with the world.
  b. They all went out with the exception of Mr. X.
  c. We got through with the loss of two men.

The non-comitative noun phrases in (26), above, might have been included with comitative noun phrases in a wider case category – call it C'-case – by adding CAUSE to the defining features. But this would result in too broad a category, including, among others, noun phrases that are not in *with*-phrases, like *the depression* and *the rain* in (31):

(31) a. The depression led to unemployment.
  b. His clothes were soaked because of the rain.

It would also vastly complicate the linking rules discussed in Section 4, below. Likewise, adding additional features, like Location and Time, to the definition of the C-case would throw the doors open too wide. A case that includes Locatives like those in (27) would have to include other Locatives as well, and perhaps many other types of prepositional phrase, too. Such a mammoth case category would most probably not permit a parsimonious statement of linguistic regularities.

It has been suggested by Dwight Bolinger (personal communication, 1980) and Richard Hudson (personal communication, 1992) that perhaps all or almost all *with*-phrases have a common meaning component, namely, that of togetherness in space and time.[10] Indeed, in many examples of the above non-comitative uses we may sense a certain affinity with ACCOMP: there is some association between the noun phrase introduced by *with* and another noun phrase. In phrases that are not arguments of the predicate, like (1), and in obligatory *with*-phrases, as in (29), one also finds related senses of *with*. This fact could figure in an explanation of the diachronic development of the meanings of this word. But I think it is inadvisable to introduce an overall case – say, the "Associative" – subsuming the Comitative and other constructions. For the reasons stated above, such a move has little to commend itself.

It seems therefore preferable not to regard the examples in this section as Comitatives. The noun phrases in (27)a–d are clearly Locative (a case that will be dealt with briefly in Chapter 8), and perhaps temporal noun phrases like those in (27)e–f should be included in this case too. In Chapter 2, Section 6, it is argued that in the present system there is no motivation for the principle that every noun phrase has to be assigned a case; the noun phrases in (26), (28), (29), and (30) may turn out to be instances of such case-less noun phrases.

3.3 C-case with INSTR and an agentive feature

A noun phrase in a *with*-phrase may have both INSTR and CAUSE (Section 2.2). In (32), for instance, *a knife* is causally involved in the action of cutting and hence has CAUSE as well as INSTR.

(32) Jack cut the cake with a knife.

The knife in (32) has INSTR and CAUSE, whereas *Jack* has CAUSE and greater strength of CONTROL. INSTR is not an agentive feature, and the two agentive features of *Jack* outweigh the feature CAUSE of *the knife* (scc Chapter 2, Sections 4.2–4.3). Therefore, although *the knife* expresses a core argument (Section 2.1), *Jack* will be A-case, and *the knife* will be only C-case.

Instruments of various types – especially Means of transport, Ingredient, and sometimes also Material – are in motion in the course of performing the activity denoted by the predicate verb, that is, they have the feature CHANGE. This feature is also outweighed by the agentive features of their human user, and hence they, too, are not assigned the A-case.

3.4 C-case with ACCOMP and an agentive feature

When a noun phrase having ACCOMP$_s$ is associated with an A-case subject, as in (4)a, it will have an agentive feature alongside ACCOMP. In addition to ACCOMP$_s$, the oblique noun phrase in (33)a has CAUSE, that in (33)b has CHANGE, and that in (33)c has CONTROL (see Chapter 2, Section 2.2).

(33) a. The bridegroom cut the cake with his bride.
      b. Our neighbor fell off the roof with his cat.
      c. Cynthia is lying on the beach with her sister Rose.

His bride is as much CAUSE of cutting as the bridegroom, *his cat* undergoes CHANGE just like *our neighbor*, and *her sister Rose* has CONTROL (over "lying") just like *Cynthia*.

It might appear that since all the oblique noun phrases in (33) have agentive features, the two noun phrases in each sentence might be readily interchanged. In fact, such interchange is often possible:

(34) a. The bride cut the cake with her bridegroom.
      b. Our neighbor's cat fell from the roof with him.
      c. Rose is lying on the beach with her sister Cynthia.

A speaker who feels that the bride has more CONTROL than the bridegroom may opt for (34)a instead of (33)a. *The bride* and *the bridegroom* have equal strength of CAUSE and of ACCOMP assigned to them, and the feature CONTROL would therefore tip the balance (see Chapter 2, Section 2.1 on the concept of strength, and Chapter 2, Sections 4.2–4.3 on assignment of the A-case). The choice between (33)b–c and (34)b–c may be dictated by pragmatic and discourse factors, which we cannot go into here (see Chapter 2, Section 5.1). Another example of interchange is

(35) a. Linda ate spaghetti with Burt.
      b. Burt ate spaghetti with Linda.

A subtle difference may be felt between these two sentences. In (35)a, Linda may have instigated the event or may be a more dominant participant in it than Burt, whereas the roles may be reversed in (35)b. Other things being equal, the noun phrase having CONTROL with greater strength will be assigned the A-case, that is, *Linda* in (35)a and *Burt* in (35)b.

Another way of reading (35) is to assign equal CONTROL to Linda and Burt; the speaker may have been influenced only by pragmatic factors in choosing between (35)a and (35)b (just as in (33)b–c and (34)b–c, where, as stated, there appears to be no difference in CONTROL). If so, both noun phrases will be A-case as well as C-case. The same is true of (36), where both *the snow* and *the ice* have the features ACCOMP and CHANGE, and in the absence of any difference in strength and of any additional agentive feature, both are in the A-case.[11]

(36) The snow melted with the ice.

That *Burt* in (35)a and *the ice* in (36) should be A-case, just like the subjects of these sentences, might seem to contravene the principle, stated in Chapter 2, Section 4.4, according to which only a core argument can be assigned the A-case. Observe, however, that the lexical entry for *eat* specifies only that there is a core argument referring to the "ingester" and both *Burt* and *Linda* answer this description; hence either one of these can express the "ingester" core argument and they can both be candidates for the A-case. Likewise, *melt* has a core argument referring to the material that melts, which may be expressed by either *the snow* or *the ice*.

To summarize, for noun phrases having an agentive feature in addition to ACCOMP there are the following possibilities:

(i) Both noun phrases have ACCOMP and CAUSE. The noun phrase having greater strength of CONTROL will be assigned the A-case and become subject (e.g., (35), on one of the interpretations, and (34)a). Because of the feature ACCOMP, the subject noun phrase will also be C-case; the other noun phrase will be only C-case.

(ii) Both noun phrases have ACCOMP and another agentive feature, and, unlike the preceding examples, no difference in strength of CONTROL is intended (as for instance (35), on the other interpretation, and (36)). In this instance, both noun phrases are A-case as well as C-case. The question of which of the A-case noun phrases will become subject will be taken up in the following section.

Table 3.2. *Multiple occurrences of A-case and C-case*

a)	Sentence	A-case	C-case
	Jack cut the cake with a knife.	Jack	a knife
	Linda ate spaghetti with Burt. *Linda* intended to be dominant:	Linda	Burt Linda
	Linda ate spaghetti with Burt. None intended to be dominant:	Linda Burt	Linda Burt
	The snow melted with the ice.	the snow the ice	the snow the ice

b)	Sentence	Noun phrase in	
		subject	*with*-phrase
	Jack cut the cake with a knife.	A-case	C-case
	Linda ate spaghetti with Burt. (*Linda* intended to be dominant)	A-case C-case	C-case
	Linda ate spaghetti with Burt. (Neither intended to be dominant)	A-case C-case	A-case C-case
	The snow melted with the ice.	A-case C-case	A-case C-case

While noun phrases with ACCOMP and with INSTR may have CAUSE as an additional feature, the feature MANN by itself will not occur with CAUSE.

Table 3.2 summarizes the various possibilities discussed in this and the preceding section.

A special kind of CAUSE is that in (37), which occurs with ACCOMP + distr.

(37) a. Don's mood changes with the weather.
     b. The raft rose with the water level.

The weather does not cause its own "changes" but rather Don's changes of mood; the water level does not cause its own rising but that of the raft. In addition, *the weather* accompanies the mood in its changing phases and the water level accompanies the rising raft.

4. Linking

A noun phrase in the C-case, whatever its feature composition, may be expressed by a *with*-phrase. Other linkings of the C-case are conditional on the feature composition of the noun phrase. This parallels the A-case, which is typically linked to the subject, but there are alternative structures to which it may be linked, depending on the feature composition (Chapter 2, Section 5).

4.1 Noun phrases with ACCOMP as subjects

We have noted previously that when two noun phrases having the feature ACCOMP are in the A-case as well as in the C-case – see (33)–(36) – the subject will be selected on the basis of pragmatic factors. Another way of resolving the conflict is by expressing both noun phrases as a conjoint subject:

(38)   a.   The snow melted with the ice.
       a'.   The snow and the ice melted.
       b.   Linda ate spaghetti with Burt.
       b'.   Linda and Burt ate spaghetti.

In all these sentences each of the two noun phrases is ACCOMP + distr. Two noun phrases having ACCOMP − distr can be conjoined only where the activity inherently requires the participation of two personae (see Section 2.3), as in (39), which should be compared to (40):

(39)   a.   Lionel wrestled with the thug.
       a'.   Lionel and the thug wrestled.
       b.   Louise discussed the matter with her sister.
       b'.   Louise and her sister discussed the matter.

(40)   a.   Leopold came to the party with his threadbare jacket.
       a'.   *Leopold and his threadbare jacket came to the party.
       b.   Lisa shopped with the baby yesterday.
       b'.   *Lisa and the baby shopped yesterday.

When two noun phrases with $ACCOMP_0$ are conjoined, a slight change of meaning results. In (41)b, the two conjoined objects no longer have $ACCOMP_0$; to wit, the coffee and the milk may have been served separately, even at different times.

(41)   a.   Barbara served the coffee with milk.
       b.   Barbara served the coffee and milk.

Not every conjoined subject has C-case arguments. Sentence (38)a', above, is a paraphrase of (38)a, and (38)b' of (38)b, but (42)b is not a paraphrase of (42)a:

(42)   a.   The Romans and William the Conqueror invaded England.
       b.   The Romans invaded England with William the Conqueror.

The difference between (38) and (42) is captured by the analysis proposed previously. Each of the noun phrases conjoined in (38)a' and (38)b' has the feature ACCOMP, but the conjoined noun phrases in (42)a, like those in (41)b, do not have ACCOMP, and this is why (42)a does not have (42)b as a paraphrase.

C-case noun phrases that do not have ACCOMP (i.e., that have only INSTR or MANN) cannot be linked with the subject (sentences with a subjectivized instrument will be dealt with in the next chapter).

4.2 Linking ACCOMP with a prepositional phrase

When an object of *with* has ACCOMP + distr, *with* may be paraphrased by *together with*. But this preposition cannot substitute for *with* when the noun phrase has ACCOMP − distr. Compare (43) with (44).

(43) a. They went to the show together with their friends.
  b. The ship sank together with the lifeboats.

(44) a. *Leo cooks together with exotic spices.
  b. *Leopold came to the party together with his threadbare jacket.
  c. *Lionel wrestled together with the thug.
  d. *Lisa shopped together with the baby yesterday.

Together with always connects the two noun phrases that have ACCOMP. In (45)a, *together with* indicates that the friend assists Shirley; its object refers back to the subject and accordingly is ACCOMP$_s$. In (45)b, by contrast, *together with* indicates that the milk goes with the coffee, and the oblique noun phrase is ACCOMP$_o$.

(45) a. Shirley cooks the meal together with her friend.
  b. Barbara served the coffee together with milk.

There are additional phrases that may be used for ACCOMP + distr: *accompanied by* − which is used only for animates − and *alongside*, which is also more restricted stylistically.

4.3 Linking of noun phrases having MANN

A *with*-phrase with MANN may be paraphrased by an adverb or by the phrase *in a ... manner*:

(46) a. Carl came into the room with caution.
  b. Carl came into the room cautiously.
  c. Carl came into the room in a cautious manner.

(47) a. Bob solved the jigsaw puzzle with patience.
  b. Bob solved the jigsaw puzzle patiently.
  c. Bob solved the jigsaw puzzle in a patient manner.

Paraphrases like (46)b and (47)b are possible only if there is an appropriate adverb in the language, and those like (46)c and (47)c are only possible if there is an appropriate adjective. Apart from this there are no constraints on the use of these paraphrases, as far as I can see.

4.4 Linking INSTR *with* use/using *and* by means of

A sentence with a noun phrase having the feature INSTR may be paraphrased with this noun phrase as direct object of *use*; see (48)a–b. Now, the direct object in (48)b, *the knife*, does not assist in the activity referred to by the verb *use*, and according to our definition of INSTR (Section 2.1) it would therefore not merit this feature. It is proposed, however, to regard (48)b as a derived form of the construction in (48)c. This permits assigning INSTR to *the knife* in (48)b as well as in (48)c. The same goes for (49)–(51).

(48) a. Jack cut the cake with the knife.
b. Jack used the knife to cut/in cutting the cake.
c. Jack cut the cake using the knife.

(49) a. He cooked the meat with his left hand.
b. He used his left hand to cook/in cooking the meat.
c. He cooked the meat using his left hand.

(50) a. I changed the light bulb with a ladder.
b. I used a ladder to change the light bulb.
c. I changed the light bulb using a ladder.

In one respect, *use* is less restricted than *with*. Where an Ancillary instrument has only a minor role in the event, *with* may be odd – see (51)a – and *use* . . . *in Ving* (where *V* stands for any verb) will be appropriate (Richard Hudson, personal communication, 1992).

(51) a. ??They built the house with a tape measure.
b.   They used a tape measure in building the house.

With before a noun phrase having INSTR may often be paraphrased by *by means of*, as in

(52) a. Jack cut the meat by means of a knife.
b. Jack cut the meat by means of a specially honed knife.
c. Jack cut the meat by means of a pair of scissors.

This example shows that *by means of* sounds more natural with an Instrument that is not quite standard, as in (52)b–c.

There are pragmatic constraints on the use of *use* and *by means of*. First, the subject of the sentence has to be human:

(53) a.   The car scraped the tree with its fender.
b. *The car used its fender to scrape the tree.
c. *The car scraped the tree by means of its fender.

Second, *use* will not ordinarily be deployed with a human object because of its connotation of exploitation, unless something similar to abuse is intended (Bolinger, personal communication, 1980). This connotation appears to be weaker with *by means of*:

(54) a. The prisoner won the appeal with a highly paid lawyer.
     b. ?The prisoner used a highly-paid lawyer to win the appeal.
     c. ?The prisoner won the appeal by means of a highly-paid lawyer.

(55) a. The little boy went to school with his mother.
     b. *The little boy used his mother to go to school.
     c. *The little boy went to school by means of his mother.

That the general is said, in (56)b–c, to use paratroopers to capture a hill presumably reflects the usual attitude of generals to their men.

(56) a. The general captured the hill with a squad of paratroopers.
     b. The general used a squad of paratroopers to capture/in capturing the hill.
     c. The general captured the hill by means of a squad of paratroopers.

The use of *by means of* is more limited than that of *use*. *By means of* is acceptable in (57) but not in (58).

(57) a. Jack cut the meat by means of a knife.
     b. He retrieved the information by means of a computer.
     c. ?We informed him of the accident by means of the/a phone.
     d. They sent the message by means of (a) satellite.

(58) a. *We washed the dishes by means of soap.
     b. *We covered the wood by means of varnish.
     c. *Burt ate spaghetti by means of a spoon.
     d. *The boy drank the juice by means of a straw.
     e. *They built the house by means of bricks.
     f. *The farmer baked bread by means of white flour.
     g. *I changed the light bulb by means of a ladder.
     h. *He fought the flames by means of a fireproof vest.
     i. *The little girl is playing by means of her dolls.
     j. *The biologist experimented by means of some rabbits.
     k. *He was summoned by means of airmail.

These sentences become acceptable with the instrument as object of *use* or *using* (but see next section); for instance:

(59) a. We used soap to wash the dishes.
     b. Burt used a spoon to eat spaghetti.
     c. They used bricks to build/in building the house.

     d. I used a ladder to change the light bulb.
     e. The biologist used some rabbits in experimenting.
     f. The little girl used dolls to play (with).

What accounts for the difference in acceptability between (57) and (58)? In each of the sentences in (57) the object of *by means of* has the feature CAUSE + act. A complex mechanism like a phone is also felt to have some degree of activity (see Section 2.2 and Table 3.1). The oblique noun phrases in (58), by contrast, do not have CAUSE + act; those in (58)a–b are CAUSE − act and those in (58)d–k do not have CAUSE at all.

It appears therefore that *by means of* is restricted to noun phrases with CAUSE + act. But things are not that simple, because the oblique noun phrases in (60), which are Proper parts and have CAUSE + act, do not admit *by means of*.

    (60) a. *He peeled the apple by means of his left hand.
       b. *She shoved the plate away by means of her elbow.

It appears that *by means of* differs from other realizations of INSTR noun phrases in that it somehow highlights the instrument, stressing its active, independent involvement. Presumably, this is why *by means of* is limited to CAUSE + act. The Tools in (57) can be viewed as, in some sense, independent of the Agent and as having CAUSE + act like the Agent. But in (60) the Agent has CAUSE + act only by virtue of its Proper part – how else can one act except by one's limbs? – and it would be strange to regard both the Agent and its Proper part as independent causes.

That *by means of* highlights the instrument may also explain why this prepositional phrase is preferably used when attention is drawn to the instrument. Cutting meat is usually done with a knife (just as most activities are carried out with one's limbs), so *by means of* in (52)a sounds somewhat stilted. With non-standard instruments, as in (52)b–c, this prepositional phrase seems more appropriate.

Sentences with Means of transport as object of *by means of* also sound odd, although they, too, have CAUSE + act.

    (61) a. ??She came home by means of a plane.
       b. ??She went to town by means of a car.

The reason for this seems to be different. The preferred construction here is *by plane* and *by car*, and when this is replaced by *by means of* and its object it sounds very awkward. Note that by adding a modifier, as in (62), the sentence becomes much better. This is because the alternative with *by* is not preferable; more on this in Section 4.6.

    (62) a.   She came home by means of a specially chartered plane.
       b. ??She came home by a specially chartered plane.

4.5 Linkings of noun phrases having INSTR *and* MANN

A further complication arises with noun phrases that have the feature MANN in addition to INSTR. These give rise to a conflict of linking rules. In (47) we saw that *with patience*, also having MANN, can be paraphrased by *patiently* and by *in a patient manner*. Presumably this is why the linkings with *use/using* and *by means of*, which are appropriate only for INSTR, result in odd-sounding sentences.

> (63) a.   Bob solved the jigsaw puzzle with patience.
>   b.   ?Bob used patience to solve the jigsaw puzzle.
>   c.   *Bob solved the jigsaw puzzle by means of patience.

That there is some degree of INSTR here is attested to by the following sentence where patience appears alongside the hammer in doing the job (Nilsen 1973: 30, quoting an unpublished paper by Ash):

> (64) With hammer, nails, wood, and patience you can build a table.

The greater the strength of the feature INSTR relative to that of MANN, the more acceptable formulations with *use . . . to* and *by means of* will be. In (63), *patience* is primarily MANN and only to some extent INSTR; that is, the feature MANN has much greater strength than INSTR, and paraphrases with *use . . . to* and *by means of* sound odd. Now contrast (63) with (65)–(66). Force and kind words are more of an instrument than patience is, and therefore the relatively weak MANN does not obviate paraphrases with *use*, as shown in (65)–(66). Here again, *by means of* is more restricted.

> (65) a.   Ann grabbed Don's arm with force.
>   b.   Ann used force to grab Don's arm.
>   c.   ??Ann grabbed Don's arm by means of force.

> (66) a.   You ought to persuade him with kind words.
>   b.   You ought to use kind words to persuade him.
>   c.   ??You ought to persuade him by means of kind words.

Interestingly, (65)c and (66)c sound somewhat better than (58), although they, too, have CAUSE − act. Perhaps Abstract instruments are conceived of as having some activity after all, and our analysis in Section 2.2 should accordingly be amended.

4.6 Other linkings of INSTR *noun phrases*

When the INSTR noun phrase refers to a Means of transport or Means of communication it may be expressed by a *by*-phrase. Examples are the sentences in (7) and (11), repeated here (see also Quirk *et al.*, 1985, Section 5.45).

(7) a. She came home by plane.
    b. She went to town by car.

(11) a. We informed him of the accident by phone.
     b. They sent the message by satellite.
     c. He was summoned by airmail.

However, this statement needs to be qualified. First, it should be noted that, while the *by*-phrase is the preferred construction for Means of transport and communication, it is by no means the only one; other instrumental expressions, though awkward, may often be admissible:

(67) a. She went home with a plane/a car.
     b. She used a plane to go home.
     c. We informed him of the accident, using a phone.

See also (57)c–d.

Second, the *by*-phrase is indicated only when the noun phrase is not modified by an adjective or otherwise. For Means of transport this is shown in (68)b–c. With such modifiers, the sentence has to be formulated – like other types of instruments – with *with*, *by means of*, or *use*; see (68)d–f.

(68) a. She went to Paris by plane.
     b. ??She went to Paris by a private plane.
     c. ??She went to Paris by the company's plane.
     d. She went to Paris with a private/the company's plane.
     e. She went to Paris by means of a private/the company's plane.
     f. She used a private/the company's plane to go to Paris.

The same holds true for Means of communication.

(69) a. We informed him of the accident by phone.
     b. They transmitted the message by radio/letter.
     c. ??We informed him of the accident by a portable phone.
     d. ??They transmitted the message by John's new radio.
     e. *They transmitted the message by (an) elaborate letter.
     f. They transmitted the message with/by means of a portable radio/John's new radio/an elaborate letter.

Means of transport differ from Means of communication in respect to the productivity of the *by*-phrase construction. The *by*-phrase is limited to a small number of commonly used Means of transport.

(70) a. She came home by car/train/boat/foot.
     b. *She came home by roller skates/surf board/parachute.

For Means of communication, by contrast, the construction is productive.

(71) They transmitted the message by radio/letter/fax/satellite/electronic mail/ ...

One can imagine using the phrase *send the parcel by bleepost*, should a service by this name become available.

Instead of *by*, some Means of communication and transport may take *via*:

(72) a. They went to China via plane.
　　 b. I sent the message via airmail/telephone.
　　 c. I went to China via Japan.

As shown in (72)c, this preposition is not limited to Means of transport and communication. The *Oxford English Dictionary* (second edition) has a 1977 entry: "... concluded via contracts, attorney ...."

There are some isolated instances of INSTR noun phrases that are neither Means of transport nor of communication and are linked to a *by*-phrase, as in (73). The INSTR noun phrase in (73)b is an Abstract instrument.

(73) a. This has been knitted by hand/machine.
　　 b. The news was spread by word of mouth.
　　 c. I know this by experience.

The use of *by* in passives will be discussed in the next chapter.

Noun phrases with INSTR of the type Ingredient may be objects of the preposition *out of*:

(74) a. They built the house out of bricks.
　　 b. The farmer baked bread out of white flour.

When a noun phrase is both Comitative – due to the feature INSTR – and Locative, a locative preposition may be preferable. Examples are (75)a–b, where the noun phrase refers to Means of transport, and (75)c, where it refers to a Tool:

(75) a. They shipped the merchandise on a raft.
　　 b. I am carrying the milk in a pail.
　　 c. We made ice cubes in the freezer.

Finally, there are a few verbs that take direct objects that are INSTR. These refer to body parts (Jespersen, 1933: 109):

(76) a. Mary nodded her head.
　　 b. She shrugged her shoulder.
　　 c. He pointed his forefinger at Arthur.
　　 d. He struck his hand upon his knee.

The direct object in (77)a has also been analyzed as Instrument, in view of the near-synonymous (77)b.

(77) a. He hit the stick against the fence.
    b. He hit the fence with the stick.

However, as already noted (Chapter 2, Section 8), two sentences may have the same meaning and yet have different case assignments, in accordance with their syntactic structure. An alternative to the customary analysis is that *the stick* in (77)a is the affected object (consider that the stick, too, gets hit), as it is in (78).

(78) He threw the stick against the fence.

In stating linking rules for INSTR phrases we have had to resort to some of the types of Instrument discussed in Section 2.2: Proper part, Ingredient, and Means of transport and of communication. In accordance with our Principle of Linguistic Relevance these will therefore be part of our system. Perhaps they should be formalized as features, but this is an issue of secondary importance.

4.7 Without-*phrases*

A sentence with a *with*-phrase can often be negated by substituting *without* for *with*, and this does not result in a change of feature composition. The oblique noun phrases in (79) are ACCOMP + distr, INSTR, and MANN, respectively.

(79) a. Linda ate spaghetti with/without Burt.
    b. They tried to eat spaghetti with/without a spoon.
    c. They ate up all the spaghetti with/without great effort.

Without is ruled out for non-comitative noun phrases (see Section 3.2).

(80) a. The river teems with/*without fish.
    b. He finds fault with/*without her.
    c. He started with/*without fright.
    d. The burden of proof lies with/*without the accused.
    e. They supply us with/*without rations.
    f. It's all the same with/*without me.
    g. He dealt with/*without the matter.

Substitutability of *with* by *without* might seem to provide us with a convenient test for the C-case; however, such a test would fail on two counts: (i) There are non-comitative *with*-phrases where such substitution is possible; and (ii) There are sentences with a C-case noun phrase where it is not.

There are instances where the oblique noun phrase is not in the C-case, because it is not an argument of the predicate verb (cf. (1)), and nevertheless *without* can substitute for *with*:

(81) He is a man with/without strong feelings.

When the predicate inherently requires a noun phrase with ACCOMP
— distr, as in (82)a–b, the latter cannot be negated by substituting *without* for
with.

(82) a. Lionel wrestled with/*without the thug.
b. Len corresponds with/*without his uncle.

That (83)b is unacceptable is perhaps due to (83)a being idiomatic.

(83) a. She walked with the tide.
b. *She walked without the tide.

In (84) *without* requires an interpretation that differs from that for *with*. In
(84)a the *with*-phrase has a noun phrase that has INSTR, whereas *without* in
(84)b takes an object that has ACCOMP (this, at least, is the preferred
interpretation).

(84) a. The car scraped the tree with its fender.
b. The car scraped the tree without its fender.

In (85) *without* is ruled out by pragmatic factors.

(85) Mix this paint with/*without yellow paint.

4.8 Do we need a C-case?

Most of the linking rules discussed in the foregoing have been stated in terms
of features: ACCOMP is linked with a prepositional phrase with *together with*,
INSTR with *use*, *by means of*, and so on. One might argue therefore that these
features are all that is needed to state linguistic regularities, and that the
construct of a C-case is superfluous and – following the Principle of
Linguistic Relevance (Chapter 1, Section 6.3) – should not be included in the
system.

There is one linking rule that applies to every noun phrase in the C-case,
whatever its feature composition: it can be expressed by a prepositional
phrase with *with*. True, this rule could also have been stated for every
comitative feature separately, and the concept of a C-case is therefore not
indispensable. But in view of the, albeit minor, simplification of rules
afforded by the introduction of a C-case, and considering the large overlap
between noun phrases of various comitative features (Section 2.5) and their
affinity in meaning (Section 3.1), it seems advisable to introduce such a case.
The same issue might be raised in regard to the A-case, where the linking
rules could also have been stated, though less parsimoniously, in terms of
agentive features, their number and strengths. There can be no fixed and
principled guidelines as to what is to count as a case, and ultimately this is a
decision that rests with the theorist.

Table 3.3. *Sentences used in paraphrasability study*

Source sentence:
The pantomimist gave a show with the clown.
ACCOMP paraphrases.
conjoint subject:
The pantomimist and the clown gave a show.
interchange:
The clown with the pantomimist gave a show.
together:
The pantomimist, together with the clown, gave a show.
INSTR paraphrase.
use:
The pantomimist used the clown to give a show.

5. Studies of linking

In our rating studies in Chapter 1, Sections 2–3, we found that the cognitive notions Instrument, Accompaniment, and Manner may be present in a construction to different degrees. This raises the question of whether the corresponding features – ACCOMP, INSTR, and MANN – are also graded, or in other words, whether the fact that we perceive them to be a matter of degree is reflected in any linguistic phenomenon. According to the Principle of Linguistic Relevance, a feature is to be regarded as graded only if gradedness makes a linguistic difference (Chapter 1, Section 6.4).

The empirical studies reported in this section are relevant to this issue. In the preceding section, rules of linking have usually been stated in absolute terms: a feature can either be linked to a construction or it cannot. We now examine the question whether the graded structure of the notions Accompaniment and Instrument results in similarly graded linking rules for ACCOMP and INSTR.

Respondents were asked to judge the appropriateness of paraphrases of the *with*-phrases. The sentences were those for which ratings had been obtained in our previous study on the notions Accompaniment and Instrument (Chapter 1, Section 2).[12]

5.1 A paraphrasability study

5.1.1 Materials
There are various ways of paraphrasing sentences with comitative noun phrases (see Table 3.3):

(i) When the oblique noun phrase has ACCOMP, it may be conjoined with the subject (Section 4.1).

(ii) The oblique noun phrase having ACCOMP is interchanged with the subject noun phrase (Section 3.4).

(iii) When the oblique noun phrase has ACCOMP, *with* may be replaced by *together with* (Section 4.2).

(iv) When the oblique noun phrase has INSTR, *with* + noun phrase may be replaced by *use* + noun phrase + *to* (Section 4.4).

A study conducted in cooperation with Neta Bargai addressed itself to the question of whether the degree of paraphrasability mirrored the degree to which – according to our previous study – the notions Accompaniment and Instrument are expressed. These notions presumably parallel closely the features ACCOMP and INSTR as defined in Section 2.1, above.

5.1.2 Procedures

Four rating forms were prepared, one for each type of paraphrase. In each of the forms, the ten sentences deployed in our previous study (Chapter 1, Section 2.2; and shown also in Table 3.4, below) were each paired with their paraphrase.[13] The sequence of sentences was the same as that in the previous study.

Respondents were asked to indicate to what extent the two sentences were synonymous. Instructions were as follows:

> Please indicate for each of the following sentence pairs whether the two sentences – (a) and (b) – mean the same. Please circle one of the numbers from 1 (= yes, definitely mean the same) to 7 (= no, definitely do not mean the same).

The following sentence pair was given as an example of two sentences definitely having the same meaning:

(a) The book is under the newspaper.

(b) The newspaper is on top of the book.

Each respondent rated two of the forms. There are six ways of pairing off the four forms:

use and conjoint subject
use and *together*
use and "interchange"
conjoint subject and "interchange"
conjoint subject and *together*
"interchange" and *together*

There were thirty-six respondents, six for each of the above six pairings (with three of the six being given one of the sequences of forms – e.g., *use* before *together* – and three being given the other sequence, *together* before *use*). In all, then, each of the four paraphrase forms was filled out by eighteen respondents, and each was the first in the sequence for half the respondents and the second for the other half.

Table 3.4. *Median ratings of paraphrasability – conjoining and interchange*

	Paraphrase	
Source sentence	conjoining	interchange
1. The pantomimist gave a show with the clown.	1.50	5.00
2. The blind man crossed the street with his dog.	2.25	4.00
3. The engineer built the machine with an assistant.	2.75	5.50
4. The acrobat performed an act with an elephant.	4.50	6.17
5. The general captured the hill with a squad of paratroopers.	2.50	4.50
6. The officer caught the smuggler with a police dog.	3.17	6.50
7. The prisoner won the appeal with a highly paid lawyer.	3.50	5.90
8. The Nobel prize winner found the solution with a computer.	4.50	6.25
9. The sportsman hunted deer with a rifle.	5.90	6.86
10. The hoodlum broke the window with a stone.	6.25	6.60

Notes:
1 yes, definitely
7 no, definitely not

5.1.3 Results: (i) Conjoining and interchange

Table 3.4 presents the judgments of respondents on the degree to which two sentences are paraphrases of each other. The figures in the table are medians of the individual judgments.

The sequence of sentences in the table is that obtained in the rating studies of the first chapter, from the sentence best expressing the notion of Accompaniment to the one expressing it least. The ratings of paraphrasability by a conjoined subject correspond very closely to the rankings in our previous rating study; that is, the more a given sentence was judged to express the notion Accompaniment, the better a paraphrase of a conjoined sentence it was considered to be. Spearman rank–order correlations between these two ratings were high: 0.88.

The largest discrepancy between the ratings in the two studies was for sentence 4 (*The acrobat ... with an elephant*), the paraphrases of which were rated much lower than would be expected from the previously obtained ratings of the notion Accompaniment. The reason may be that the activities of a circus elephant in a show typically differ from those of an acrobat, and respondents might have felt that by conjoining *elephant* with *acrobat* this difference was ignored.

Sentences where the subject was interchanged with the oblique noun phrase were regarded as relatively poor paraphrases; see the high medians in Table 3.4. It seems that respondents were aware that in these paraphrases the emphasis was changed or that features of different strength were involved. Nevertheless, judgments of paraphrasability correlated highly with Accompaniment ratings, the Spearman rank–order correlation coefficient being 0.82. The correlation between the ratings in the two columns of Table 3.4 was 0.88.

Table 3.5. *Median ratings of paraphrasability* – together with *and* use to

Source sentence	Paraphrase	
	together with	*use to*
1. The pantomimist gave a show with the clown.	2.50	5.00
2. The blind man crossed the street with his dog.	1.14	3.50
3. The engineer built the machine with an assistant.	1.40	4.30
4. The acrobat performed an act with an elephant.	4.25	5.00
5. The general captured the hill with a squad of paratroopers.	2.75	2.50
6. The officer caught the smuggler with a police dog.	4.50	4.17
7. The prisoner won the appeal with a highly paid lawyer.	2.90	4.00
8. The Nobel prize winner found the solution with a computer.	3.50	2.50
9. The sportsman hunted deer with a rifle.	4.00	3.00
10. The hoodlum broke the window with a stone.	5.00	2.17

Notes:
1 yes, definitely
7 no, definitely not

5.1.4 Results: (ii) together with *and* use

Table 3.5 presents the median judgments of respondents concerning replacement of *with* by *together with* and by *use ... to*. The sequence of sentences in this table is the same as that in Table 3.4, that is, from the sentence best expressing the notion of Accompaniment to the one expressing it least.

The table shows that the more the sentence is regarded as expressing the notion of Accompaniment, the better paraphrases with *together with* were judged to be: the medians become larger as we move down the table, and the larger the score, the lower the paraphrasability. The Spearman rank–order correlation between these two variables was 0.73.

Conversely, the medians for *use ... to*, which expresses the notion of Instrument, become smaller as we move down the table. Recall that in the rating study reported in Chapter 1, ratings of Instrument were found to be inversely related to ratings of Accompaniment. The Spearman rank–order correlation of paraphrasability by *use ... to* and rating for Instrument was 0.78. That the correlation is not higher may be due to the pragmatic factors discussed in Section 4.4: *use* is not readily applied to humans (sentence 7) – with the possible exception of soldiers (sentence 5) – or even to animals (sentences 2, 4, and 6).

The findings of this study, then, reinforce the conclusions of the rating study in the first chapter. The question of whether a given notion is represented in a sentence does not have a simple yes-or-no answer; rather, this is a matter of degree. Furthermore, as in the rating study, there was a partial overlap of categories: one and the same sentence can exemplify two different notions, and rate high on both; see, for instance, sentences 2, 5, and 8 of Table 3.5.

Table 3.6. *Acceptability of Arabic prepositions*

Source sentence	Acceptability with	
	ma'a (ACCOMP)	*biwasita* (INSTR)
1. The pantomimist gave a show with the clown.	1.27	3.61
2. The blind man crossed the street with his dog.	2.20	2.20
3. The engineer built the machine with an assistant.	1.32	4.64
4. The acrobat performed an act with an elephant.	1.81	2.90
5. The general captured the hill with a squad of paratroopers.	1.27	2.42
6. The officer caught the smuggler with a police dog.	3.81	2.00
7. The prisoner won the appeal with a highly paid lawyer.	3.42	2.06
8. The Nobel prize winner found the solution with a computer.	4.62	1.17
9. The sportsman hunted deer with a rifle.	2.75	2.00
10. The hoodlum broke the window with a stone.	4.68	1.60

Notes:
1 appropriate
5 inappropriate

5.2 An acceptability study

In English (and in several other languages), a noun phrase in the C-case, irrespective of its feature composition, can appear (with few exceptions; see Section 4.6) in a *with*-phrase. There are languages that have different prepositions for INSTR and ACCOMP. Thus, Arabic has a preposition for Accompaniment, *ma'a* (meaning, roughly, "with"), and the preposition *biwasita* for Instrument. The question addressed in this study was whether in such a language the gradient of Accompaniment and Instrument found in Chapter 1, Section 2.2, would be reflected in both prepositions.

In this study, respondents were asked to judge the acceptability of the Arabic paraphrases.[14]

5.2.1 Procedures
Separate rating forms were prepared for each of the above prepositions in Arabic. The sequence in which the sentences were presented to respondents was the same as in the rating study. Respondents were native speakers of Arabic. Each respondent was given one of the two forms. Instructions were worded as follows (translated from Arabic):

> Please indicate for each of the following sentences whether it is formulated correctly, by circling one of the five points on the scale from Appropriate to Inappropriate.

Data were obtained from twenty-three respondents to the form with the ACCOMP preposition and from twenty-four respondents to the form with the INSTR preposition.

5.2.2 Results

Acceptability ratings of the two paraphrases are presented in Table 3.6, where the sequence of sentences is the same as that in Tables 3.3 and 3.4, that is, from the sentence rated as most clearly expressing the notion of Accompaniment to the one rated as expressing it least. It will be seen from the table that rankings obtained in the previous rating study correspond very closely to those of the acceptability ratings (the present study); the Spearman rank–order correlation for ACCOMP preposition (*ma'a*) and Accompaniment ratings was 0.78, and for INSTR preposition (*biwasita*) with Instrument ratings was 0.93. (The ratings for these two prepositions are of course negatively correlated: −0.82.)

It will be observed that sentences 2, 4, 5, 6, 7, and 9 are judged to be fairly acceptable with both prepositions. This finding parallels those of the previous rating study, where a certain degree of overlap of the notions Accompaniment and Instrument was found for sentences 2–7.

5.3 Kinds of Instruments

In conclusion, attention is drawn to a serendipitous finding in the studies reported in the preceding, as well as in the rating study of Chapter 1.

The list of ten sentences included two which were thought to express the prototypical Instrument: sentences 9 and 10 in the above tables (... *with a rifle* and ... *with a stone*). Inspection of the results, however, shows that they differ in respect to instrumentality. In Table 3.6, sentence 9, ... *with a rifle*, was rated as somewhat more acceptable with the ACCOMP preposition and somewhat less acceptable with the INSTR preposition than sentence 10, ... *with a stone*. Parallel results were obtained with native speakers of English. Paraphrase by *together with* is less objectionable for ... *with a rifle* than for ... *with a stone*, and paraphrase by *use* is better for ... *with a stone* than for ... *with a rifle* (Table 3.5). Finally, in the study in Chapter 1, *a stone* appeared to be more of an instrument than *a rifle*, as reflected by ratings of Accompaniment as well as of Instrument (but this effect was very slight).

It appears, then, that a simple tool like a stone is more INSTR than a relatively more complex mechanism like a rifle, a point that will be taken up again in the next chapter.

6. Conclusions

Three additional features were introduced in this chapter: INSTR, ACCOMP, and MANN. These features frequently co-occur and merge into one another, which is why they have been taken to define a new case category: the C-case. The C-case is linked to the *with*-phrase, but there are other possibilities of expressing it, depending on the feature composition. Of the two noun phrases in a sentence that have ACCOMP, one will become the subject if it has the required agentive features. A classification has been proposed of noun phrases having INSTR, and some of the classes may have specific linking effects.

4   Non-comitative instruments

> The correct first assumption is that speakers mean *what* they say –
> the trick is to find out the "what" on the basis of the language, not of
> ontology.
>
> Dwight Bolinger

The title of this chapter may strike one as a misnomer, because the feature
INSTR (Instrument) is a sufficient condition for assignment of the Comitative,
or C-case (Chapter 3, Section 3.1). However, the title refers to the notion
Instrument, not to the feature of that name. As will be seen in the following,
there are tools and appliances to which this notion pertains and to which the
feature INSTR is not assigned. It will also be shown that features may be
determined in part by the linguistic structure of the sentence.

1. The "Instrument" in subject position

Sentences like (1) are usually taken to show that, in the absence of an agent,
the Instrument may be realized as sentence subject; the Instrument follows
the Agent in the subject selection hierarchy.

(1) The knife cut the cake.

It appears, however, that this analysis is flawed. Note, first, that contrary to
the specification of the subject selection hierarchy, not every instrument can
become subject. A noun phrase that has the feature INSTR can become subject
only if, like *the knife* in (1), it also has the feature CAUSE.[1] The types of
Instrument that we have called Secondary tool, Ingredient, Ancillary
instrument, and Instrument-undergoer do not have CAUSE (Chapter 3,
Section 2.2) and, as shown in (2), do not permit subjectivization.

(2) a.   The boy drank the juice with a straw.
     a′. *A straw drank the juice.
     b.   They built the house with bricks.
     b′. *Bricks built the house.
     c.   I changed the light bulb with a ladder.
     c′. *A ladder changed the light bulb.
     d.   The clown juggled with six balls.
     d′. *Six balls juggled.
     e.   The biologist experimented with some rabbits.
     e′. *Some rabbits experimented.

Assignment of CAUSE to a noun phrase depends of course on the verb. Thus, while bricks cannot build a house, (2)b', they certainly can break a window.[2]

That the feature CAUSE is a necessary condition for subjectivization of instruments suggests that it is this feature, which is a diagnostic of the A-case (i.e., the extended Agent), that licenses subjectivization of *the knife* in (1). I propose therefore that noun phrases referring to instruments in subject position are A-case. The instrumental noun phrases in (2) cannot become subjects because, lacking CAUSE, they are not eligible for the A-case.

Some authors voice similar views. Jakobson (1936/1971: 36) notes that in Russian sentences like "The lorry killed the child," where the inanimate noun is in the nominative, there is a "gewisse[r] Beigeschmack der Personifizierung," that is, they smack of personification. Fillmore (1971) notes the similarity between Agent and Instrument and suggests that both may comprise a hyper-case. Simmons (1973: 63–113) introduces the notion causal-actant which collapses the Instrument and the Agent. Cruse (1973: 16) states that "inanimate objects can, as it were, acquire a temporary 'agentivity' by virtue of their kinetic (or other) energy." Grimes (1978) speaks of the "agentive roles" Agent, Instrument, and Force. Allerton (1982: 68) views certain types of instruments in subject position as subvarieties of the Agent. Quirk, Greenbaum, Leech, and Svartvik (1985: 701) state that "[b]oth agentive and instrument may be said to denote the semantic role of AGENCY." Jackendoff (1990: 142–43, 259) observes: "For the most part, instrumental subjects (*The key opened the door*) are grammatically just inanimate Agents."

A consequence of the close relation between Instrument and Agent is the fact that (as mentioned earlier) the same suffix, *-ant*, serves for nouns denoting Agents – e.g., *participant*, *applicant* – and instruments: *deodorant*, *disinfectant* (Marchand, 1969: 251–52).

The data in (2) are awkward for the hypothesis of a subject selection hierarchy. The *with*-phrases in (2)a–c are clearly instrumental, and if the hypothesis predicts that the Instrument follows the Agent in the hierarchy, then (2)a'–c' should be acceptable. The hypothesis can only be maintained by introducing the condition that it pertains only to instruments having the feature CAUSE, in other words, that only agent-like instruments can become subjects. From there it is only a small step to my proposal that when an instrument appears in subject position, as in (1), it is in the A-case.

The subject of (1) refers to an instrument. Does it, then, have the feature INSTR (in addition to CAUSE)? *The knife* has the same function in (3)a as in (3)b, and one might be tempted therefore to accord to this noun phrase the same feature in both. Once an instrument, always an instrument.

(3) a. The knife cut the cake. (=(1))
     b. Jack cut the cake with the knife.

But this reasoning takes into account only the reality that is described by the sentence, and not how this reality is conceptualized by the sentence. As we have repeatedly had occasion to observe, when two sentences describe the same reality, the corresponding noun phrases do not necessarily have the same cases. What counts in assigning cases and features to noun phrases is the relation of the latter with the predicate. Thus, in (4) *a little statuette* is not INSTR, in spite of its being used as an instrument.

(4) Felix bought a little statuette. He used it as a paperweight.

That a knife serves as an instrument, both in general and in the event portrayed by (3)b, does not commit us to assign the feature INSTR to *the knife* in (3)a. Here the noun phrase has a different syntactic function. Due to the feature CAUSE, *the knife* in (3)a is A-case and hence the sentence subject, and the fact that it serves as an instrument is part of our knowledge of the world but is not expressed in the sentence.[3]

The proposed analysis also accords with intuitive judgments. In a study with preschool children, Braine and Wells (1978; Experiment V) found that the instrument – in, e.g., *The fan blows the curtain* and *The fire heats the pot* – is conceived of as an "actor."

The subjectivized instrument, then, does not have INSTR. This parallels the analysis of other C-case noun phrases:

(5) a. Linda ate spaghetti with Burt.
     b. Linda ate spaghetti.

Linda in (5)a has the feature CAUSE and is A-case as well as C-case, and the same may be true of *Burt* (Chapter 3, Section 3.4). In (5)b *Linda* also has the feature CAUSE (and is in the A-case, which makes it eligible for subject position), but it no longer has ACCOMP.[4] Even if we know (from the linguistic or extralinguistic context) that Burt joined Linda, the sentence *by itself* does not mention that anyone accompanied her.

2. Constraints on subjects

Our analysis of subjectivization enables us to explain certain linguistic phenomena, which are incompatible with the hypothesis of a subject selection hierarchy.

2.1 The deliberation constraint

2.1.1 The constraint

The subject selection hierarchy ought to apply to Instruments across the board, but in fact, subjectivization of the instrument is subject to severe constraints. One of these is discussed at length in Schlesinger (1989), from where the following examples are taken or adapted. Compare (6)a'–b' with (7)a–b.

(6) a.   He was cutting sandalwood with the chisel.
    a'. The chisel was cutting sandalwood.
    b.   He was scribbling fast with the pen.
    b'. The pen was scribbling fast.

(7) a.   *The chisel was cutting sandalwood into a statuette.
    b.   *The pen was scribbling a poem.

Why are the sentences in (7) odd? Intuitively, this is because one cannot entrust inanimate objects with creative activities that involve deliberation. Such lowly activities as cutting and scribbling in (6) may be ascribed to chisels and pens, but when the result is a work of art, we balk: the deliberation required is too great. One can speak of inanimates as agents in an extended, somehow metaphorical sense, but when too much sophistication enters the picture, the metaphor breaks down; we are loth to let our imagination run wild. This has been called the **deliberation constraint**.

At the first blush this account does not seem to square well with our analysis of the subjects in (6). If a noun phrase has the feature CAUSE it is eligible for the Λ-case and for subjecthood, whether or not what is predicated of it demands deliberation. An explanation of this constraint requires a hypothesis regarding an effect of linguistic structure on the way the message is conceived.

2.1.2 Semantic saturation

The **semantic saturation** hypothesis states that the syntactic function of a noun phrase results in assigning to it features that are typical of this function. Thus, when a given entity is encoded as subject, it will be conceived of as more agent-like than when it is encoded as a noun phrase having some other syntactic function. In other words, there is a "drift" toward more central members of the category: a subject noun phrase will be saturated by the semantic features of the prototypical agent.

This hypothesis conflicts with the conception of a clean division between the formal linguistic structure and the structure of the meanings conveyed by them. Instead, the specific linguistic structures in which messages are encoded affect the hearer's conception of the messages through the semantic saturation process.

The possibility of linguistic structure influencing the message has so far received only scant attention. The literature contains only passing references to it, like the one by Talmy (1985b: 101) that subjecthood may tend to confer "some initiatory or instigative characteristics." Van Oosten (1977: 460–61) states that "when the patient is made the subject of the sentence it, or a property it has, is understood to be responsible for the action of the verb"; responsibility is a typical property of the agent.[5] Quine (1973: 86) writes: "Red is a color" has the same form as "Fido is a dog," which suggests that

somehow colors are bodies; and: "Language thrives on analogical formation
... As one came increasingly to think in referential ways, one came to
objectify colors along with bodies on the strength of superficial grammatical
parallels."

2.1.3 An explanation of the constraint

Returning to (6)a′ and (6)b′, we note that, due to semantic saturation, the
subjects – *the chisel* and *the pen* – are endowed with the feature CONTROL,
which is found in prototypical agents. The same feature would be assigned
also to the subjects in (7). However, the activities referred to here are so
sophisticated that the degree of CONTROL required to perform them is very
large, and it strikes us as incongruous to ascribe so much CONTROL to
inanimate objects like chisels and pens. We are ready to put up with only a
slight measure of metaphorical extension, and this is exceeded in (7).[6]

In (6), by contrast, little CONTROL has to be ascribed to the subjects,
because the activities they perform are very simple: cutting sandalwood and
scribbling (and our definition of CONTROL in Chapter 2, Section 2.2.1, does
not confine this feature to animates). Another constraint that may be
explained by referring to semantic saturation of the subject with CONTROL is
discussed in the following section.

2.2 The mediation constraint

In Section 2.1 we have seen that an inanimate Agent may be accorded
CONTROL. However, it cannot be said to use an instrument in performing the
activity. An inanimate entity wielding an instrument is too strange an idea to
pass as a metaphorical expression. When an inanimate entity is in subject
position, the sentence can therefore not contain an instrumental *with*-phrase.
This "mediation constraint" (Schlesinger, 1989) holds both for natural
forces, as in (8)a, and for tools and appliances, as in (8)b.

> (8) a.   The wind broke the window.
>   a′. *The wind broke the window with a twig.
>   b.   The tape recorder made an announcement.
>   b′. *The tape recorder made an announcement with two
>   loudspeakers.

For (8)a′ to be acceptable, the wind would have to have CONTROL not just over
breaking the window, but over *break the window with a twig*, and this would
require an inordinately high degree of CONTROL.

Moreover, even in the absence of a *with*-phrase, the sentence may be
unacceptable when the activity is understood to have been carried out with an
instrument:

> (9) a.   He made a hole in the wall with a hammer and a chisel.
>   b.   *The hammer made a hole in the wall with a chisel.

    c. *The hammer made a hole in the wall.
    d. The chisel made a hole in the wall.

(10) a. The hunter wounded the deer with a bow and arrows.
    b. *A bow wounded the deer with arrows.
    c. *A bow wounded the deer.
    d. Arrows wounded the deer.

Example (9)c is acceptable only in the sense that one hits the hammer against the wall and damages it. Sentence (10)c is acceptable only when taken to mean that the impact of the bow – not the arrow – wounded the deer. But on the reading suggested by (9)a and (10)a, respectively – namely, that the hole was made by means of a hammer hitting a chisel and the deer was wounded by the bow propelling arrows – (9)c and (10)c are unacceptable, even though no instrument is mentioned.[7]

An "instrument" in subject position, then, cannot wield another instrument. An exception is the case where the latter is a Proper part of the former or is integral to its operation, as in (11). Here less CONTROL is required than in the case of the "use" of an external instrument. Moreover, the oblique noun phrase has the feature MANN to a certain extent. The mediation constraint therefore does not apply here:

(11) a. The bike hit the wall with its front wheel.
    b. The car scraped the tree with its fender.
    c. The apparatus bores holes with a laser beam.
    d. The movie frightened him with its horrible ending.

That this exception applies to "proper part" in an extended sense is shown by (12) (from Siewierska, 1991: 68), where the sandstorm may be said to have control over the sand or dust it carries with it.

(12) The sandstorm covered everything in its wake with a centimeter of dust.

An alternative explanation of the mediation constraint in (8)–(11) is discussed and refuted in Schlesinger (1989).

2.3 Semantic saturation and contraction

The two constraints discussed in the foregoing may be due to a feature assigned to the subject by semantic saturation; the constraint accordingly results indirectly from the syntactic structure of the sentence. Another possibility is that it is an indirect consequence of the lexical entry of the verb in the sentence.[8] The lexical entries for the verbs *cut* and *scribble* prescribe that there is an argument (the "cutter" and "scribbler," respectively) with the feature CONTROL, and this feature is contracted by the instrument (Chapter 2, Section 3.3.1). In (6) only a low strength of CONTROL is required, and the sentence is acceptable. In (7), by contrast, much greater CONTROL is required by the activity, and by no stretch of imagination can we grant this to the inanimate tool.

A similar explanation may be given for the mediation constraint: When natural forces and inanimate objects contract the feature CONTROL, it seems incongruous that CONTROL should be had over an activity that involves the use of an instrument or causing others to behave in a certain way.

Semantic saturation and contraction, then, are two processes that may converge in producing the same constraints. But the contraction account does not fit all instances of constraints equally well. It would be somewhat forced to assume that all the verbs in the examples in Section 2.2 have lexical entries that specify the feature CONTROL. For instance, it is common for inanimate objects to inflict injuries, and therefore the lexical entry for *wound* presumably does not have an argument with CONTROL, which may then be contracted by *a bow* in (10)b–c. Here the semantic saturation account has to be resorted to.

3. Degree of CONTROL in the inanimate subject

The constraints discussed in the preceding depend on the nature of the activity carried out by the entity referred to by the subject. Furthermore, the acceptability of subjectivization of the instrument is a function of the nature of the instrument.

3.1 Four determinants

There appear to be at least four determinants of the acceptability of sentences with subjectivized instruments.

3.1.1 Complexity

At the end of the previous chapter it was noted that a complex tool (like, e.g., a rifle) is regarded as less of an instrument than a more simply constructed one, when the complexity is relevant to the activity mentioned. This is because a complex tool is viewed as functioning in a sense more independently, having more CONTROL, and thus being more agent-like (Schlesinger, 1989). The first sentence in each pair in (13) is therefore decidedly better than the second:

> (13) a.   The crane picked up the crate.
>   a'. The fork picked up the potatoes.
>   b.   The piper plane sprayed the fields.
>   b'. The spray gun sprayed the fields.
>   c.   The dishwasher cleaned the dishes.
>   c'. The rag cleaned the dishes.

3.1.2 Essential property

The more the success of the activity depends on properties of the instrument, the more the latter can be credited with CONTROL. In each of the following pairs the first sentence sounds much better than the second.

(14) a.   The magic key opened the door.
     a'.   The key opened the door.
     b.   This pencil draws very thin lines.
     b'.   The pencil draws lines.
     c.   This spray kills cockroaches instantly.
     c'.   The spray killed the cockroaches.

3.1.3 Independence

To the extent that an instrument can perform the activity without the intervention of a human agent, it will be assigned more CONTROL and be more suitable as sentence subject. The sentences in (15) sound much better than those in (16):

(15) a.   The clock was ticking so loudly that it woke the baby.
     b.   The letter of introduction opened all doors to him.

(16) a.   The stick hit the horse.
     b.   The pencil drew lines.

Operation of this factor often coincides with that of the complexity factor. The dishwasher in (13)c, for instance, may function independently after being switched on.

3.1.4 Saliency

The greater the saliency of the instrument relative to the human agent, the greater the CONTROL that can be assigned to it. This factor overlaps to a large extent with that of Independence: the more an instrument can operate independently of a human agent, the more salient it will be relative to this agent. Saliency (without Independence) is responsible for the difference in acceptability between the following two sentences:

(17) a.   *The baton conducted Copland's symphony.
     b.   This is the baton that conducted Copland's symphony on its opening night.

The deliberation constraint rules out (17)a, but (17)b (which might be said, for instance, by a guide in a museum) is acceptable, because attention is drawn away from the conductor to the baton.

3.2 An empirical study – Method

To obtain further empirical evidence for the operation of the four variables discussed in the preceding, a psycholinguistic study was conducted. Respondents judged to what extent each of these variables was involved in active sentences with animate subjects, as in (18)a. Another group of respondents were asked to judge the acceptability of the corresponding sentences, with the instruments as subjects, as in (18)b.

> (18) a. The waiter washed the dishes with a dishwasher.
>   b. The dishwasher washed the dishes.

The hypothesis was that the greater the rated complexity, saliency, etc. of the instrument in sentences like (18)a, the greater the acceptability of sentences like (18)b. This study was conducted in cooperation with Dalia Kelly.

3.2.1 Generation of sentences

To avoid the possibility of the investigator inadvertently biasing the results by choosing sentences that would bear out the hypothesis, it was decided to obtain the Hebrew sentence material used in the study from Hebrew speakers who were naive as to the hypothesis tested.

For the purpose of eliciting sentences, four types of forms were prepared, one for each of the variables Saliency, Essential property, Independence, and Complexity. Respondents were asked to construct sentences having the structure agent-action-instrument and which expressed one of these notions to various degrees. Instructions for each of these forms briefly explained the relevant notion, giving example sentences. Here is the gist of the instructions:
For *Saliency*:

> The farmer ploughed the field with a wooden plough.
> The farmer ploughed the field with a tractor.

> These two sentences differ, among others, in the degree to which the instrument is salient relative to the human being. The tractor is more salient relative to the human being than the plough.
> Please write down sentences in which the instrument is salient. Please try to compose sentences on various topics.

After completion of this task, the informant was asked to write down sentences in which there was little saliency of the instrument.

For the other three factors, instructions were similar, with the necessary changes for the notion involved:
For *Essential property*:

> The janitor opened the secret door with a key which he took from his pocket.
> The thief drove the horses with a whip.

In the first sentence the success of the activity is dependent on the specific character of the key (a different key would not have opened the door). In the second sentence this is not the case. Almost any kind of whip would permit the action to take place.

Another example:

The gardener exterminated the bacteria with a spray.
The maid cleaned the house with water and soap.

For *Independence*:

He washed the dishes with a dishwasher.
The police stopped traffic with a barrier.

In both sentences the activity (washing dishes and stopping traffic) can continue without the assistance of human beings. The one who operates the machine can leave the room; his presence is not requested for washing the dishes; and likewise in the case of the second sentence.

For *Complexity*:

He washed the dishes with a dishwasher.
He washed the dishes with a rag.

The instrument in the first sentence is more complex and sophisticated than the instrument in the second sentence.

3.2.2 *Selection of sentences*

The next step in sentence selection was to ask "judges" to go over the list of sentences generated in the first stage, delete any sentence that did not contain an agent, an action, and an instrument, and, where necessary, to reformulate those that did, so as to conform to the agent–action–instrument structure. Each of the sentences generated in the first stage was given to two judges, who screened them independently of each other.

Eighteen students of the Psychology Department participated in the first two stages, as part of their course requirement.

The following guidelines served for the selection of the final list of sentences from those generated and screened in the previous stages.

If one of the two judges struck a sentence off the list, it was omitted.

If the judges suggested two different formulations of a sentence, the clearer, less ambiguous formulation was adopted. For example, the Hebrew preposition *be'emtsaut* ("by means of") was preferred to the prefix *b-* ("by"), because the latter might be interpreted as a locative preposition.

When a stylistic change was suggested by one of the judges, it was adopted, even when the other judge did not suggest any change.

Deletion of a subordinate clause was accepted, even if suggested by only one of the judges.

Of two very similar sentences proposed by the two judges (e.g., *He washed his socks* and *He washed the washing*), only one (arbitrarily chosen) was retained.

3.2.3 *Instrument rating form*

Four rating forms were constructed, one for each of the variables Saliency, Essential property, Independence, and Complexity. Each of the rating forms included thirty Hebrew sentences randomly chosen from the lists resulting from the three stages described in the foregoing. Instructions asked the respondents to rate each sentence in respect to one of the above variables. The meaning of each of the variables was illustrated by means of two example sentences. Ratings were on a five-point scale:

> Saliency: to what extent the instrument is salient relative to the person mentioned in the sentence (1 – not salient at all, 5 – very salient).
>
> Essential property: to what extent the success of the activity depends on the specific properties of the instrument (1 – not dependent at all, 5 – very dependent).
>
> Independence: to what extent the presence of a person is required during the entire activity (1 – necessary, 5 – not necessary at all).
>
> Complexity: to what extent the instrument is complex and sophisticated (1 – not complex at all, 5 – very complex and sophisticated).

The sequence of the sentences in the rating forms was randomly determined.

3.2.4 *Acceptability rating forms*

In these forms, sentences without agents were rated. The original sentences were reformulated; for instance, for the Acceptability scale, (19)a was rephrased without agent, as in (19)b.

> (19) a. The biologist examined the virus with a microscope.
>   b. The microscope examined the virus.

Four rating forms were constructed, one for each of the variables Saliency, Essential property, Independence, and Complexity. Each of the rating forms included the thirty sentences of the corresponding Instrument-rating forms, reformulated in the manner indicated above. Instructions asked the respondents to judge the acceptability of each sentence on a scale from 1 (totally unacceptable) to 5 (definitely acceptable).

The sequence of the sentences in the Acceptability scale was the same as that in the Instrument-rating form.

Table 4.1. *Correlations between Instrument and Acceptability ratings*

| | First study | Replication study | |
		Form 1	Form 2
Saliency	0.60	0.49	0.21
Essential property	0.38	0.69	0.11
Independence	0.61	0.61	0.60
Complexity	0.47	0.38	0.27

3.2.5 *Respondents*

The rating forms were administered to groups of undergraduate students at The Hebrew University, Jerusalem, whose native language was Hebrew or who had been speaking Hebrew for at least fifteen years. The Instrument rating form for Saliency was taken by twenty-four respondents, that for Essential property by twenty-five respondents, that for Independence by twenty-two and that for Complexity by twenty-seven respondents. The numbers of respondents taking the Acceptability rating forms were twenty, twenty-four, twenty-four, and twenty-two for the Saliency, Essential property, Independence, and Complexity forms, respectively.

3.3 *Results of the empirical study*

Pearson correlation coefficients were computed for the mean ratings of the thirty sentences on the Saliency Instrument-scale and their means on the Saliency Acceptability-scale. The same was done for each of the other three variables, Essential property, Independence, and Complexity. The correlation coefficients are given in the left-hand column of Table 4.1. All correlations were statistically significant at the 0.01 level.

3.4 *A replication study*

In the previous study, each of the four variables was studied separately, the sentences in each form pertaining to one variable only. In the second study we used rating forms containing sentences from all four of the groups of sentences included in the previous study.

From each of the four sentence lists of the first study, eighteen sentences were drawn randomly. The four sets of eighteen sentences were divided into two parallel rating forms as follows. Within each of the four lists, the eighteen sentences were paired off according to the mean ratings of the Instrument-rating scale in the first study; one sentence, randomly chosen, of each pair was included in Form 1 and the other in Form 2. Each of the resulting two forms thus included thirty-six sentences: nine sentences for each of the four variables (but, due to an oversight, a sentence was missing in one of the two parallel forms).

Four Instrument-rating forms, one for each of the four variables, were constructed for each of the two parallel forms in the same way as in the first study.

The requirements for Hebrew language proficiency were the same as in the first study; see Section 3.2.5. For Form 1 there were twenty-eight respondents for the Saliency scale, twenty-three for the Essential property scale, thirty for the Independence scale and twenty-seven for the Complexity scale. The corresponding numbers of respondents for Form 2 were twenty-five, twenty-five, twenty-seven, and thirty, respectively.

Pearson correlation coefficients were computed for each form separately between (i) the mean rating (over nine sentences) on Saliency in the present study, and (ii) the mean Acceptability rating obtained for the corresponding sentences in the first study. Correlations for the other three variables were computed in the same way. The correlation coefficients are given in Table 4.1.

While all the correlations for Form 1 were statistically significant at the 0.02 level, for Form 2 only the correlation for Independence was significant. I have no explanation for the difference between these forms in size of the correlation coefficients. At any rate, the fact that the results of the previous study were replicated provides support for the linguistic analysis in Section 3.1, which revealed four factors contributing to subjectivizability of the instrument.

4. Conjoining of subject noun phrases

Two noun phrases in the same case can normally be conjoined, as in (20)a. However, a sentence with an instrumental noun phrase typically cannot be reformulated as one where the latter is conjoined with the subject; see (20)c.

> (20) a.   Jack and Jill cut the cake with the knife.
> b.   The knife cut the cake.
> c.   *Jack and the knife cut the cake.

Fillmore's (1968: 22) explanation of the unacceptability of (20)c is based on the assumption that *the knife* in (20)b is in a different case from *Jack* in (20)a, and (20)c runs afoul of the principle that two noun phrases in different cases cannot be conjoined. This explanation is incompatible with our claim that the instrument in subject position is in the A-case.

But there is evidence against Fillmore's account. There are instances that do not involve two different cases, on the customary analysis, and where conjoining is nevertheless ruled out, or at least awkward:

> (21) a.   The general captured the hill with a squad of paratroopers.
> b.   A squad of paratroopers captured the hill.

    c. ??The general and a squad of paratroopers captured the hill.

(22) a.   The prisoner won the appeal with a highly paid lawyer.
        b.   A highly paid lawyer won the appeal.
        c. ??The prisoner and a highly paid lawyer won the appeal.

In (21)b and (22)b *a squad of paratroopers* and *a highly paid lawyer* are clearly agents; nevertheless they cannot be conjoined with an agentive subject – see (21)c and (22)c. In part, this may be due to the fact that the activities referred to by the verbs have slightly different meanings for the two noun phrases: the general has a different role in capturing the hill from his soldiers, and the lawyer's role in winning the appeal differs from that of his client. But this cannot be the whole story, as shown in

(23) Floods and guerrilla forces ravaged the area.

The sense in which the floods may be said to ravage the area clearly differs from that in which guerrilla forces ravage it, and yet the sentence is grammatical.[9] Note, further, that these two noun phrases have different cases, and conjoining should therefore be inadmissible, according to Fillmore's principle. Noun phrases which are customarily assigned different cases are also conjoined in (24) and (25):

(24) a. Carol and her expensive necklace attracted much attention.
        b. Carl and the old grandfather clock in the corner attracted much attention.
        c. John and the new Renault won the race.
        d. Dave and the computer played a game of chess (with each other).

(25) a. The cheering crowd and the passing train drowned out their voices.
        b. The noise of the Niagara Falls and the chattering tourists drowned out the rumbling of the distant thunderstorm.

The Fillmorian same-case principle would block conjoining in (24) and (25). It appears therefore that it is not the different case categories that account for unacceptability of conjoining in (20)c, (21)c, and (22)c. I will now propose a different explanation for the oddness of these sentences.

In Chapter 3, Section 4.1, we saw that noun phrases having the feature ACCOMP + distr may be realized as conjoined subjects; (20)a is an example. The reverse also seems to hold: Noun phrases conjoined as subjects tend to be conceived of – if only because of semantic saturation – as having ACCOMP + distr. Thus, in (23) the floods are understood to do the damage together with the guerrillas. Let us now make the further, very plausible, supposition that two noun phrases in a sentence can have ACCOMP + distr only if they have a similar feature composition. This accounts for the oddness of (20)c. *Jack* in (20)a, denoting an animate entity, has more CONTROL over the activity of cutting than *the knife* in (20)b, and the difference in strength of this feature is so large that these two noun phrases cannot have ACCOMP + distr, and hence they cannot be conjoined. Likewise, the general and his subordinates in (21) differ appreciably in the degree of CONTROL they exercise, and so do the lawyer and his client in (22).[10]

In Section 3 it was shown that Independence and Complexity, among others, determine the degree of CONTROL that may be assigned to a noun phrase when it is in subject position. Accordingly, we find that inanimate noun phrases with a high degree of Independence and Complexity can conjoin with animate agents. The floods in (23) are conceived of as functioning independently; hence, when they are in subject position and semantic saturation accords a high degree of CONTROL to *floods*, our credulity is not strained, as it is in (7), for instance. *Floods* and *guerrilla forces* can therefore be conjoined. The necklace in (24)a and the grandfather clock in (24)b presumably aroused interest each in its own right, and due to the property of Independence, they may be assigned a high degree of CONTROL. Complexity contributes to the acceptability of (24)c–d, where the inanimate noun phrases are of great Complexity and may therefore be assigned – through semantic saturation – a large measure of CONTROL so that they can have ACCOMP + distr and conjoin with the animate noun phrases.

Consider now (25). Very little CONTROL is needed to drown out sounds. The crowd and the tourists just cheer and chatter, and may be quite unaware of the effect. The verb *drown out* also does not seem to involve much CONTROL in typical situations, so that we need not assume that this feature is contracted in (25). Furthermore, both the train – in (25)a – and the noise – in (25)b – have Independence, which enhances the degree of CONTROL that they can be assigned. It follows that there is no great difference in feature composition between the two conjoined noun phrases in (25)a–b, and they can thus be assigned ACCOMP + distr.

It appears therefore that our explanation in terms of difference in feature composition gives a better account of the data than Fillmore's same-case principle.

5. Passives with instruments

5.1 Two forms of passives

The active sentence (26)a can passivize as in (26)b–c (Chapter 3, Section 2.4).

(26) a. Jack cut the cake with the knife. (= (3)b)
   b. The cake was cut with the knife by Jack.
   c. The cake was cut with the knife.

The feature analysis of *the knife* in (26)b–c is the same as that of its active counterpart, (26)a: It is both CAUSE and INSTR.

Let us turn now to a different type of passive sentence. In Section 1 we discussed active sentences where the "instrument" is the subject, like (27)a. The passives of such sentences have *by*-phrases, as in (27)b, rather than *with*-phrases.

(27) a.   The knife cut the cake. (= (3)a)
b.   The cake was cut by the knife.

In (27)b, as in (26)b–c, *the knife* has CAUSE. But here the similarity ends:

(i)   Unlike in (26)b–c, *the knife* in (27)b does not have INSTR. The arguments adduced for not assigning INSTR to (1) (Section 1) apply also to the passive of (1).

(ii)   Due to semantic saturation and through contraction, *the knife* in (27)b has CONTROL, like the knife in (1); see Section 1. *The knife* in (26)b–c, by contrast, does not have CONTROL.

Let us turn now to the cases assigned to *the knife* in passive sentences. In (27)b it has CAUSE and some CONTROL, whereas the surface subject (*the cake*) has only CHANGE, and CAUSE carries more weight than CHANGE (Chapter 2, Section 4.3). Therefore *the knife* is in the A-case (recall that the A-case may be linked to the *by*-phrase; see Chapter 2, Section 5.2).

In (26)b, the feature CAUSE in *the knife* is outweighed by the features CAUSE and CONTROL in *Jack*. The same holds true of the active sentence (26)a (see Chapter 3, Section 3.3).

In (26)c *the knife* has INSTR and CAUSE. Due to INSTR, it is assigned to the C-case (and in accordance with the linking rules stated in Chapter 3, Section 4, it appears in a *with*-phrase). Due to CAUSE it is assigned also to the A-case. *The cake* has only CHANGE, which is outweighed by CAUSE and therefore is not A-case. This raises a problem: why is *the knife* in (26)c, which is in the A-case, not the subject? (Recall that *the knife* is a core argument of *cut*; Chapter 3, Section 2.1.)

It appears therefore that there is a linking rule for the A-case in addition to those introduced in Chapter 2, Section 5: a noun phrase in the A-case may be linked to a *with*-phrase in a passive sentence.

The surface subjects of passive sentences will be dealt with in Chapter 6, Section 4.1.

In their discussion of (28)a and (28)c, Quirk *et al.* (1985, Section 9.50) state that *by* excludes a human agency ("a storm may have caused the branch to cause the damage"), whereas *with* excludes natural cause ("and would suggest that human agents had used the branch broken from a tree to inflict the damage").

(28) a.   My car has been damaged with the branch of a tree.
b.   Somebody damaged my car with the branch of tree.
c.   My car has been damaged by the branch of a tree.
d.   The branch of a tree damaged my car.

This squares well with the analysis proposed here. The active sentence corresponding to (28)a is (28)b. The latter has a human noun phrase with CAUSE and CONTROL, which is consequently in the A-case. Such a human Agent is implied also by the "agent-less" passive (28)a, and therefore a different, natural cause is excluded, as Quirk *et al.* observe.

By contrast, the active form of (28)c is (28)d, where *the branch of a tree* is the Agent (Section 1) of the sentence, and thus there is no room for another Agent. In the corresponding passive sentence, (28)c, a human Agent is therefore also preempted, as observed by Quirk *et al.*

The following section presents evidence for our analysis of the passive with *by*.

5.2 Constraints on by-*phrases*

Support for the foregoing claim that the instrument in a *by*-phrase is in the A-case comes also from the observation that sentences where the instrument is in the *by*-phrase are subject to the same constraints as those where it is in subject position. The deliberation constraint rules out the sentences in (7) and likewise the corresponding passives with *by*:

(29) a. *The sandalwood was being cut into a statuette by the chisel.
      b. *The poem was being scribbled by the pen.

Similarly, the mediation constraint applies also to passive sentences with *by*. Just as (8)a′ and (8)b′ are ruled out by the mediation constraint, so are (30)a–b. Sentences (30)c–d are the passives of the unacceptable (9)b–c.

(30) a. *The window was broken by the wind with a twig.
      b. *An announcement was made by the tape recorder with two loudspeakers.
      c. *A hole was made in the wall by the hammer with a chisel.
      d. *A hole was made in the wall by the hammer.

Note that substituting *with* for *by* in (29) and in (30)d results in perfectly acceptable sentences:

(31) a. The sandalwood was being cut into a statuette with the chisel.
      b. The poem was being scribbled with the pen.
      c. A hole was made in the wall with the hammer.

The reason that in (30)a–c substitution of *with* for *by* does not render acceptable sentences is that there would be two slightly different uses of *with* in the same sentence:

(32) a.   *The window was broken with the wind with a twig.
      b.   ??An announcement was made with the tape recorder with two loudspeakers.
      c.   ??A hole was made in the wall with the hammer with a chisel.

Further, *with the wind* in (32)a is inappropriate because the wind is a natural force and there is no other agent. The sentences with *by means of* in (33)a–b, however, seem to be slightly better than (30)b–c, respectively.

(33) a. ?An announcement was made with the tape recorder by means of two loudspeakers.

b. ?A hole was made in the wall with the hammer by means of a chisel.

6. Semantic saturation and language acquisition

Formulation of the semantic saturation hypothesis was inspired by theoretical work on native language acquisition. The semantic assimilation hypothesis (Schlesinger, 1988) claims that formal grammatical categories are acquired by gradual extension of the child's semantic categories. On encountering a subject that is not an Agent, for instance, the language learning child notes certain similarities between the semantic relations of the entity referred to by this subject with the Agent relation. The "newcomer" is then assimilated into the primitive Agent category, which is gradually extended in this manner until it ultimately becomes the formal syntactic category subject.

This developmental theory leads to certain expectations concerning the mature linguistic system. If grammatical categories develop out of semantic ones on the basis of semantic similarity, the "flavor" of the semantic category may be expected to be retained even in non-prototypical instances of the mature syntactic category. Thus, subjects which according to our theory are peripheral will be conceived of, even by adults, as being somehow agent-like. This is the semantic saturation hypothesis.

In this chapter we have found evidence for semantic saturation in instruments in subject position. From an objective viewpoint, an instrument is the CAUSE of an activity but has no CONTROL over it. However, when the instrument is in the A-case and becomes the sentence subject, it becomes saturated with CONTROL, which is the feature that is characteristic of more central instances of the Agent category. This process functions in the explanation of the constraints discussed in Sections 2.1–2.2.

The results of psycholinguistic experiments obtained in a doctoral thesis by Ainat Guberman of The Hebrew University also accord with this hypothesis. Extending the findings of de Villiers (1979), Guberman found that a new linguistic construction can be more easily learned by kindergarten children for sentences with action verbs than for those with mental or stative verbs (when verb frequency is controlled for). Further, in a lexical decision task, latencies for action verbs were found to be significantly shorter than those for mental and stative verbs, both for 10–11-year-olds and for adults (again with verb frequency controlled). Finally, Guberman found that verbs were judged to be more active than related nouns (e.g., *to swim* was judged to involve more activity than *a swim*).

In Chapter 7, Section 5, further relevant findings will be reported.

7. Conclusions

Cases are constructs that belong to the linguistic system; they are not categories in the cognitive space. Therefore, when two differently structured sentences describe the same situation, the corresponding noun phrases do not necessarily have the same case. Thus, a noun phrase referring to an instrument is in the C-case when it is the object of *with*, but (by dint of the feature CAUSE) in the A-case when it is the sentence subject.

Another principle illustrated in this chapter concerns the effect of linguistic structure on the feature composition of noun phrases. A noun phrase referring to an instrument may have the feature CAUSE, and when it is the subject of a sentence it will be endowed with the feature CONTROL which is typical of subjects. This semantic saturation process functions in the explanation of certain constraints on the subjectivization of instrumental noun phrases.

5 Predicates

This chapter discusses the nature of predicates. It is important to keep in mind that the concept of predicate that we will be concerned with here is the one used in case grammar, where one distinguishes between the predicate verb and its arguments. This concept needs to be clarified before a new case category is introduced in the next chapter.

1. What is a predicate?

Predicate and argument pertain to the cognitive level (the terms have been taken over by linguists from logic). The decision as to what is the predicate and what are the arguments of a sentence is logically prior to case assignment and the determination of the syntactic functions by which they are to be realized (see also Chapter 2, Section 5.3). The question to be examined now is: by which objective criteria may the predicate be identified?

1.1 Predicates and verbs

In the literature on case grammar it is usually assumed implicitly that the predicate is the main verb of the sentence. This happens to be true for English sentences, but there are languages, like Hebrew, for instance, where a sentence does not necessarily have a verb. Furthermore, it will not do to define the predicate as the main verb, even in English, because, as mentioned, predicate is a cognitive category and its definition is logically prior to determining how it is to be expressed. There are numerous instances where a given state of affairs may be expressed by means of words from different grammatical categories; for example:

(1) a. John is afraid to marry.
    a'. John is afraid of marriage/wedlock/matrimony.
    b. John is stupid.
    b'. John is a fool.
    c. The train is moving.

    c′. The train is in motion.
    d. John sleeps.
    d′. John is asleep.

Other languages furnish many more examples. In Hebrew the equivalent of the English *he has a book* is, translated literally, *there is a book to him*. In Japanese, there is an expression for *I see a tree* in which the tree is the subject (*the tree appears to me*). In Greenlandic, one says *the arrow flies away from me*, where in English one says *I shoot the arrow* (Waisman, 1962; see also Schlesinger, 1977: 91–95). As Sapir has remarked, "[o]ur conventional classification of words into parts of speech is only a vague, wavering approximation to a consistently worked out inventory of experience. . . . 'it is red' is related to 'it reddens' very much as 'he stands' to 'he stands up' or 'he rises'. It is merely a matter of English or of general Indo-European idiom that we cannot say 'it reds' in the sense of 'it is red'. There are hundreds of languages that can" (Sapir, 1921: 117). Lyons (1977: 432–33) quotes authorities on Nootka and Kwakiutl as stating that in these languages there are lexemes that are neutral with respect to the verb–noun distinction.

1.2 Predicates and ontological categories

At the first blush one might say that in cognitive space there is a distinction between actions and states on the one hand and objects on the other, and that this determines what becomes the predicate and what becomes the argument. Thus, Jackendoff (1990: 22) speaks about "major ontological categories . . . such as Thing, Event, State, Action, Place . . .", and: "Things must be expressed by noun phrases" (250).

But there are numerous states of affairs that appear to belong to more than one category, or are boundary cases. Consider (2). Ruling involves an activity, and (2)a describes an event, but there is more to being a ruler than that event: it involves being in a certain "position"; see (2)b.

    (2) a. John ruled the island.
         b. John was the ruler of the island.

Similarly, social events – symposia, conventions, etc. – have aspects of both thing and event or activity (although there is no English verb corresponding to *symposium*). The thing–event dichotomy thus does not provide a firm basis for the predicate–argument distinction.

1.3 Evidence from meteorological terms

In speaking about rain, the English speaker may have the following options to choose from:

    (3) a. Rain is falling/coming down/pouring down/ . . .
         b. It is raining.

Table 5.1. *Verbs for meteorological phenomena in ten languages*

	Span.	Germ.	French	Engl.	Ital.	Roman.	Hungar.	Arab.	Russ.	Hebrew
rain	+	+	+	+	+	+	+	+	—	—
snow	+	+	+	+	+	+	+	—	—	—
hail	+	+	+	+	+	—	—	—	—	—
lightning	+	+	+	—	—	+	+	—	—	—
dew	+	+	—	—	—	—	—	—	—	—

Note:
+ means that the language has a verb for the phenomenon
— means that none exists

In (3)a *rain* is an argument, whereas in (3)b the verb *rain* is a predicate. In some languages there is no verb for rain. Rain, snow, lightning, and other meteorological phenomena have two aspects: they are thing-like and event-like.

Why does English have verbs used impersonally for some phenomena – like *it rains/snows/hails* – but none for lightning and dew? We say that there is lightning and that dew falls, but not *it lightnings*, or *it dews*. The absence of a verb for dew might seem to be accounted for by the fact that one does not see dew forming (as one sees rain or snow falling), but if so, why are there languages that do have a verb for the formation of dew, namely, German and Spanish?

In a small crosslinguistic study we compared five weather terms in the following ten languages: Hebrew, Russian, Arabic, Hungarian, Romanian, Italian, English, French, Spanish, and German. The five terms were found to fall into three groups:

1. *Rain and snow* There are verbs in eight of the ten languages for rain – that is, all except Russian and Hebrew – and in seven of them for snow – all except Russian, Hebrew, and Arabic. (That Arabic has a verb for rain and none for snow may of course be due to the warmer climate in which Arabic-speaking peoples live.)

2. *Hail and lightning* Only five of the ten languages have verbs for hail: Italian, English, French, Spanish, and German. Five languages have a verb for lightning: Hungarian, Romanian, French, Spanish, and German.

3. *Dew* The only languages of the ten that have a verb for this are Spanish and German.

Table 5.1 shows that these three groups form an implicational scale: If a language has no verb for Group 1, then it will have no verbs for the terms in Groups 2 and 3; and if it does not have verbs for the terms in Group 2 it will have none for that in Group 3. The existence of such a scale suggests that these phenomena lie along a gradient of activity, those involving more activity being more likely to be expressed by verbs.

Looking at individual terms and not at groups, we note that the only exceptions to a perfect implicational scale are due to *lightning* – which differs from all the other terms in that it does not refer to any precipitation (Richard Hudson, personal communication, 1993).

1.4 Communicative effects of form class

Does the form class of the word describing a situation affect the way it is perceived? According to the Whorfian hypothesis there is such an influence of language on cognition. One of Whorf's (1956) examples is taken from the area of meteorological phenomena. He argues that speakers of a language that refers to lightning by a noun differ in the way they conceive of the phenomenon from speakers of a language that refers to it by a verb. The structure of one's language affects the way one conceives of reality.

Many years of empirical research have failed to provide conclusive evidence for an effect of grammar on cognition (see Schlesinger, 1992, for a review). However, there is evidence for a weaker hypothesis: grammatical form class affects the way the hearer conceives of the referent. Ainat Guberman (1992) has shown that verbs are conceived of as portraying more activity than the corresponding nouns (e.g., *to walk* more than *a walk*), both by children and by adults. This is a communicative effect: the linguistic form of the message affects the way the message is understood. This in itself does not imply the stronger claim that the linguistic system affects the way the world is conceived of in general (and not just in the communicative situation), which is the gist of the Whorfian thesis.

1.5 The nature of the predicate

We have seen that the predicate cannot be defined ontologically (for instance, as the action or state talked about) or linguistically, as being the main verb. The terms predicate and argument[1] apply to propositions, to statements about states of affairs, not to the states of affairs in and by themselves. They pertain not to reality, but to the way we communicate about it.

Languages may take different perspectives in respect to reality, as we have seen in the foregoing discussion of meteorological phenomena. The speakers of some languages are provided with only a single choice in communicating about, say, rain, whereas other languages leave their speakers a choice between two ways of communicating about the same phenomena. The speaker's choice of predicate is constrained by the options afforded by his language. In other words, the first step in constructing a linguistic expression of one's intentions must already take into account the resources provided by the language. This is generally recognized in regard to the choice of lexical items (when one intends to talk about a female horse one has *mare* at one's disposal, but for a female cat one has to resort, in English, to a two-word phrase); the foregoing shows that it is no less true of syntactic constructions.

2. Phrasal predicates

In the preceding we have seen that the predicate is not defined in terms of grammatical categories. We now note that it need not be confined to a single word. In (4) the italicized phrase as a whole is the predicate.

(4) a. Sophie *is timid*.
     b. Sophie *has a lapdog*.
     c. Sophie *is a lawyer*.
     d. Sophie *seems upset*.
     e. Sophie *keeps trying*.

The verbs *be, become, can, have, seem,* and *keep* impart information mainly in conjunction with their complements, and very little in isolation. It is proposed therefore that in each of the sentences in (4) the italicized phrase as a whole be regarded as the predicate – we will call this a *phrasal predicate* – and the subject as the argument of this predicate.

The verbs in (4) – *is, has, seems,* etc. – also have a special syntactic property: they do not allow clefting (**It is a lawyer that Sophie is,* **It is upset that Sophie seems*; see Quirk, Greenbaum, Leech, and Svartvik, 1985, Section 18.26), or questions like **What did Sophie seem/keep?*. The verbs in (5), however, do admit these constructions, but they are like those in (4) in respect to dearth of independent informational content.

(5) a. John *deserves a medal*.
     b. Two and two *equal four*.
     c. John *resembles Uncle Paul*.
     d. The car *lacks a hand brake*.
     e. John *needs a new suit*.
     f. He *weighs 100 pounds*.
     g. The blue dress *becomes her*.

The verbs in (5), like those in (4), do not convey information independently. Ask yourself what you know when you read these sentences without the verb complement:

(6) a. John deserves . . .
     b. Two and two equal . . .
     c. John resembles . . .
     d. The car lacks . . .
     e. John needs . . .
     f. He weighs . . .
     g. The blue dress becomes (in the sense of fit) . . .

These (truncated) statements apply almost universally: Everybody weighs a certain weight, resembles someone, etc. The verbs in (6) are incomplete predicates; the direct objects in (5) are parts of the predicates. I propose therefore that the sentences in (5), too, have phrasal predicates (italicized).[2]

In Chapter 2, Section 6, non-agentive subjects were discussed. It now becomes clear that most of these nonagentive subjects are arguments of phrasal predicates, as shown by the examples in (5).

The subjects in (7) are in the A-case. The verbs in these sentences, too, have little informational content, and the italicized phrases are therefore phrasal predicates (see Quirk *et al.*, 1985, Section 10.30, on empty verbs with eventive objects, like (7)a, f, and g).

(7) a. Humpty Dumpty *engaged in a dialogue.*
    b. The lobsters *executed a quadrille.*
    c. The White Queen *carried out an attack.*
    d. He *began/finished his vacation.*
    e. He *tries a new brand of cigarettes.*
    f. He *made a comment.*
    g. He *gave a talk.*
    h. He *had an argument* with her.

There are several other verbs that do not constitute predicates by themselves but only as part of a phrase: *appear* (in *appears to be . . .*), *belong to, comprise, contain, cost, do* (in *do a favor* or *do a dance*), *have, look* (in, e.g., *looks sad*), *match* (as in *the curtains match the carpet*), *relate to, result from, suit, undergo.*[3] The lexical entry of the verb must specify what constitutes a predicate of which the verb is a part.

Some verbs may have informational content in one of their uses and very little in another. In (8)a, (8)b, and (8)c the verbs by themselves are the predicates, whereas in (8)a'–c' the same verbs are in phrasal predicates.

(8) a. The steward *seats* the passengers.
   a'. The hall *seats four hundred persons.*
    b. The boy *sleeps* in the room.
   b'. This room *sleeps two.*
    c. He *lives,* though reported dead. (Allerton, 1982: 61)
   c'. He *lives in Alaska.*

The verbs *seat, sleep,* and *live* in (8)a'–c' carry little information by themselves. Every – or nearly every – room can sleep or seat a certain number of people, and everyone lives somewhere. The lexical entries for the verbs in (8), then, each have two subentries, one of which – those for the expressions in (8)a'–c' – has specifications of what constitutes a predicate of which the verb is a part.

It should come as no surprise that there is a fuzzy boundary between verbs that do form predicates by themselves and those that do not. Take the verb *own*. It is very difficult to find anyone who does not own something or other, but *own* usually signals that it is an object of some value that is being owned (ordinarily it would be odd to say that someone owns a safety pin). So this verb does have some informational content in isolation (that is, when the direct object is omitted), though very little. The verb *break* does not give much information, as long as it is not clear whether one is talking about breaking the rules, a vase, a seal, or a promise.

There are many more verbs like this. As pointed out by Samuel Johnson in the Preface to his *Dictionary* (Johnson, 1755/1963: 14), there is

> a class of verbs too frequent in the English language, of which the signification is so loose and general, the use so vague and indeterminate, and the senses detorted so widely from the first idea, that it is hard to trace them through the maze of variation, to catch them on the brink of utter inanity, to circumscribe them by any limitation, or interpret them by any words of distinct and settled meaning: such as *bear, break, come, cast, fill, get, give, do, put, set, go, run, make, take, turn, throw*.

The rest of the verbs are at the further end of what is, after all, a gradient.

3. Events and States

We distinguish two kinds of predicates: Events and States. These concepts will be needed for the definition of a case category in the next chapter. The sentences in (9) (= (4)a–d and (5)) describe States, whereas those in (10) (= (7)a–d) refer to Events.

(9) a. Sophie is timid.
    b. Sophie has a lapdog.
    c. Sophie is a lawyer.
    d. Sophie seems upset.
    e. John deserves a medal.
    f. Two and two equal four.
    g. John resembles Uncle Paul.
    h. The car lacks a hand brake.
    i. John needs a new suit.
    j. He weighs a hundred pounds.
    k. The blue dress becomes her.

(10) a. Humpty Dumpty engaged in a dialogue.
    b. The lobsters executed a quadrille.
    c. The White Queen carried out an attack.
    d. He began/finished his vacation.

Events and States are well-worn terms in the linguistic literature, but there is little agreement as to the criteria by which they ought to be distinguished (see, e.g., Van Voorst, 1992; Siewierska, 1991: 45–51). Instead of a single Event category, many writers (e.g., Dowty, 1979) now recognize three categories: Activity, Achievement, and Accomplishment. These distinctions within the Event category are not crucial for our present purpose. The above three categories are subsumed by what Mourelatos (1981) calls "occurrences," instead of which the more familiar term Event will be used here.

3.1 Criteria for the Event–State distinction

Among the various criteria for distinguishing between Events and States proposed in the literature, I have found the following to be the most helpful and they will be referred to in some of the discussions further on.

3.1.1 Events are transient

Events are characterized by transience – they begin and end; see, for example, (10). States may last indefinitely long. In (9)a–b, being timid and having a lapdog do not have a natural point of beginning in time and a natural end point. On hearing (9)c we know that Sophie has not been a lawyer before she had reached the age of twenty (at least), but this is outside information and is not included in the predicate *be a lawyer* itself.

Information about beginning and end points in time may be supplied by knowledge of the world and even by parts of the sentence outside the predicate. But only the information in the predicate itself is relevant in determining transience, and the sentences in (11), for instance, will therefore be taken to describe States.

> (11) a. As a young man, Bruno *was a law student* at Harvard.
>   b. Sophie *was timid* at the party.

The transience criterion is not always easy to apply, though, because there is no clear dividing line between the information contained in the predicate and real world knowledge.

3.1.2 Events implicate change

If any one of its obligatory arguments – either the subject or the direct object – undergoes change, the predicate is an Event predicate. If not, it is a State predicate. By saying that Sophie is timid or that she is a lawyer, one does not intimate that she is undergoing any change; and that she has a lapdog, (9)b, implies no change in her or in the lapdog. By contrast, engaging in dialogue, executing a quadrille, carrying out an attack, and beginning a vacation – see (10) – each involve a change in the situation. When the copula in (9)d is replaced by a "resulting copula" (Quirk *et al.*, 1985, Section 16.21), such as *becomes*, *gets*, *turns*, etc., we also have an Event predicate. This criterion is obviously closely related to the previous one.

It should be noted that "change" is used here in a somewhat broader sense than that of the feature CHANGE (cf. Chapter 2, Section 2.2.2). Neither the noun phrase *he* nor the noun phrase *his vacation* in (10)d will be assigned the feature CHANGE, but there is a change in the situation as a whole.

3.1.3 The What happened? test

Whenever the sentence is an appropriate answer to the question *What happened?* or *What is/will be happening?*, it has an Event predicate. This is a rough-and-ready test for eventhood, which is related to the two preceding criteria. The sentences in (10) pass this test.

3.1.4 States do not take the Comitative

There is a constraint on the arguments a State predicate can have. Unlike Event predicates, a State predicate cannot have an argument in the Comitative case.

(12) a. *John deserves a promotion with diligence.
b. *John resembles his father with elegance.

An exception are expressions referring to the intensity of the State; these may be viewed as a kind of Manner (MANN):

(13) a. John resembles his father faintly.
b. John truly deserves a promotion.
c. The dress fits her splendidly.

3.2 Borderline cases

Transience is a graded concept, and the boundary between Events and States is a fuzzy one. In (14) we have a gradient from States to Events, and in (15), too, there is a gradient from relatively permanent to more transient situations.

(14) a. He has blue eyes.
b. He has a stomach ulcer.
c. He has a lapdog.
d. He has a headache.
e. He has a cup of coffee before leaving.

(15) a. He was a scion of a noble family.
b. He was a well-known writer.
c. He was a neighbor of my aunt.
d. He was a fool when he accepted the job.
e. He was certain there would be trouble.

Processes involve change. Yet a process need not be transient, and when this is the case – as in (16), for instance – there is a conflict between the two criteria discussed in the preceding section.

(16) a. The trees are growing.
     b. The moon revolves round the earth.

The predicates in (16) are best conceived of as both Events and States, but they are neither prototypical Events nor prototypical States.

On the face of it, (17) does not describe an event. However, in accordance with our treatment of modals in Chapter 2, Section 3.3.3, we conceive of predicates like this as Events with an added modal verb (just as the negation *not* does not turn an Event into a non-Event). Like Events, predicates with modal verbs – *can, would, may, should*, etc. – admit Comitatives:

(17) Jack and Jill should have gone up the hill more carefully and with special mountaineering equipment.

3.3 State–Event ambiguity

A given predicate may ambiguously refer to either a State or an Event:

(18) a.   Bruno is studying Law.
     a'. Bruno is a law-student.
     b.   Steve plays football.
     b'. Steve is a football player.

The first sentence in a pair may be intended to mean more or less the same as the second one, and then its predicate refers to a State. Alternatively, the predicates in (18)a and (18)b may refer to Events. Bruno may be doing some studying without being enrolled as a student, and Steve may be playing football from time to time without deserving the appellation football player; these are intermittently recurring Events.

The verbs *shine, glitter*, and *sparkle* can refer either to a State or to a more short-lived Event:

(19) a.   Gold shines.
     a'. A flashlight briefly shone in his face.
     b.   This champagne sparkles.
     b'. He held the test tube against the light and the liquid sparkled.
     c.   Diamonds glitter.
     c'. His eyes glittered.

Similarly, the sentences in (20) may have either an inchoative meaning – the water is in the process of becoming stagnant, the old lady is in the process of bending her knees – and then they describe Events. Alternatively, they may refer to the State that is the outcome of that Event: the water is in a stagnant condition and the lady is in a kneeling position. The ambiguity may be avoided by using *kneel down* instead of *kneel* in (20)b. In some contexts one may refer to both the Event and the State by a sentence like (20)a.

(20) a. The water stagnates.
     b. The old lady kneels.

The interpretation of (21) as an Event or as a State may depend on the context: when driving the car, it may mean that it is now moving effortlessly, i.e., the sentence will have an Event predicate. In a different context, the sentence may refer to the car's driving characteristics, that is, it may have a State predicate.

(21) The car drives easily.

3.4 The linguistic expression of States and Events

Let us see now how the Event–State distinction relates to that of phrasal and non-phrasal predicates.

State predicates are typically phrasal predicates; the phrasal predicates in (9), for instance, are States. By contrast, Event predicates are typically non-phrasal, as in

(22) a. The water evaporates.
     b. She accepted the gift.
     c. The inflation caused unemployment.

This correlation has many exceptions, however. There are States expressed by non-phrasal predicates, like (23); and conversely, there are Events expressed by phrasal predicates, as in (10) and in (24).

(23) a. The lamp hangs from the ceiling.
     b. The lamp glimmers/shines.
     c. The rotting plants smelled/reeked/stank.

(24) a. He is being rude to her.
     b. He had his dinner.

In the next chapter we will examine some consequences of the Event–State distinction.

6 The Attributee

1. The subjects of States

In this chapter a new case is introduced, which is assigned to the subject of a State predicate.

1.1 Attributee – feature and case

The subjects of Events are assigned the A-case (that is, our extended Agent case; see Chapter 2). Subjects of States, by contrast, are frequently non-agentive. Consider the State predicates in (1).

(1) a. John deserves a medal.
   b. Two and two equal four.
   c. John resembles Uncle Paul.
   d. The car lacks a hand brake.
   e. John needs a new suit.
   f. He weighs a hundred pounds.
   g. The blue dress becomes her.
   h. The play lasts three hours.
   i. The lamp hangs from the ceiling.
   j. The lamp glimmers/shines.
   k. The rotting plants smelled/reeked/stank.

These predicates designate attributes of their respective subjects. The subjects in (1) will therefore be called **Attributees** of their predicates, and this is the term proposed for the case category of the subjects of State predicates.

"Attributee" is both a feature, ATTRIBUTEE, and a case. The Attributee case is assigned to any noun phrase that has the feature ATTRIBUTEE; the case is defined by a single feature, unlike the A-case and the C-case, which are defined by clusters of features. It is plausible to assume that the feature ATTRIBUTEE is a primitive and is both universal and innate.[1]

The lexical entries of *deserve*, *equal*, and the other verbs in (1) each specify that one of the arguments has the feature ATTRIBUTEE. So do the lexical entries of *be*, *have*, *seem* and one of the subentries of *keep*, for these verbs also take Attributee subjects, as shown in (2) (from the preceding chapter).[2]

(2) a. Sophie is timid.
    b. Sophie has a lapdog.
    c. Sophie is a lawyer.
    d. Sophie seems upset.
    e. Sophie keeps trying.

The Attributee case is linked to the sentence subject. In Chapter 2, Section 6, non-agentive subjects were discussed. It now appears that those subjects that are not in the A-case are – with very few exceptions – in the Attributee case. It is of interest in this connection that children distinguish between the "actor" category and the "subject of attribution" (Braine and Wells, 1978; see also Atkinson-Hardy and Braine, 1981). Guberman (1992) found that preschool children could not be trained to distinguish sentences with *be* or *has* as main verb (such as *the baby is in the crib*), from sentences with stative verbs (such as *the baby sleeps*), whereas they managed to learn to distinguish between the former and sentences with dynamic verbs (such as *the baby lifts her head*).

There are exceptions to this rule, however. Besides those mentioned in Chapter 2, Section 6, there are sentences whose subjects are the expletive *it*, appearing in meteorological predicates (see Chapter 5, Section 1.3) of which (3) is an example. The subject *it*, being semantically empty, does not have any features; hence it is neither an Attributee, nor is any other case assigned to it. The predicate in (3) thus has no core argument.

(3) Last week it rained in Spain on the plain for two hours.

In the previous chapter (Section 3.2), instances were discussed that are on the borderline between Events and States. There are two ways in which one might assign cases to the arguments of such predicates. One might wish to separate the sheep from the goats by imposing some criterion; but this would probably have to be rather arbitrary. It might be best therefore to assign the subject of the doubtful sentences to the Attributee case. These will obviously be non-prototypical instances of this case; gradients of case categories are discussed in Chapter 9.

1.2 *Contraction of* ATTRIBUTEE

The lexical entry of a verb referring to a State – like those in (1) – contains the information that it has an argument with the feature ATTRIBUTEE. As stated in Chapter 2, Section 3.3.1, a feature registered in the lexical entry may be contracted by any noun phrase expressing the relevant argument. Thus, the verbs *shine*, *glitter*, and *sparkle* are typically used to refer to States, and their lexical entries therefore specify that they have arguments with ATTRIBUTEE (the thing that shines, glitters or sparkles). Now, there are sentences where these verbs refer to Events, and not to States, e.g.,

(4) a. *A flashlight* briefly shone in his face.
   b. When he held the test tube against the light, *the liquid* sparkled.
   c. *His eyes* glittered.

The feature ATTRIBUTEE will be contracted by the italicized noun phrases, and since this feature is linked to the subject, they will be subjects.

1.3 Sentences with two Attributees

It has been shown (Chapter 2, Section 4.3) that in exceptional instances a sentence may have two noun phrases in the A-case. Occasionally one may also come across a sentence having two noun phrases in the Attributee case. The verb *resemble*, for instance, has two arguments that are Attributees. If Dan resembles David, then David resembles Dan, and (5)a therefore tells us just as much about David as about Dan.

Resemblance is not always symmetrical, however. For instance, (5)a' states something about the clouds; one would hardly ever compare an elephant to a cloud (see also Tversky, 1977, on the asymmetry of judged similarity). But the lexical entry for *resemble* will specify that there are two arguments with the feature ATTRIBUTEE, and consequently *an elephant* contracts this feature and is also Attributee. Similar observations apply to *match* in (5)b and (5)b'.

(5) a. Dan resembles David.
   a'. These clouds resemble an elephant.
   b. The wallpaper matches the carpet.
   b'. The tie matches the suit.

When a sentence has two noun phrases in the A-case, the subject is selected from among them according to pragmatic considerations (Chapter 2, Section 5.1); likewise, the subject of a sentence with two Attributees will be determined by pragmatic factors.

2. Noun phrases that are both A-case and Attributee

According to our approach (see Chapter 3, Section 3.4), a noun phrase may be assigned more than one case. We turn now to examples of noun phrases that are Attributee and at the same time A-case.

2.1 Noun phrases having CAUSE − act − aff

The following sentences have State predicates, and their subjects are Attributees:

(6) a. This room sleeps four.
    b. The auditorium seats two thousand people.
    c. His new book sells well.
    d. Our baby scares easily.

Now, the subjects of (6) have the feature CAUSE − act − aff (Chapter 2, Section 2.4), and they are therefore also A-case.

2.2 Noun phrases having CONTROL

Sentences with some stative verbs have Attributees as subjects. The sentences in (7), for instance, refer to States; no change is implied.

(7) a. Bill was sitting in his favorite chair.
    b. Ben was reclining on the couch.
    c. Barbara remained in her room.

Now, the subjects of (7) have CONTROL (see Chapter 2, Section 2.2.1). They are therefore A-case in addition to being Attributees.

In an experimental study employing a sorting task, Guberman (1992) found that kindergarten children do not distinguish between sentences like (2) and sentences with other stative verbs. They do distinguish, however, between sentences with activity verbs and those with stative verbs.

Sentences with the feature CHANGE in the Attributee noun phrase are discussed in Section 4.1, below.

2.3 Noun phrases with contracted agentive features

State predicates may involve verbs the lexical entries of which specify that an argument has one or more agentive features. For instance, the verb *surround* has a lexical entry with the features CAUSE and CONTROL, because of the verb's normal use in sentences with human agents; as, e.g., in (8)a. In (8)a', the noun phrase *pine trees* contracts these features from the lexical entry, and is therefore A-case. Similarly, *point*, as typically used, will have a human agent – see (8)b – and as a consequence will have agentive features in its lexical entry. This will be contracted by *the arrow* in (8)b', and the latter will therefore be A-case.

(8) a.   The police surrounded the field.
    a'. Pine trees surround the field.
    b.   The doorman pointed at the exit.
    b'. The arrow points at the exit.

In addition to being A-case by dint of the contraction of agentive features, *pine trees* in (8)a' and *the arrow* in (8)b' are Attributee, because these sentences describe States.

In sum, each of the lexical entries of the verbs in Sections 2.1–2.3 has an argument with agentive features as well as ATTRIBUTEE and they are therefore both A-case and Attributee. A subject can be Attributee when the predicate is a State predicate; it can be A-case with any predicate, whether it is a State or an Event.

2.4 The Comitative with State predicates

One of the criteria for distinguishing between States and Events proposed in Chapter 5 (Section 3.1) is that State predicates do not admit the Comitative. But this is true only of State predicates that do not have A-case subjects; when the subject is A-case as well as Attributee, the Comitative is not ruled out (remember that the Comitative in our system includes Instrumental and Manner):

> (9) a. Belinda sat on the balcony with her best friend.
>   b. Ben was reclining on the couch in a magisterial manner.
>   c. Barbara remained in her room with reluctance.
>   d. Bob is standing with a brace.
>   e. This room sleeps four with difficulty.

In (9)a–d the subject has CONTROL, and in (9)e, *this room* is CAUSE − act − aff (Chapter 2, Section 2.4). Hence these subjects are in the A-case, in addition to being Attributees. (But see Section 4.3, below.)

There is an important exception to this, however. When assignment of the A-case is due merely to contracted features, it does not license the Comitative:

> (10) a. The police surrounded the field with their dogs.
>   b. *Pine trees surround the field with the hedges.
>   (in the sense of "pine trees and the hedges surround …")
>   c. The doorman pointed at the exit with great emphasis.
>   d. *The arrow points at the exit with great emphasis.

Only as a personification of the arrow will (10)d be acceptable.

There is an exception to this exception: Proper parts are permissible as Comitatives even when the sentence has merely an A-case with contracted features, as in

> (11) a. Trees obstruct the view with their thick foliage.
>   b. The arrow points at the exit with its blunted point.

3. Implicit Events and States

Consider what may be presumed to have led to the situations described in the following sentences:

> (12) a. Dinner is ready.

   b. The victim is dead.

   c. The lock is rusty.

For each of the States described by the predicates of these sentences there is an Event from which it resulted. Preparing dinner is an Event preceding the State of dinner being ready; a process of dying (and, possibly, an act of killing) preceded and led up to the victim's being dead; and a chemical process resulted in the lock being rusty. However, only the resulting States are explicitly referred to in (12); the Events are only implicit. It is proposed that implicit States and Events are not to be taken into account in the analysis. The predicates in (12) are regarded as States for the purpose of case assignment, and the noun phrases are in the Attributee case. (Further applications of this principle will be discussed in the next chapter, Sections 3 and 4.2.)

    The unit of analysis is the clause. Adding to (12)a a clause referring explicitly to the preceding Event does not affect the analysis of the clause that mentions only the State; see (13)a. The same holds for (12)b; cf. (13)b.

   (13) a. Claire prepared dinner, and it is ready.

         b. The victim is dead, having been shot by Clarence.

    The predicates in (12) describe States resulting from Events; those in (14) describe States leading to Events, and there, too, the Events are implicit and disregarded in the analysis.

   (14) a. This room sleeps four.

         b. The auditorium seats two thousand people.

That the room has the property of sleeping four may lead to the Event of four people being accommodated in it, or perhaps to the Event of more people being put up in it and feeling cramped. These Events are not explicitly referred to in the sentence. Anyhow, *the room* is analyzed as A-case because it has the feature CAUSE −act −aff (Section 2.1).

    There are also predicates where the State is implicit and only the Event is explicitly referred to. These fall into two classes:

(i) Inchoate predicates:

   (15) a. The orange ripens.

         b. The snow freezes.

         c. The door opens.

         d. The boy stood up.

         e. The frog turned into a prince.

         f. The pauper became a millionaire.

These sentences describe Events that result in States (the orange is ripe; the snow is frozen; the boy is standing, etc.; (15)e–f have phrasal predicates), which are implicit and therefore are not taken into account in the analysis.

The subjects of these predicates have the feature CHANGE and thus are A-case (Chapter 2, Section 2.2.2).

(ii) Accomplishments:

> (16) a. Doris broke the vase.
> b. Diana painted the wall.
> c. David built a house.

In (15) the resulting States are those of the subjects. The Events of (16), by contrast, result in States where the object is affected (a vase that is broken, a wall that is painted) or effected (a house that did not exist before). Such predicates are called Accomplishments in the Vendler-Dowty scheme (Dowty, 1979).[3] Since the Events, and not the States, are explicit, the subjects of (16) are in the A-case.

Some verbs – notably *swarm*, *abound*, *stream*, *drip*, and *crawl* – may describe either an Event or a State, depending on the constructions they appear in:

> (17) a. The garden swarms with bees.
> a′. Bees swarm in the garden.
> b. His jacket is dripping with water.
> b′. Water is dripping from his jacket.
> c. The bed was crawling with bugs.
> c′. Bugs were crawling in the bed.

In (17)a, the State of the garden is focused on; the fact that this State is caused by the Event of bees swarming recedes into the background. When the Event is focused on, (17)a′ rather than (17)a will be used. In (17)a′ it is the State resulting from this Event that recedes into the background. It follows that the subject of (17)a is Attributee, while that of (17)a′ is A-case. Similar observations seem to apply to the other pairs in (17).

The distinction between (17)a and (17)a′ has usually been held to be one of degree of affectedness: (17)a says that the garden is full of bees, whereas (17)a′ merely says that there are bees in it, maybe only in part of it. This difference is closely related to the State–Event distinction: In saying that something is in a certain State one normally means that it is wholly, not partially, in this State. See also the discussion of (22) further on.

4. Passive sentences

In Chapter 2, Section 5.2 we discussed the features associated with the *by*-phrases of passive sentences. We now turn to the subjects of passive sentences.

4.1 The subjects of passives

There are passives that have no corresponding actives; for instance:

(18) a. The answer to this question is well known.
    b. His gesture was well intentioned.
    c. He is related to the Prime Minister.

These predicates have an adjectival reading (cf. Antonopoulou, 1991; Siewierska, 1984). The fact that they can be modified by adverbs like *very*, *rather*, and *somewhat* also shows that these predicates are adjectival (Sidney Greenbaum, personal communication, 1992). The sentences in (18) describe States, and their subjects are Attributees.

The predicates in (18) require lexical entries for *well known* (perhaps as a subentry of *know*), *well intentioned* and *related to*, which list arguments with the feature ATTRIBUTEE as obligatory.

The analysis of passives that do have corresponding active forms is more complicated. The sentences in (19) describe Events; their surface subjects have the feature CHANGE.

(19) a. The dishes were washed.
    b. The key was inserted into the lock.
    c. The little hut has just been painted.
    d. The farm is sold.

But in addition these sentences also tell us something about the current state of the entities denoted by the surface subjects. The Event of washing the dishes results in the State of the dishes being, if not clean, at least washed.

Now, in Section 3 it was claimed that only what is expressly stated in the sentence is taken into account in the analysis. It might be argued therefore that only the Event of washing and not the current State of the dishes should be reflected in feature composition. I propose that the rule of Section 3 does not apply to passives like (19), because here the State is made explicit in the sentence. The lexical entries for *wash*, *insert*, *paint*, and *sell* will have subentries for *washed, inserted, painted*, and *sold*[4] which – just like the verbs in (18) – each contain an argument with the feature ATTRIBUTEE; whenever something undergoes the Event of being "V-ed" it is in a State of, well, having been "V-ed" (V stands for verb).

In active sentences the state of the direct object – for instance of the dishes in *washed the dishes* – may of course be inferred from what is said, but it is not focused on. In some passive sentences, attention will be focused on the Event, and the resulting State will be of little interest. In others, the State will be at the forefront of attention. At any rate, a passive sentence refers both to an Event and a State, and therefore its surface subject has the feature ATTRIBUTEE. It will accordingly be in the Attributee case.

Usually the surface subject will also have the feature CHANGE – as in (19) – and then it will be A-case. There are verbs, however, that do not imply CHANGE – for instance the verb *see* – and the surface subjects of passive sentences with these verbs will not be in the A-case.

It appears, then, that there is an additional linking rule for the Attributee case. It may be linked not only to the subject of an active sentence (Section 1.1), but also to the (surface) subject of a passive sentence.

Passives with *by*-phrases will be analyzed similarly. The feature composition of the surface subjects in (20) is the same as that in (19), namely, ATTRIBUTEE and CHANGE (with the latter tending to be more prominent than in the corresponding truncated passives). Because of ATTRIBUTEE, the surface subjects of (20) are in the Attributee case, like those of (19). The feature CHANGE in the subjects of (20) is outweighed by the features of the oblique noun phrases, namely, CAUSE and CONTROL, either one of which carries more weight than CHANGE (Chapter 2, Section 4.3). The A-case is therefore assigned to these oblique noun phrases (recall that there is a linking rule that the A-case may be linked to a *by*-phrase).

(20) a. The dishes were washed by the maid.
b. The key was inserted into the lock by the burglar.
c. The little hut has been painted by Rhoda.

Evidence for this analysis is provided by a comparison of (19) with sentences with tough-movement, (21). The predicates of (21) are State predicates and their subjects are Attributee, and it is reasonable to assign the same case to the subjects of (19).

(21) a. The dishes are easy to wash.
b. The key is hard to insert into the lock.
c. The little hut was fun to paint.

In our discussion of (17) we observed that a statement about a State is normally understood wholistically. According to our analysis, (22)a refers not only to an Event, but also to a State. In line with this, (22)a is interpreted as saying something about campfires in general, whereas (22)b only refers to some campfires. See Pinker (1989: 70, 89ff.) for an essentially similar analysis.

(22) a. Campfires are made by Boy Scouts.
b. Boy Scouts make campfires.

The claim that the subject of the passive is an Attributee receives further support from certain phenomena discussed in the two following sections.[5]

4.2 *Constraints on passivization*

There are two constraints on passivization. The first constraint, which has been discussed in Chapter 2, Section 5.2, pertains only to passives with *by*-phrases:

First Constraint on Passivization:

> Only a noun phrase that has the features CAUSE + act, CAUSE + aff, or CONTROL can appear in the *by*-phrase of a passive sentence.

Another constraint has been repeatedly dealt with in the literature and is illustrated in (23). (Examples (23)a and (23)g are from Dixon, 1991: 304–305.)

(23) a. *The office was left by Fred at five o'clock.
     b. *The corner was turned by Kate.
     c. *The lake was swum by Sally.
     d. *His/Sam's feet were shuffled by Sam/him.
     e. *A loud cough was coughed by John.
     f. *A brick was seen by John's mother in the bath.
     g. Mary was seen entering the building at six o'clock.

The subjects of (23)a–f do not make "good" Attributees. There is no reason to attribute *was left by Fred* . . . to the office; the office is not in a special state as a result of Fred's leaving it. Nor is the brick affected by having been seen, and so on. A noun phrase can be an Attributee if it is intended to tell us something new about its referent, to attribute something to it. In (23)a–f this condition is not met. The feature ATTRIBUTEE is contracted by the noun phrases in (23), and since they do not have genuine Attributees, the sentences are unacceptable.

Sentence (23)f should be compared to (23)g, which suggests possible negative consequences for Mary (Keenan, 1985), and is therefore acceptable. Mary may be in a different state as a result of her having been seen at the spot (her name may appear in the gossip columns or she may be in for questioning by the police).

We can therefore formulate a constraint that pertains to all passive sentences – those with a *by*-phrase as well as agent-less passives:

Second Constraint on Passivization:

> The surface subject of a passive sentence must be a genuine Attributee.

Due to its high frequency of occurrence in English, passivization has become routinized, and occasionally we find that a noun phrase figures as subject in spite of its not being a "good" Attributee, as for instance in (24).[6] The incongruity of having the subjects of (24) treated as Attributees no longer grates on our ear.

(24) a. The distance between the two points was paced by the surveyor.
b. The square was thronged by the scouts.
c. Money is needed by the organization.

So far, we have discussed passives of sentences with a direct object. An active sentence with a prepositional object may also be passivized, as in

(25) The bed has been slept in.

Again, passivization of prepositional objects is blocked when it results in a sentence whose surface subject is not a "good" Attributee:[7]

(26) a *The bridge has been walked under.
b. *The stadium was arrived at.
c. *The tunnel was carefully gone into by the engineers.
d. *The lake has been camped beside by Mary.

In (25) the subject is in a new state (others may not want to sleep in the bed until the sheets have been changed, etc.). By contrast, the subjects in (26) are not honest-to-goodness Attributees.

Passives of sentences with prepositional objects, like (25), are somewhat less frequent than passives of direct objects. As a consequence, routinization has not progressed so far, and the requirement that the subject should be a genuine Attributee is more closely adhered to. This can be seen by comparing (27)a–c with (27)a'–c', respectively.

(27) a.   The tunnel was carefully explored by the engineers.
a'. *The tunnel was carefully gone into by the engineers.
b.   The town hall was surrounded by the police.
b'. *The town hall was stood around by the police.
c.   Three baskets were scored by John.
c'. *Three baskets were aimed at by John.

Active sentences with State predicates usually do not passivize. The active sentences in (1), above, have no corresponding passives:

(28) a. *A medal is deserved by John.
b. *Four is equalled by two and two.
c. *The play is lasted by three hours.
d. *A hand brake is lacked by the car.
e. *A hundred pounds are weighed by him.
f. *She is become by the blue dress.

In (28), both the First and the Second Constraints on Passivization are violated: The noun phrases in the *by*-phrases do not have the required features, and the subjects are not "good" Attributees. The same holds true of the passive sentences (29)a'–b', where *four people* and *two thousand people* are not "good" Attributees, and although the subject noun phrases in the active

(29)a–b are in the A-case, they have the feature CAUSE − act − aff, which does not license linking to the *by*-phrase.

(29) a.   This room sleeps four people.
      a′. *Four people are slept by this room.
      b.   The auditorium seats two thousand people.
      b′. *Two thousand people are seated by the auditorium.

Each of these violations is sufficient by itself to block passivization. When the sentences in (28) are reformulated without *by*-phrases (*A medal is deserved*, etc.), only the Second Constraint applies.

Only the First Constraint is violated by (30)b. As argued in Section 1.3, above, in connection with (5), (30)a tells us something not only about Dan – thus making *Dan* a "good" Attributee – but also about David; and this is true of the corresponding passive in (30)b as well. Hence, if (30)b is unacceptable, this is not due to the subject. Rather, it is the First Constraint that blocks passivization: *Dan* has neither CAUSE nor CONTROL. (Jespersen, 1961: 300, found in the literature only one instance of *resemble* in the passive.)

(30) a.   Dan resembles David.
      b.   *David is resembled by Dan.

We have seen that the feature composition of the *by*-phrase contributes to the unacceptability of the sentences in (28). In (31), by contrast, the *by*-phrase makes the sentence acceptable.

(31) a.   Landlords who live in London own the apartments.
      b.   The apartments are owned by landlords who live in London.
      c.   *The apartments are owned.

The subject of *own* in (31)a has CONTROL, and so has the noun phrase in the *by*-phrase of (31)b. As pointed out by Keenan (1985: 249–50), (31)b is much better than (31)c. The reason is, I suggest, that *the apartments* is a "good" Attributee in (31)b – the sentence provides some information about the apartments – but not in (31)c: That an apartment is owned (by someone) hardly tells us anything.

Verbs that passivize also admit tough-movement; see (20)–(21) (Section 4.1). Verbs that do not permit passivization, like those in (28)–(30), block tough-movement (Allerton, 1982: 82–85).

The constraints discussed here are language-specific. Keenan (1985: 250) points out that in some languages stative verbs such as those in (28) are indeed passivizable, and he quotes from Kinyarwanda (a Bantu language): *Four kilos are weighed by this book, Much joy is had by this child, A bad death was died by this chief.* Hebrew is even less tolerant in respect to passivization than English, and so are Slavic languages, which "do not allow recipients/ benefactives or prepositional objects to function as passive subjects" (Siewierska, 1988: 254).

4.3 A semantic saturation account

We have already seen that semantic saturation may impose constraints on constructions (Chapter 4, Section 2). The semantic saturation process affords us an alternative explanation for the unacceptability of those passives which have been accounted for in the previous section in terms of the Second Constraint on Passivization.

The surface subject of a passive sentence is the direct object of the corresponding active sentence. It is very common for the direct object to refer to the entity that is affected by the event referred to by the predicate verb, and accordingly the subject of passive sentences will very frequently be affected by the event. The semantic saturation hypothesis predicts a semantic "drift" of a syntactic category toward its central members, viz., the category "subject of passive" will be saturated with this frequently encountered notion of affectedness. When the subject, on the normal reading, is not affected there is a conflict with semantic saturation and as a consequence the sentence will sound odd. The subjects of (23)a–f, (26), and (28) are not affected, and their oddness is therefore accounted for by semantic saturation.

It is reasonable to assume that the less frequent a syntactic structure is, the more pronounced the effect of semantic saturation will tend to be. Frequently used structures may be expected gradually to lose their semantic "flavor" and to be less given to semantic saturation than those that are less often used. Like metaphors, the meaning of a construction may fade. As a result, sentences like (24) may be acceptable, whereas those with less frequent constructions, like (26), are not. This explanation is similar in spirit, though not in formulation, to those proposed by Bolinger (1977a: 10; 1977b), Ziv and Sheintuch (1981), and Dixon (1991: 304–305).

The following objection might be made here. On the semantic saturation account one would expect active sentences with an unaffected direct object – such as the active counterparts of (23) – to sound odd; and this is patently false. Consider, however, that active sentences are much more frequent than passive ones. Therefore routinization has progressed still further, which is why no similar constraints apply to them.

Recall that sentences describing states which have subjects that are also in the A-case may have an oblique noun phrase in the Comitative (Section 2.4). For passive sentences this rule does not seem to hold: only when the noun phrase has the feature INSTR (i.e., Instrument), as in (32)a, not when it has MANN or ACCOMP (Manner, Accompaniment), as in (32)b–c. Why are (32)b–c unacceptable?

(32) a.   This knife has never been cut with (by me).
     b.   *Care has never been played Russian roulette with (by anyone).
     c.   *John has never been travelled with (by his wife).

Sentence (32)b is ruled out because a noun phrase referring to Manner is not a good Attributee. Sentence (32)c, however, tells us something about John; John is a good Attributee. To explain why (32)c is odd, we have to resort to semantic saturation. The subject of a passive sentence is more often than not affected. Due to semantic saturation, sentences where this is not the case sound extremely odd. Being "travelled with" is not something that necessarily affects a person, which is why one would normally avoid a sentence like (32)c. (Semantic saturation may be an additional factor in ruling out (32)b.)

Neither *travel* nor some of the verbs in (23) may be assumed to have a feature "affected" registered in their lexical entries, and the phenomena discussed here cannot therefore be explained as being due to contraction of such a feature.

Semantic saturation thus accounts for some of the data discussed in Section 4.2 and for (32)c. But semantic saturation cannot be the whole story, as will be seen presently.

4.4 Instances not accounted for by semantic saturation

The subjects in (33) do not appear to be in any way affected. One would expect them therefore to be unacceptable, due to semantic saturation. Nevertheless these sentences are perfectly acceptable:

(33) a. Mt. Everest has been repeatedly climbed since the fifties.
b. This game was already played by the ancient Greeks.
c. The barn can be seen from my window.

These sentences describe States, and their subjects are Attributees. Mt. Everest has the property of being a much-climbed mountain, the game is a Greek game, and the barn is said to be at a certain location relative to the window.

Compare also the following:[8]

(34) a. *A steak is being had by John for supper.
a′. A steak can be had at the store for two pounds.
b. ?Publicity is shunned by Ellen.
b′. Publicity should be shunned.
c. *A mile was run by John.
c′. A mile was first run in 4 minutes by John.

Antonopoulou (1991: 68) remarks that (34)b′ is acceptable because it is "attributing a property" to publicity.

Even passives of prepositional objects are acceptable, even when they are not affected, when there is a "good" Attributee:

(35) a. *This bridge has been walked under by my brother.
a′.   This bridge has been walked under by generations of lovers.

     b. *Fame is aspired to by Emily.
     b'. Fame is aspired to by everyone.
     c. *The book has been referred to by John.
     c'. The book has been referred to by several authors.

What might a semantic saturation account of the acceptability of (34) and (35) be like? It, too, would have to appeal to the fact that a state is described, but would have to argue that the subject is affected in the sense of having passed into this state due to the event referred to by the predicate. Such an account is clearly more labored, and the explanation proposed in Section 4.2 may therefore appear preferable. It should be borne in mind, however, that (as far as the phenomena dealt with in Section 4.2 are concerned) the two explanations are not mutually exclusive. There may be some truth in both of them and they may converge on the same set of phenomena.

The distinction between noun phrases that are genuine Attributees and those that are not, may have the disadvantage that it is not formally defined; its advantage is that it seems to work better than others that have been proposed. Thus, the well-known rule that stative verbs do not passivize has many exceptions. Pinker (1989: 50) illustrates this by the following examples, among others, of passives with stative verbs:

(36) a. This book is owned by the library.
      b. The drastic measures are justified by the situation.
      c. The morning star was believed to be different from the evening star.

These sentences are acceptable because their subjects are obviously "good" Attributees: we are told something about the status of the book and the measures and about the changing conceptions of the morning star.

Jackendoff's (1972) Thematic Hierarchy Condition predicts that when the surface subject in a passive sentence is Goal or Location, the noun phrase in the by-phrase must be the Agent. This might account for some of the sentences that are not passivizable – see, for instance (28)–(29), where the noun phrase in the by-phrase is not an Agent – but others, e.g., (35)a, are left unaccounted for. Pinker (1989: 57) adduces the following counter-example to Jackendoff's rule:

(37) The mountain was capped by snow.

The subject of this sentence expresses the notion Location, but the noun phrase in the by-phrase is not an Agent.

4.5 Passives with contracted features

A passive sentence is acceptable even if the required features of the noun phrase in the by-phrase are contracted. Consider

(38) a. The fence encircles/surrounds/encloses the playground.
b. The playground is encircled/surrounded/enclosed by the fence.

Judging by the situation referred to, one would not accord to *the fence* any one of the agentive features. But (38)b is not blocked by the First Constraint on Passivization, because *encircle*, *surround*, and *enclose*, being frequently used to denote activities of persons, have lexical entries specifying that they have an argument with CAUSE and CONTROL. The subject of (38)a and the oblique noun phrase in (38)b contract agentive features registered in the lexical entries of the verbs *encircle*, *surround*, and *enclose*. These arguments become A-case and consequently can be linked to the subject or to a *by*-phrase. Another example is

(39) Gas lighting was replaced by electricity.

Electricity has neither CAUSE nor CONTROL when it replaces gas; but since *replace* is typically used with human subjects, these features are contracted from the lexical entry.

Contraction operates only within a subentry, not across subentries (Chapter 2, Section 3.3.2). This explains the unacceptability of (40)c.

(40) a. The police contained the demonstrators.
b. The yard contains a swimming pool.
c. *A swimming pool is contained by the yard.

The lexical entry of *contain* specifies that this verb has an argument with CAUSE and CONTROL, as shown in (40)a (after Rice, 1987: 422). If these features were contracted by *the yard* in (40)b–c, both these sentences would be acceptable. But they are not contracted, because the usages of *contain* in (40)a on the one hand and (40)b–c on the other are so different that they must be based on different subentries of the verb.

Contraction does operate in (41)b–c. The lexical entry for *hold* presumably has an argument with the feature CONTROL – see (41)a – and this is contracted by *a bookcase* in (41)b–c, where *hold* presumably does not belong to a different subentry. Although (41)c thus does not infringe the First Constraint on Passivization, it is blocked by the Second Constraint: *A hundred books* is not a genuine Attributee in (41)c.[9]

(41) a. He is standing there holding these books.
b. This bookcase holds a hundred books.
c. *A hundred books are held by this bookcase.

The same explanation probably applies to (42)c. In (42)a, *the boy* has CAUSE and CONTROL. These features are contracted by noun phrases in other sentences, e.g., by *the bridge* in (42)b. If (42)c is nevertheless unacceptable, this is because it tells us little about the river, so that the surface subject of (42)c is not a good Attributee.

(42) a.   The boy straddled the fence.
    b.   The bridge straddles the river.
    c.   *The river is straddled by the bridge.

5. Conclusions

An additional case category is introduced in this chapter: the Attributee. This is the case of one of the arguments of a State predicate. The Attributee is linked to the subject of an active sentence and to the surface subject of a passive sentence. Some Attributee noun phrases are also Agents.

Certain constraints on passivization have been discussed, some of which can be accounted for as resulting from semantic saturation.

7   Mental verbs

In the preceding chapters we saw that the subject of a sentence may be either in the A-case (the extended agent) or in the Attributee case. This chapter deals with subjects of mental verbs (sometimes called psychological verbs). It will be shown that no additional case category needs to be introduced for sentences with mental verbs; rather, these can be accommodated by the cases discussed in previous chapters.

1. Experiencer and Stimulus – the problem

In English there are two types of sentence structure in which a mental verb may appear. There are sentences where the subject refers to the **Stimulus** of the experience (sometimes called the Theme, but here we will use the former term). In the other kind of sentence the subject is the **Experiencer**. These two types are illustrated in Table 7.1. (For the sake of clarity, Experiencers will usually be given names beginning with an **E**, while names beginning with **St** will designate the Stimulus.)

Table 7.1 introduces some terms it will be convenient to use: A distinction is made between **S-sentences**, in which the subject is the Stimulus, and **E-sentences**, in which it is the Experiencer. The mental verb in an S-sentence will be called **S-verb**, and the verb in an E-sentence will be called **E-verb**. S-verbs include: *fascinate, irritate, annoy, bore,* and *thrill*. E-verbs include: *respect, like, hate, admire,* and *detest*.

That either the Stimulus or the Experiencer may be the subject poses a problem for any subject selection hierarchy. Such a hierarchy stipulates which case role takes preference over the other, and the pair of sentences in Table 7.1 suggest that there is no such preference hierarchy. If it is the Experiencer that is linked to the subject, it is hard to see why it should not also be the subject of S-verbs like *fascinate*; conversely, if the Stimulus is linked to the subject, there is no reason why it should not be the subject of E-verbs like *respect*. This problem is notorious; Dowty (1982: 112) speaks of "the infamous class of psychological verbs."

Jackendoff (1990: 140–41) captures the difference between S-verbs and E-verbs by their specifications: E-verbs have the specification REACT (for

Table 7.1. *The Experiencer in direct object and in subject position*

S-sentence (Stimulus as subject):
   Stella fascinates Erna.
     S-verb

E-sentence (Experiencer as subject):
   Ed respects Stan
     E-verb

"reacting"), and S-verbs have AFF (for "affecting"). This is merely a description of the state of affairs; in fact, Jackendoff does not deal primarily with problems of linking and does not presume to solve the problem we have raised in the preceding.

According to Dowty (1991: 579), both the Experiencer and the Stimulus have an equal number of what he regards as agentive features – the Experiencer is sentient, the Stimulus is a cause – and both these arguments are therefore equally entitled to agenthood. This treatment, too, does not say what determines whether a verb takes the Stimulus or the Experiencer as subject.

Grimshaw (1990) accounts for the difference between the two kinds of verbs in terms of two analyses. The thematic analysis is in terms of Experiencer and Theme, whereas the aspectual analysis accords Cause to the Stimulus in S-sentences. Both the (thematic) Experiencer and the (aspectual) Cause are associated with the subject, and linking is determined by the interaction of the two analyses.

In the present chapter I show that case assignment and the consequent subject selection in E-sentences and S-sentences can be explained in terms of features without resorting to two tiers of analysis, as Grimshaw does. It seems to me that the problem arises because the analysis has so far been made in the wrong terms. Experiencer and Stimulus (or Theme) are concepts that pertain to reality; they are useful labels for the relational notions in sentences with mental verbs, but they need not be deployed as features or cases. When E-sentences and S-sentences are analyzed in terms of the concepts introduced in the preceding chapters, the problem has a straightforward solution.

2. The subjects of mental verbs

Some subjects of mental verbs are Experiencers; others are Stimuli. That the Stimulus may be the subject of the sentence is due to the fact that it causes the mental experience; it has the feature CAUSE and accordingly is in the A-case. A problem arises with the Experiencer, however, which does not cause the experience but "has" it. We will first deal with the features of the Experiencer due to which it becomes the subject of E-sentences. After that, the Stimulus in S-sentences will be discussed.

2.1 Experiencers with Event predicates

Some E-verbs can be used in two ways. An E-verb may refer either to the mental experience undergone by someone or to the behavior accompanying this experience and expressing it. Compare the following two uses of *admire*:

(1) a. Ellen is in the gallery, admiring the painting and expounding its merits to John.
   b. Ellen admires Gauguin and wishes she could see one of the originals.

In (1)a, *admire* describes a transient Event, rather than a State, whereas in (1)b it refers to a State. In (1)a Ellen engages in a process of which she is the CAUSE and over which she has CONTROL; *Ellen* is therefore in the A-case and thus eligible for subject position. The case of *Ellen* in (1)b will be discussed in the next subsection.

That (1)a describes an Event is also shown by the *What-happened?* test (Chapter 5, Section 3.1.3). The sentence would be an appropriate answer to the question "What is happening?"

Another diagnostic is the progressive. Note that *admire* in (1)a is in the progressive, whereas in (1)b it cannot take this form (but see Quirk, Greenbaum, Leech, and Svartvik, 1985, Section 4.29). The E-verb *think* is an Event predicate and in (2) it has the progressive form. Here Ernest has some CONTROL over the activity of thinking and this noun is therefore in the A-case.

(2) Ernest is thinking about his exams.

In this instance, however, the *What-happened?* test fails. The distinction between Event and State, we have noted in Chapter 5, Section 3.2, is not clear-cut; rather, there is a gradient between the two and there may be borderline instances.

A further test of Eventhood is provided by the imperative. Sentence (3)a – quoted from fire department guidelines – is a request to acquaint oneself with fire extinguishers; (3)b–c are requests to turn one's attention to a topic. These are transient Events that have a beginning and an end. Sentence (3)d is a request to behave in a certain way. Where a sentence in the imperative is not easily construed as referring to overt behavior – as in (3)e, for instance – it sounds odd.

(3) a. Know to use fire extinguishers!
   b. Think about it!
   c. Observe how Mary talks to John!
   d. Respect your parents!
   e. ??Like Stockholm!

Note that neither the *What-happened?* test nor the progressive test identify (3)a and (3)d as referring to Events.

Private, inner experiences – such as liking, believing, and thinking – cannot be shared with others. Therefore sentences with Experiencer subjects typically cannot have a *with*-phrase with an ACCOMP noun:

(4) a. *Ethel liked the symphony with Estelle.
   b. *Ernest thought with Erika that the tenth power of two is twenty.
   c. *Ethel believes with Ernest that the earth is flat.

When the verb refers to an activity, however – and only then – a *with*-phrase with an ACCOMP noun may be appropriate. In (5) *admire* is understood as involving an activity, such as communicating the admiration to each other. This is another indication that the predicate refers to an Event. *Ellen* in (5) is in the A-case.

(5) Ellen is admiring the painting with Edwin.

2.2 Experiencers with State predicates

The E-sentences in (1)a, (2), and (3)a–d describe Events. But typically E-sentences refer to States. In (1)b – repeated here as (6)a – and in (6)b the experiences are not transient; the Experiencer subjects are said to be in a State, not to come to be in it; no activity is involved.[1]

(6) a. Ellen admires Gauguin and wishes she could see one of the originals.
   b. Evans knew Gauguin.

The subjects of State predicates are Attributees. The Attributee is linked to the subject (Chapter 6, Section 1.1), which is why the Experiencers in (6) are subjects.

Several observations support the analysis of some E-sentences as States and their Experiencer subjects as Attributees.

(i) In common with other State sentences (Chapter 5, Section 3.1.4) E-sentences do not permit Comitative arguments (unless they refer to activities, as in Section 2.1, above) – (7)a–b. The only exceptions – again in common with other State sentences – are expressions pertaining to degree, as in (7)c:

(7) a. *Ed respects Stan with enthusiasm/enthusiastically.
   b. *Ed likes Stan with an effort.
   c. Ed hates Stan with intensity/intensely.

(ii) Constructions with *force ... to* are admissible only with Events involving activities, not with States; cf. also the imperatives in (3). Thus (8)a imposes an interpretation involving activity; (8)b evokes, at best, associations of a police state; and (8)c, where an activity interpretation is not easily come by, sounds odd.

(8) a.   She forces Ed to respect his stepmother.
    b.   ?They forced Erwin to remember the storm.
    c.   ??They forced Esther to like the stew.

The adverb *deliberately* behaves similarly.

In Chapter 5, Section 3.3, it was observed that sentences with non-phrasal predicates like (9)a may be ambiguous between an Event reading and a State reading: Bruno may either be a law student – the predicate is a State – or happen to engage for a while in such study without being a regular student, and then the predicate is an Event. In the first case, but not in the second, (9)a will be interpreted like (9)b. No such ambiguity attends E-sentences, because these tend to be interpreted as States. Sentence (9)c will therefore always be understood like (9)d.

(9) a. Bruno is studying law.
    b. Bruno is a law student.
    c. Ed loves music.
    d. Ed is a music lover.

With reference to perceptual E-verbs, which we have not mentioned so far, some of them, like *listen* and *look* or the transitive *taste*, as in *taste the soup*, and *smell* as in *smell the violets*, quite obviously refer to Events and have an A-case subject. Others, like *hear* and *see* and the intransitive *taste* and *smell*, behave like Event predicates in some respects: they refer to transient experiences resulting from a change in the environment, and occasionally they can be in the progressive or the imperative. However, *force ... to* and *deliberately* are not applicable to these verbs.[2] Only when *see* and *hear* are understood as involving an activity ("go to see/hear") will (10) be fully acceptable. The question of the case the subjects of these verbs should be assigned to must therefore be left open for the time being; perhaps they are both A-case and Attributee (like the subjects in Chapter 6, Section 2).

(10) a. ??She forced Emily to hear the Stravinsky concert.
     b. ?She forced Emma to see the strawberry shrub.
     c. ??Emily heard the Stravinsky concert deliberately.
     d. ?Emma saw the strawberry shrub deliberately.

To summarize the discussion so far, E-verbs either refer to Events, and then their subjects are in the A-case, or – more typically – they refer to States, and then the subjects are Attributees. In some instances it may be uncertain whether a verb refers to an Event or a State (or both), but this is of little consequence, because whatever case is assigned to them, A-case or Attributee, they are eligible for subject position. And besides, as will be shown further on (Section 4.1), the Experiencer normally has CONTROL even in sentences with State predicates, and due to this feature they are assigned to the A-case.

2.3 Stimuli with Event and with State predicates

Unlike E-sentences, which often refer to States, S-sentences typically describe Events. In (11) Erna undergoes a change, and occurrence of change is typical of Events (Chapter 5, Section 3.1.2). Stella is the CAUSE of this Event, and accordingly this noun is in the A-case (recall that CAUSE outweighs CHANGE; Chapter 2, Section 4.3).[3]

> (11) Stella irritates Erna.

This contrast between E-sentences, which typically refer to States, and S-sentences, which refer to Events, may be illustrated by the verb pair *fear* (E-verb) and *frighten* (S-verb). You may fear the devil all your life, but when the devil frightens you, he will have done something (according to your lights) to instill fear into you; an event will have occurred. Compare (12)a with (12)b (where ?? means: odd as an answer to the preceding question). The *What-happened?* test identifies the answer in (12)a as an Event.

> (12) a. – What happened?
>   – The devil frightened me.
>   b. – What happened?
>   – ??I fear the devil.

Some S-sentences, however, refer to States. S-verbs that may be included in State predicates are *worry*, *perturb*, *preoccupy*, *please*, and *concern*. Examples given by Grimshaw (1990: 113) are:

> (13) a. The weather pleases us.
>   b. The matter concerns us.

Sentence (13)a says that the weather is pleasant (to us); that is, it describes a State; and so does (13)b. The subjects in (13) are therefore in the Attributee case. But they are also in the A-case, because they have the feature CAUSE.

One and the same verb may figure in an Event sentence as well as in a State sentence. Thus (11) may refer to the Event of Stella behaving in an irritating manner, perhaps even intentionally, and the subject (*Stella*) will be in the A-case. Alternatively, Stella may be unaware of irritating Erna; Stella may just be an irritating person, and the sentence refers to a State – Stella having the property of being considered irritating (at least by Erna) – and the subject is Attributee (besides being in the A-case due to the feature CAUSE).

3. The objects of mental verbs

So far the subjects of mental verbs have been discussed, and we have seen that they are either in the A-case or in the Attributee case. Turning to the objects of mental verbs, the following question arises.

In S-sentences the Stimulus is the subject and has the feature CAUSE + aff.

It might be argued that this feature should also be assigned to the Stimulus when it is the object, that is, when it appears in an E-sentence (like *Stan* in *Ed respects Stan*). This would mean that the Stimulus-object in E-sentences is in the A-case, whereas the Experiencer-subject is, typically, an Attributee. Hence the Stimulus in E-sentences would compete with the Experiencer for subject position.

Recall, however, the principle that feature assignment is governed solely by those aspects of the situation that are made explicit in the sentence (Chapter 6, Section 3). The sentence *Ed respects Stan* does not say that there is any characteristic of Stan that causes this feeling in Ed; if there is such a characteristic, this is left implicit and thus does not affect feature assignment. The lexical entries of E-verbs do not specify that the argument pertaining to the Stimulus has CAUSE.[4]

That the Stimulus is not assigned CAUSE when it is the direct object in an E-sentence is quite evident in sentences with verbs of cognition. In (14)a one would not be tempted to assign CAUSE to *Stan*. In (14)b this noun should not be assigned CAUSE any more than in (14)a.

(14) a. Ed knows/recognizes/remembers/forgot Stan.
     b. Ed likes/respects/admires/detests Stan.

Due to the absence of CAUSE in the Stimulus-object, (15)a is quite acceptable, although (15)b is odd. The Stimulus subject always has CAUSE, and applying this feature to a potentiality, as in (15)b, is problematic (but (15)c is acceptable because *the possibility*, unlike the storm, is actual). Significantly, some E-verbs have a Stimulus-object whose existence is only a potentiality – *expect*, *fear*, and *hope for*, for instance, refer to events that may happen but have not actually occurred – whereas there are no S-verbs, to my knowledge, that take a non-actual subject.

(15) a. Ernestine fears a possible storm that might occur next week.
     b. ??A possible storm that might occur next week frightens Ernestine.
     c. The possibility of a storm occurring next week frightens Ernestine.

It is in line with this analysis that middle verbs do not take Stimulus-subjects. The subject of a middle verb has the feature CAUSE (Chapter 2, Section 2.4), and for (16)b–c to be acceptable, the Stimulus, *Stan*, would have to have this feature.

(16) a. Everybody hates/respects Stan.
     b. *Stan hates easily.
     c. *Stan respects well.

The Experiencer is the Attributee in E-sentences referring to States (Section 2.2). What is the case of the Experiencer in S-sentences? In (11), repeated here, *Erna*, the Experiencer, is in a State, so perhaps *Erna* should be Attributee? If this were so, *Erna* would compete with *Stella* – which is A-case – for subject position, and this would necessitate a new linking rule giving the A-case precedence over the Attributee.

(11)   Stella irritates Erna.

But recall that the Attributee has been defined as the case of a noun phrase which is described by a State predicate; in (11) *Erna* is not a candidate for this case because the predicate describes an Event. The problem, then, arises only with State predicates, like *concern*, *worry*, *perturb*, and *please*, as for instance in:

(17)   a.   The state of the economy concerns Eleanor.
        b.   The strawberries please Eleanor.

I would argue, however, that even in (17) the Experiencers should not be analyzed as Attributees. It is not the State Eleanor is in which is focused on here but rather the effect of the Stimulus. The sentences in (17) do not pretend to attribute anything to the Experiencers, hence the latter are not Attributees. The lexical entries of S-verbs, then, do not contain an argument with the feature ATTRIBUTEE.

4.   CONTROL in the Experiencer and the Stimulus

4.1   CONTROL in the Experiencer

Mental processes are conceived of as being in a sense under the control of the experiencer (Huddleston, 1970; Dixon, 1991: 269). Hatred is an emotional response, but it is not an uncontrollable one. When Elaine hates Stewart, she can try to overcome her hatred: she has CONTROL. In general, the Experiencer-subject has the feature CONTROL even when the predicate refers to a State. Because of this feature it is assigned to the A-case, in addition to being in the Attributee case.

The assignment of CONTROL to the Experiencer seems to be justified by the *should-not* test suggested in Chapter 2, Section 2.2.1:

(18)   a.   Elaine, you should not hate Stewart.
        b.   You should not respect Stan (because he is a coward).

Because the Experiencer has CONTROL, it can appear in a *by*-phrase of a passive sentence (Chapter 2, Section 5.2):

(19)   a.   Stewart is hated by Elaine.
        b.   Stan was respected by all his colleagues.

That children treat Experiencers like Agents is suggested by a study by Maratsos, Kuczaj, Fox and Chalkley (1979). They found that two-to-three-year-olds tended to overgeneralize the past inflection *-ed* to mental verbs (*seed, feeled*) as much as to action verbs (*goed, buyed*). Further, when given sentences with mental verbs, they reacted to "Who did it?" questions as naturally as to such questions asked about sentences with action verbs.

Possibly, CONTROL should be assigned to the Experiencer not only when it is the subject in an E-sentence but also when it is the direct object in an S-sentence, as in (11). The Stimulus in an S-sentence – and not the Experiencer – is assigned to the A-case, because it has the feature CAUSE in addition to CONTROL.

4.2 CONTROL *in the Stimulus*

An S-sentence, we have noted, may describe either an Event or a State (Section 2.3). The CONTROL exercised by the Stimulus subject will typically be of much greater strength (see Chapter 2, Section 2.1) in Events than in States. Take the above example (11). An Event reading of the sentence would be that Stella irritates Erna by, say, talking too much. A State reading would be that Stella's personality is such that she irritates Erna. Clearly, Stella has more CONTROL on the former reading than on the latter.

When the Stimulus is the subject of an S-sentence, then, it has CONTROL to varying degrees. Not so when it is the direct object of an E-sentence as in

(20) Elaine hates Stewart.

That Stewart can do anything about the matter is at least doubtful. He may not even be aware of the feelings harbored by Elaine, and if he is, there may be nothing he can do about them: they may be due, say, to Elaine's character. As pointed out by Lee and Kasof (1992), Stewart may be hated (or liked, respected, etc.) even long after he has died. The sentence says something about Elaine's feelings; all the rest is conjecture. This is an instance of a State resulting from an Event, where the Event is implicit, and only explicit States and Events affect case assignment (see Chapter 6, Section 3). The Stimulus in an E-sentence, then, is not assigned CONTROL.

Further evidence for this conclusion is provided by the *should-not* test. Unlike the Experiencer of an E-sentence which passes this test (see (18) in Section 4.1), the Stimulus of an E-sentence does not pass it:

(21) a. *Stewart, you should not be hated by Elaine.
      b. *Stan should not let himself be respected by Ed.

(Sentence (21)b will be acceptable, if at all, only on the Event reading; cf. (8)a.)[5]

4.3 Passives of S-sentences

In the preceding we have seen that the Stimulus in S-sentences may have CONTROL with varying degrees of strength. There is a linguistic way of signalling strength of CONTROL of the Stimulus. In addition to the regular passive with the agent in a *by*-phrase, English has a passive with what Svartvik (1966: 102–104) calls "quasi-agents." In (22), the Stimulus appears in prepositional phrases with *with, at, about, in, over,* and *of.* In passive sentences these prepositions are reserved almost exclusively for mental S-verbs.

(22) a. Ed was thrilled with the scene.
    b. Ed was amazed at the spectacle.
    c. Ed is worried about the recession.
    d. Ed is interested in baseball.
    e. Ed is perturbed over the situation.
    f. Ed was tired of looking at the bare walls.

(See also Quirk, *et al.,* 1985, Section 3.76.)

Especially common is the participle form with *with* (*annoyed, bothered, disgusted, fascinated, maddened, pleased, bored, occupied, obsessed*) and with *at* (*surprised, astounded, dumbfounded, astonished, horrified, perturbed, irritated, exasperated*).

Now, some S-verbs admit of two alternative passives – one with a *by*-phrase and one with a different prepositional phrase:

(23) a. Eric was bothered with his neighbors.
    a'. Eric was bothered by his neighbors.
    b. Estelle was surprised at him.
    b'. Estelle was surprised by him.
    c. Erna was annoyed with Stella.
    c'. Erna was annoyed by Stella.

The two sentences in each pair seem to differ in the amount of CONTROL of the Stimulus: *by*-phrases are the regular realizations of the A-case, and the underlying subject thus is perceived of as having more CONTROL than that in the passive with other prepositions.

That the difference between *by* and other prepositions corresponds to a difference in CONTROL is also confirmed by (24)a, which is an exceptional construction because, as pointed out, the passive with a preposition other than *by* usually occurs only with a mental verb. *John* in (24)b – even when he is the bridegroom and not the priest – appears to have decidedly more CONTROL than *John* in (24)a:

(24) a. She was married to John.
    b. She was married by John.

5. Studies of rated CONTROL

In a series of psycholinguistic studies (Schlesinger, 1992) I have attempted to obtain confirmation of the claims made in Section 4 about CONTROL in the Experiencer and the Stimulus. In these studies, respondents were asked to rate the degree of CONTROL of each of the two participants in a situation described by either an E-sentence or an S-sentence. One of the studies will be briefly reported here.

Ratings of features tap the respondents' cognitive space; they can inform us only indirectly about linguistic features. In assigning features, we have repeatedly noted, information that is only implicit in the sentence is to be disregarded (see Sections 3 and 4.2). This provision pertains to the linguistic level. It cannot prescribe the responses of native speakers, who will presumably take into account such implicit information. Further on we will see how the results of our studies are affected by this.

5.1 Procedures

The respondents were sixty-eight native speakers of English. They were each presented with a rating form containing sixteen S-sentences and sixteen E-sentences. To control for possible effect of position and of focus, two cleft constructions were used:

> Subject-relative: *It is Paul who fascinates/respects John.*
> Object-relative: *It is John whom Paul fascinates/respects.*

Two parallel rating forms were constructed. In one form, half the S-sentences were presented in the subject-relative form and the other half in the object-relative form, and the same was done with the E-sentences. In the other form, those sentences that appeared in the subject-relative form in the first form appeared in the object-relative form, and vice versa.

Respondents were asked to indicate on a scale from 1 (little control) to 7 (much control) the degree of control exercised by each of the two participants, John and Paul, in each sentence. The meaning of the term "control" was explained by an example. Full details of the procedures are given in Schlesinger (1992).

5.2 Results and discussion

As hypothesized, the subject was perceived as having greater CONTROL than the object, in both E-sentences and S-sentences. The differences, presented in Table 7.2, were significant ($p < 0.001$). The effect was somewhat larger for subject-relative than for object-relative sentences, but this variable does not concern us here.[6]

In other studies reported in Schlesinger (1992), these findings were

Table 7.2. *Control in S-sentences and E-sentences*

S-sentence	Stimulus	Experiencer
	subject	object
subject-relative	5.06	4.13
object-relative	5.19	3.86

E-sentence	Experiencer	Stimulus
	subject	object
subject-relative	5.42	3.58
object-relative	5.13	3.81

Notes:
1 = little control
7 = much control

replicated. In one of the replications, respondents were asked to rate the degree of intention of each participant instead of control. Intuitively, Intention seems to be related to Control, and in fact the results for the latter notion were replicated with the notion intention.

As stated in Section 4.2, while the Stimulus in an E-sentence may be said to exercise some measure of control, this is not stated explicitly in the sentence, and therefore the Stimulus object in an E-sentence is not assigned the feature CONTROL. Respondents in our rating task, however, were not committed to this principle of feature assignment. They presumably judged the situation rather than the way it was referred to in the sentence. This accounts for the, albeit low, ratings of control in the Stimulus in E-sentences; see Table 7.2.

The table also shows that the degree of CONTROL accorded to Experiencers in S-sentences was lower than that accorded to Experiencers in E-sentences.[7] Possible factors to the lower degree of rated CONTROL in Experiencers in S-sentences are:

(i) An Experiencer of an Event that is sprung on him may be perceived as having less CONTROL than an Experiencer of a relatively permanent State. If this is so, then Experiencers in S-sentences, which typically refer to Events (Section 2.3), will be judged as having less CONTROL than Experiencers in E-sentences which predominantly refer to States (Section 2.2); that is, Experiencers that are objects will be accorded less CONTROL than Experiencers that are subjects.

(ii) The sentences in our study have non-phrasal predicates (Chapter 5, Section 2). The subjects of non-phrasal predicates (not only of mental verbs) are mostly in the A-case and very often have the feature CONTROL. Due to semantic saturation (Chapter 4, Section 2.1), the subjects of E-sentences may acquire an additional measure of CONTROL.[8] This resulted in higher ratings of CONTROL for the subjects than for the objects of the E-sentences in our study.

Findings that parallel those on CONTROL were obtained in Kasof and Lee's (1993) study of rated saliency of subjects and objects of mental verbs. The Experiencer was found to have greater saliency in subject position than in object position, and the same was true of the Stimulus. These findings parallel those obtained in previous studies on the relative saliency of the Experiencer subject and Experiencer object and of the Stimulus subject and object. Further, Kasof and Lee found that saliency correlated with causality ratings obtained in various previous studies. Both saliency and causality typically occur in subjects, and the above differences are therefore accounted for by the semantic saturation process.

Note that previously the semantic saturation hypothesis has been deployed to account for constraints on acceptability (Chapter 4, Section 2; Chapter 6, Section 4.3). Now it is argued that semantic saturation may also affect the features in acceptable sentences.

6. The Event–State dichotomy of mental verbs

6.1 The scarcity of complementaries

We have seen that mental verbs in English fall into two large groups: one group, the E-verbs, take the Experiencer as subject, and the other, the S-verbs, take the Stimulus as subject. The former predominantly refer to States, and the latter, to Events. While there are exceptions to this rule (see Sections 2.1 and 2.3), there is some experimental evidence that people perceive these two types of verbs in this manner. Lee and Kasof (1992) have shown that E-verbs are perceived to have greater latency than S-verbs; that is, the situations referred to by S-verbs tend to be judged to occur "suddenly, in reaction to relatively few behaviors," as opposed to "gradually, in reaction to longer series of behaviors."

Now, some mental experiences may be viewed either as Events or as States, the English language providing for them both an E-verb and an S-verb. For instance:

(25) a.   Stanley frightened Ervin.
     a'. Ervin fears Stanley.
     b.   Steve comes home late and worries Eleanor.
     b'. Eleanor worries about Steve because he is late.
     c.   Stephanie pleases Erika.
     c'. Erika likes Stephanie.

Let us call such Event-State verb pairs **complementaries**.

Different (though related) verbs are involved in (25)a and (25)a'; the same verb figures in (25)b and (25)b′ (albeit in a different collocation). The pair in (25)c and 25c′ is etymologically unrelated; but note that *please* cannot be used in all the contexts that *like* can (*John pleases me* is much more restricted in use than *I like John*).

It is noteworthy that there are very few such complementaries in English; the above list is probably exhaustive.[9] There is no complementary verb for *astonish* (one has to use the passive *be astonished*), for *fascinate*, for *irritate*, and so on.

Linda Manney (1990) reports that in Modern Greek the situation is similar. Modern Greek has a morphologically marked middle voice. She reports that there are "several" active-middle pairs among verbs of emotion such that the middle voice designates an emotional response (i.e., is an E-verb), and the active voice designates the causation thereof (i.e., is an S-verb). Her examples are, translated into English: *I'm worried about his health* (middle), *His health worries me* (active); *S/he gets upset every time s/he sees the police* (middle), *Seeing the police upsets her* (active) (Manney, 1990: 235). The middles in all the above examples have "non-affected prepositional objects or sentential complements" and not accusative objects (in this they differ from English E-sentences).[10] Note that she mentions only "several" such pairs and reports that there are other middle-active pairs where the meaning of the emotion differs. Interestingly, the Greek word for *worry*, which does service both as an E-verb and an S-verb in English, is among the few Greek examples.

Why are complementaries so scarce? An explanation that comes to mind is that it seems more natural for certain mental experiences to occur as States rather than as Events, whereas other experiences may appear to lend themselves better to a description as Events rather than as States. For example, the Event of annoying or of impressing someone may be conceived of as more typical than the State of being annoyed or impressed; and conversely, it may be more natural to view someone as respecting another person (a State) than as being caused to respect him (an Event).

It is proposed, then, that differences between mental experiences coded by these two classes of verbs are reflected in linguistic structure. In line with this explanation are Lee and Kasof's findings, summarized in the preceding, on the difference in the way E-verbs and S-verbs are perceived. However, their findings are also compatible with an alternative account. The causal relationship may run in the opposite direction, that is, these verbs may be perceived in different ways – as States (E-sentences) or Events (S-sentences) – as a result of being used in different linguistic structures.

The issue can be approached from a crosslinguistic perspective. If the difference between E-verbs and S-verbs is inherent in the mental experiences they refer to, as has been conjectured above, the following two hypotheses should be confirmed:

Hypothesis A
Complementaries are infrequent in the languages of the world.

Hypothesis B
Coding mental experiences is not entirely language-specific. An experience that is coded by an E-verb in one language will tend to be coded by an E-verb in another language, and an experience coded by an S-verb in one language will tend to be coded by an S-verb in another language.

The data on Modern Greek reported in the preceding are in line with Hypothesis A, but more data are clearly needed. A modest beginning in testing these hypotheses has been made by Laura Epstein (1988) in a study comparing Spanish and English mental verbs, reported in the following.

6.2 Complementaries in Spanish

To test Hypotheses A and B, Epstein first obtained a list of Spanish mental experience verbs.

The pool of English mental verbs contained the English E-verbs and S-verbs included in a previous study (Schlesinger, 1992). Due to time limitations, only emotionally negative verbs were included in the study, i.e., verbs having senses similar to those of *hate*, *despise*, *disgust*, and *irritate*.

The Spanish verbs were (i) translation equivalents of the English verbs in the above pool, as obtained from an English–Spanish dictionary; (ii) several synonyms and near-synonyms of the Spanish verbs in (i) found in a Spanish monolingual dictionary and in a Spanish dictionary of synonyms (Barcia, 1948). After excluding rare verbs and those that have additional non-mental meanings, Epstein was left with a list of seventeen Spanish E-verbs and thirty-eight Spanish S-verbs.

The mental verbs – in both the English and in the Spanish lists – fell into several groups according to their content:

E-verbs having meanings close to –
"hate" (e.g., *detestar, abominar*)
"despise" (e.g., *desdeñar, subestimar*)
"reject" (e.g., *repudiar, ignorar*)

S-verbs having meanings close to –
"estrange" (e.g., *indisponer, alienar*)
"disgust" (e.g., *enfermar, nausear*)
"offend" (e.g., *agraviar, violentar*)
"irritate" (e.g., *exasperar, enfadar*)
"annoy" (e.g., *molestar, incomodar*)

The investigation of Hypothesis A proceeded in two stages:

Stage 1

Generation of a list of verb pairs that are, prima facie, complementaries. The set of Spanish verbs was divided into three lists: one list contained the E-verbs and each of the other two contained half of the S-verbs. Two native Spanish speakers were given each of these lists. They were asked to propose a complementary verb for each of the E-verbs, the notion of "complementary" being illustrated by examples.

A fourth list of verbs was given to three Spanish speakers, who were asked to pair off complementaries from its members. This list included E-verbs with meanings close to "hate" and "reject" and S-verbs with meanings close to "disgust," "irritate," and "annoy." (E-verbs with meanings close to "despise" and S-verbs with meanings close to "estrange" and "offend" did not hold out much promise, since there seemed to be no semantic group of S-verbs and E-verbs, respectively, that formed complementaries with them.)

Stage 2

The investigator selected from the sets of verbs obtained in the four lists of Stage 1 those verb pairs that appeared to be, prima facie, complementaries. These, together with the examples given in the instructions of the lists in Stage 1, were now screened by another Spanish speaking informant, using the following procedure.

The notion of "complementary" was first explained to the informant by means of two examples, introduced in the form of questions:

> Is it possible that John buys something from Paul but Paul does not sell it to John?
> Is it possible that Paul sells something to John but John does not buy it from Paul?

After the informant answered in the negative, he was asked:

> Is it possible that John leads Paul but Paul does not follow John?
> Is it possible that Paul follows John but John does not lead Paul?

The correct answer to the first question is obviously "no" (if Paul does not follow John, the latter does not lead, at most he attempts to do so), and the answer to the second one is "yes" (John may be unaware of Paul following him, and leading is an intentional act). The second pair, then, illustrates an implicational relation, which holds in one direction only, i.e., *lead → follow*, but not the reverse. This difference was discussed with the informant.

Next, the verb pairs that were selected as being prima facie complementaries were presented, one by one, to the informant, who was asked questions like those above about each such pair.

The results can be summarized as follows:

None of the pairs was regarded by the informant as a true complementary pair; but five of the pairs were regarded as implicational in the sense described above:

(26) a. *repulsar → repeler*
    b. *repudiar → desagradar*
    c. *aborrecer → repugnar*
    d. *aborrecer → disgustar*
    e. *detestar → desagradar*

(Some other informants, consulted after the study, claimed that (26)c is somewhat problematic.)

Informants gave various reasons for the fact that the reverse implication (*repeler → repulsar*, etc.) does not hold in (26):

(i) The E-verb describes a feeling that may arise in the Experiencer-subject without being due to characteristics of the Stimulus (in (26)a).

(ii) One of the verbs indicates a feeling of greater strength (*detestar* is much stronger than *desagradar*, hence it is not the case that *desagradar → detestar*, and the same is true of (26)d).

(iii) One of the verbs indicates a deeper and more lasting feeling (*aborrecer* is more lasting than *repugnar*, although here the informant felt that one can almost say that *repugnar → aborrecer*; on the other hand, he also had some reservations about *aborrecer → repugnar*).

Three other pairs were judged as being neither true complementaries nor implicational: *aborrecer – irritar*, *repeler – asquear*, and *odiar – disgustar*.

This study thus suggests that Spanish does not differ much from English in respect to the occurrence of complementaries. While the sample in this study is not exhaustive and the possibility cannot be ruled out that in the area of mental verbs true complementaries do exist, these are, at best, very scarce. The prediction based on Hypothesis A was thus borne out.

6.3 English–Spanish complementaries

Hypothesis B predicts that there will be no tendency for English E-verbs to have complementary S-verbs in Spanish and for English S-verbs to have complementary E-verbs in Spanish. Epstein's investigation included the following stages:

Stage 1
Generation of a list of Spanish–English verb pairs. Two lists were prepared:

(i) a list containing English E-verbs (from the original set of verbs used in Schlesinger's 1992 study) and Spanish S-verbs.

(ii) a list containing Spanish E-verbs and English S-verbs.

In both lists, the E-verbs had meanings close to "hate" and "reject" and S-verbs had meanings close to "disgust", "irritate" and "annoy" (as in the fourth list of the Spanish–Spanish study; see previous section).

Each of the two lists was given to two bilingual speakers of Spanish and English. They were asked to find pairs of complementaries. The notion of "complementary" was explained as in the Spanish–Spanish study, above, but with mixed Spanish–English examples (e.g., *A loathes B* and *B repugna A*).

Stage 2

From the two above lists those verb pairs were selected that appeared to be, prima facie, complementaries. These, together with the examples given in the instructions of the lists in Stage 1, were now screened by a bilingual informant (who had also served as informant in the Spanish–Spanish study), using the procedure adopted in Stage 2 of the Spanish–Spanish study.

It was found that two pairs (with English E-verb and Spanish S-verb) were judged to be true complementaries:

> (27) a. dislike – *desagradar*
> b. loathe – *repugnar*

In three pairs with Spanish E-verb and English S-verb the informant detected an implicational relation:

> (28) a. *aborrecer* → disgust
> b. *abominar* → disgust
> c. repulse → *repeler*

The emotions expressed by *aborrecer* and *abominar* were judged by the informant to be stronger than that of *disgust* and hence the reverse implications did not hold. The same was true of the reverse implication of (28)c (see the reason given for (26)a in the Spanish–Spanish study). An additional pair, *dislike – degustar*, was judged as being neither complementary nor implicational.

Hypothesis B thus fared tolerably well in this study. The only disconfirming instances were those in (27) and the hypothesis cannot be considered flawed by these isolated exceptions.

However, strong support for Hypotheses A and B might be obtained only by a study of a larger set of mental verbs in several additional languages unrelated to English.

7. The linguistic realization of experiences

So far we have been dealing with sentences with non-phrasal predicates as realizations of mental experiences. In fact, in English and in other languages there are various other ways of expressing these. As far as I know, no language has a construction that serves specifically for expressing the experiencer; rather, this notion is always realized by constructions also used for other notions (as, for instance, the transitive noun phrase-verb-noun phrase construction, which is used for activities).

In this section we look at some of the ways Experiencers may be expressed in English and in other languages.

7.1 English realizations of experiences

English has, for the most part, four types of sentences to refer to mental experiences (under which term we include here visceral and other bodily experiences, like being hungry or cold). These are illustrated in Table 7.3. The experiences in the table are grouped into emotional, cognitive, perceptual, and physical (i.e., bodily), but not much store should be set by this classification.

The Experiencer is always in the Attributee, whether the experience is expressed by an E-verb, an adjective (*Ed is afraid*), or a noun (*Ed has a headache*).

For other kinds of English constructions see Talmy (1985b: 99).

The form "*have* + noun" is very common in English, with the nouns frequently being nominalizations of E-verbs – *pity, admiration, desire, hope, fear, trust*, etc. – but they are also used with nouns that are not nominalizations, such as *faith, confidence, courage*.

It is of interest that nominalizations of S-verbs differ from nominalizations of activity verbs. In the latter, either the object or the subject may be the "possessor" – see (29) – whereas in nominalizations of S-verbs the "possessor" is normally the subject:

(29) a. Stan constructs the machine.
      b. The machine's construction (by Stan)
      c. Stan's construction of the machine

(30) a. Stan astonishes/irritates/worries Ed.
      b. Ed's astonishment/irritation/worry
      c. *Stan's astonishment/irritation/worry of Ed

(But: *John's embarrassment of Mary*; see Grimshaw, 1990: 118ff, for an extended discussion.)

A very frequently used E-verb is *feel*:

(31) a. Ed feels the chill.
      b. Ed feels astonishment at Stan's action.
      c. Ed feels sadness.
      d. Ed feels respect for Stan.

Table 7.3. *Coding of experiences in English*

Experience expressed as	Type of experience	Stimulus coded[a]	Stimulus not coded	Nominalization
E-verb	emotional	Ed respects Stan.		Ed's respect for Stan
	cognitive	Ed remembers Stan.		Ed's remembrance of Stan
	perceptual	Ed sees Stan.		
	physical	Ed suffers (from the cold).	Ed freezes.	Ed's suffering (from the cold)
S-verb	emotional	The war is worrying (Ed).[a]		Ed's worry (about the war)
		The affair concerns Ed.		Ed's concern (about the affair)
	cognitive	Stan astonishes Ed.		Ed's astonishment
	perceptual			
	physical	The blow hurt (Ed).		
be + adjective	emotional	Ed is afraid (of Stan).	Ed is sad.	Ed's sadness/ fear (of Stan)
	cognitive	Ed is aware of Stan.		Ed's awareness of Stan
	perceptual			
	physical		Ed is cold.	
have + noun	emotional	Ed has respect for Stan.		Ed's respect for Stan
	cognitive	Ed has memories of Stan.		
	perceptual	Ed has a glimpse of Stan.		Ed's glimpse of Stan
	physical	Ed has a headache (fom the noise).		

Note:
[a] i.e., the Stimulus may be expressed as direct or indirect object. Optional expressions are parenthesized. Note that with S-verbs it is the Experiencer, not the Stimulus, that may be optional.

Note that in (31)b–d the objects are nominalizations of verbs belonging to the categories S-verb, "*be* + adjective," and "*have* + noun" (Table 7.3), respectively. The sentences in (31) describe States, and their subjects (*Ed*) are in the Attributee case.

In some instances an experience will be coded with a part of the

Experiencer's body as the Experiencer term; see (32)a. Alternatively, the body part may be conceived of as the Stimulus, as in (32)b.

(32) a. The blow hurt Ed's hand.
b. Ed's hand hurts.

A person's body, then, can be conceived of as either a part of his personality, undergoing the experience, or an external agent, causing him or her to have an experience. But there is an alternative analysis of (32)b: *hurt* may be one of the verbs that enter into unaccusative constructions, like *open*, *melt*, and *freeze*.

In previous sections we have seen that the subjects of E-verbs and of S-verbs may be Attributees, A-case, or both. The subjects of sentences with "*be* + adjective" or with "*have* + noun" are usually Attributee, but occasionally they, too, may be A-case:

(33) John will join you in a minute; he is just having a quick glimpse of the view.

What determines in which of the four forms in Table 7.3 a given experience is coded? Obviously, the choice of the "*be* + adjective" and "*have* + noun" forms is constrained by the availability of the appropriate adjectives and nouns in the language (although this may be begging the question, for why did the language not provide the relevant forms?). But even within the possibilities of the lexicon of the language not all options are taken. Thus we say *is hungry* but not **has hunger*, whereas a person may *have pains* but not **be painful*. To throw some light on this issue, a small crosslinguistic study was conducted, which is to be reported in the following section.

7.2 A crosslinguistic study

This study included nineteen European languages and one Semitic language, Hebrew. The European languages were: English, German, Dutch, Yiddish, Swedish, Danish, French, Italian, Spanish, Portuguese, Romanian, Polish, Russian, Lithuanian, Modern Greek, Persian, Estonian, Hungarian, and Eskimo.[11]

Informants were asked to give the translation equivalents of ten types of experiences, which are expressed by the following terms in English:

(34) a. be happy
a'. be sad
b. be hungry
b'. be thirsty
c. be warm
c'. be cold
d. be healthy

    d'. be ill
    e. have a pain
    e'. have a headache

The data provided by the informants may possibly be somewhat incomplete. Occasionally an informant may have supplied one translation equivalent and have failed to come up with a less frequently used alternative expression. I will therefore not give the data in full detail, but rather outline some general trends that emerged.

While the languages studied varied widely in the means used for coding experiences, and there were not even clear signs of implicational scales, there were some general tendencies of certain experiences favoring a certain type of coding across languages. In particular, it appears that those experiences that are predominantly coded as attributes of the Experiencer are less likely to be coded as experiences the Experiencer is affected by. Further, the experiences differ in the extent languages tend to express them as "being had" by the Experiencer. These tendencies may be a reflection of the clustering of mental experiences in the underlying cognitive space, a possibility that will be discussed further on. First, we discuss the crosslinguistic data in terms of two distinctions: the attributive–affected distinction and the possessive–nonpossessive distinction.

(i) *The attributive–affected distinction* In English, all but the last pair in (34) are expressed by the construction "*be* + adjective." The Experiencer is the Attributee of the experience. Not all languages in our sample have a copular *be*, but when we look at adjectival constructions we find that these are used by most languages in this study for: happy/sad, healthy/ill, and hungry/thirsty. The exceptions are: French for hungry/thirsty, Russian for thirsty, and Eskimo for happy/sad.

Many fewer languages use attributive constructions for the other two pairs of experiences. Only Eskimo and English use it for warm and cold; Swedish uses it only for warm. None of the languages studied has the attributive relation for headache; English (*be in pain*) and Eskimo have it for pain.

There are only isolated instances of the use of E-verbs for the experiences in (34), and those reported to me were all for "cold": German (*ich fröstele/ friere*), Swedish, Danish, and Hungarian.[12]

Instead of viewing an experience as an attribute of the Experiencer, a language may use a construction that conceives of the Experiencer as affected by the experience, such as the S-sentence in English. In English, however, none of the experiences in (34) is coded in this form. Some languages with case markings use the Dative (to me it chills); Romanian and German use the accusative.[13] For the warm/cold pair, the Experiencer is frequently conceived of as affected, but this is less often the case for the pain/headache pair. Romanian uses the accusative as an alternative to an attributive construction for hungry/thirsty, but there was not a single instance in the languages studied for healthy/ill being coded as affected. Constructions with *feel*

Table 7.4. *Experiences as attributes and possessions of the Experiencer and as affecting him*

Experience	Characterization	
pain/headache	*possessive*	affected
warm/cold	possessive	affected
healthy/ill	possessive	attributive
hungry/thirsty	possessive	attributive
happy/sad		attributive

Note:
Italic print indicates that this kind of coding was particularly frequent.

(almost exclusively as alternatives to other constructions) are also frequent with warm/cold and with pain.

The crosslinguistic data permit us to propose, tentatively, the following grouping of experiences:

> Expressed predominantly as attributes of the Experiencer:
> happy/sad, healthy/ill, hungry/thirsty
> Expressed predominantly as Experiencer affected by the experience:
> warm/cold, pain/headache

As stated, these may reflect an underlying attributive–affected distinction pertaining to experiences. When the Experiencer is coded as affected by the experience, the latter is presumably conceived of as something external impinging on him. When the experience is treated by a language as an attribute of the Experiencer, it is presumably conceived as something more "internal," originating in the Experiencer.

(ii) *The possessive–non-possessive distinction* Many languages have a construction, which – like the one in English – credits the Experiencer with "having" an experience. Often this is only one of the options offered by a language for coding the experience.[14]

Three groups of experiences may be distinguished in respect to the tendency of languages to code the Experiencer as "having" an experience:

pain/headache: Most of the languages studied express these experiences by a possessive construction ("having").

warm/cold, healthy/ill, hungry/thirsty: Coding these as possessives is less frequent.

happy/sad: Hardly any instances were found of these emotions being coded as something the Experiencer "has."

It may be instructive to look at the two distinctions together, as shown in Table 7.4.

Table 7.4 suggests that in cognitive space there may be one underlying gradient. To the extent that the experience tends to be conceived of as coming from outside and the Experiencer as being affected by it, it may also be viewed as something the Experiencer "has." This gradient affects the way experiences are coded by the languages of the world, with each language choosing the "cutting point" in the gradient at which the coding switches from one construction to another. Obviously, data on more languages and more mental experiences will be needed before this conjecture can be established.

8. Conclusions

The chapter deals with the case of the subjects and objects of verbs referring to internal (cognitive, emotional, perceptual or physical) experiences, or mental verbs as they are called here. When the subject refers to the Experiencer, it is either in the A-case or in the Attributee case, or both. This is true also of sentences where the predicate consists of *be* and an adjective or of *have* and a noun (Section 7.1). When the Stimulus is the subject it is in the A-case. No new case category is needed, then, to accommodate the subjects of mental verbs.

The object of a mental verb, whether it refers to the Experiencer or to the Stimulus, is neither in the A-case nor in the Attributee case. The problem of which case is assigned to objects in general is broached in the next chapter.

8   Objects

This chapter deals with direct objects and objects of prepositions and the distinction between them. The direct object has been defined in various ways. For our purposes, it will be expedient to use this term for any noun phrase related to the main verb (unless it is a copular verb)[1] that is not preceded by a preposition, regardless of whether the sentence can passivize or not, and regardless of whether any other tests are passed by it. This definition has the merit that it is easy to apply: it is based on surface cues, and not on any theoretical presuppositions. Direct objects will be discussed first.

1. Direct objects

How can we characterize the semantics of the direct object? Let us look first at the notions expressed by direct objects. After this we will deal with the question of whether these correspond to cases.

1.1 Notions expressed by direct objects

Many direct objects – for example those in (1) – express entities that are affected by the Event referred to by the predicate verb. These are usually called Patients or Themes. Often the entity referred to by the direct object is not merely affected but actually comes into being through the Event; it is "effected," as in (2).

(1) a. They demolished the castle.
    b. They are painting the wall.
    c. They embarrassed the boy.

(2) a. They are building a castle.
    b. They are painting a picture.
    c. They invented an excuse.

Affected and effected direct objects appear to be predominant, but there are also many other types. As we have seen in the previous chapter, the Stimulus of a mental experience can be expressed as direct object; cf. (3)a.

The direct object may also express the Recipient, as in (3)b, or the Instrument as in (3)c and (3)d (Chapter 3, Sections 4.4 and 4.6; on (3)d see Jespersen, 1933: 109).

(3) a. He saw the show.
    b. He presents John with a book.
    c. He uses a fork to eat spaghetti.
    d. He pointed his forefinger at Arthur.

These examples suffice to show that the direct object is semantically heterogeneous. Can this construction be nevertheless characterized in terms of case categories?

1.2 What is the case of the direct object?

Given that there are many notions that may be expressed by the direct object, it might be thought that a semantic characterization is possible in terms of a selection hierarchy. It appears, however, that attempts to construct such a hierarchy will fail for reasons similar to those noted in regard to subject selection hierarchies (Chapter 2, Section 1). Consider the alternative formulations in (4) and (5).

(4) a. They entrusted the agent with the message.
    b. They entrusted the message to the agent.

(5) a. The merchant provided the pilgrims with food.
    b. The merchant provided food for the pilgrims.

If *the agent* and *the pilgrims* are assigned to the Recipient, then this case ought to precede the Theme (*the message* and *food*), as suggested by (4)a and (5)a; but (4)b and (5)b show this to be incorrect.

The subject of a passive sentence – e.g., (6)a – is in the Attributee case (Chapter 6, Section 4.1). Could the direct object of the corresponding active sentence, (6)b, also be an Attributee?

(6) a. The Sistine Chapel was painted by Michelangelo.
    b. Michelangelo painted the Sistine Chapel.

Such an analysis would be indicated by the maxim that when two sentences refer to the same situation, the corresponding noun phrases have to be assigned the same case. In Chapter 2, Section 8, I argued that such a procedure ought to be rejected, because it lends too much weight to the reality referred to, and too little to the linguistic form expressing it. Sentence (6)a says that *the Sistine Chapel* has undergone a change, and furthermore that it is now in a State; it has the feature ATTRIBUTEE in addition to CHANGE (Chapter 6, Section 4.1). By contrast, (6)b merely addresses itself to the Event which causes a CHANGE; the present State of the Chapel can only be inferred from the sentence and is not explicitly referred to.

In Chapter 2 we saw that, although the subject may appear to be a semantically heterogeneous category, it can be semantically characterized in terms of a cluster of agentive features. Perhaps, then, we can proceed similarly with the direct object and construct a new case category by an analysis of various instances of direct objects into features. The difficulty of such a venture should become apparent on considering the manifold relational notions that may be expressed by the direct object. Many of them seem to be reserved for the specific verb and have not been given any label in the literature. A sample of these is presented in (7). For most of these direct objects it would be hard to tell which of the currently employed case categories they instantiate. The same is true of the direct objects in phrasal predicates (Chapter 5, Section 2), such as those in (8).

(7) reports the incident   Beware the Jabberwock!
measures the width of   studies Latin
imitates the teacher   finds the pencil
avoids the question   precedes the procession
follows the guidelines   regrets the mistake
misses the train   discovers the island
denies the charges   computes the costs
describes the picture   joins the party
keeps the secret   admits the charge
touches the ceiling   explains the theorem
examines the outcome   grants permission
forgives the insult   proves his guilt
revenges the murder   reflects the light
resists temptation   refuses the offer
adopts the plan   proposes a law
suggests a change   memorizes the poem

(8) lacks money
costs much money
deserves a medal
derives benefits
equals ten
owns a house
needs a new suit
prefers tea
means nothing

Examples like these lend support to Jespersen's (1961: 230) claim that "on account of the infinite variety of meanings inherent in verbs the notional (or logical) relations of the verbs and their objects are so manifold that they defy any attempt at analysis or classification." The best one can hope to do is compose a list (which would probably have to be open-ended) of relational notions that may be expressed as direct objects, and such a list would hardly be of any theoretical interest.

After much searching, I had to give up the attempt at finding a cluster of features that might take care of the large variety of direct objects exemplified by (7).[2] An attempt to find features that characterize direct objects has recently been made by Dowty (1991), but on examination it turns out that his proposal, too, does not accommodate all direct objects. Dowty proposes two cluster concepts, which he calls Proto-Roles: the Agent Proto-Role, which is linked to the subject of the sentence, and the Patient Proto-Role, which is linked to the direct object. The latter is defined as follows: "a. undergoes change of state b. incremental theme c. causally affected by another participant d. stationary relative to movement of another participant (e. does not exist independently of the event, or not at all)." The parentheses are meant by Dowty to indicate his doubts as to whether this property ought to be included; the term "incremental theme" is explained in his paper.

Dowty's Patient Proto-Role undoubtedly accommodates a larger variety of direct objects than the traditional Patient (or Theme), which is the case usually ascribed to the direct objects in (1). But none of Dowty's properties a–e are present in any of the direct objects in (7), and hence his Proto-Patient leaves a great variety of direct objects unaccounted for.

The conclusion is forced on us, then, that many direct objects cannot be assigned to any case. As argued previously (Chapter 2, Section 6; see also Chapter 3, Section 3.2), there is no compelling reason for accepting the rule that every noun phrase has to be assigned to a case category. The present discussion should convince us that such a rule is quite untenable.

1.3 Is there a Patient case?

Although many direct objects are Patients, the Patient, as we have seen, does not characterize the direct object, nor is there a selection hierarchy in which it plays a role. This raises the question of whether the system of case categories should include the category Patient. Recall that according to the Principle of Linguistic Relevance (Chapter 1, Section 6.3) a case may be introduced only if it permits the statement of a linguistic regularity.

A possible argument for admitting a Patient case into our system might run as follows. It is a generally accepted rule that if a noun phrase refers to the entity that undergoes a change of state, it is the direct object.[3] Suppose now that we define the Patient as the case of the noun phrase undergoing a change of state, or, in our terms, as the noun phrase with the feature CHANGE. It might then be possible to formulate a linking rule to the effect that the Patient is expressed as direct object (although the reverse is clearly not the case). Such a linking rule, it might be argued, justifies the introduction of a Patient case.

Observe, however, that such a move would conflict with the analysis given in Chapter 2, Section 2.2.2 for noun phrases that have the feature CHANGE. It was proposed there that CHANGE is an agentive feature, and noun phrases having this feature are candidates for the A-case. Unless the sentence includes a noun phrase with agentive features that outweigh it (see Chapter 2, Section 4), the noun phrase with CHANGE will be subject. Among the examples given were:

(9) a. The plumber fell from the roof.
    b. The arrow disappeared.
    c. John grew up.

The subjects in (9) have been customarily analyzed as Patients (or Themes) and as underlying direct objects. This analysis would entail more complex linking rules for the subject, and moreover would require introducing an additional case category, namely the Patient. All this does not seem to me to be a price worth paying for the advantage of having a linking rule relating to some – but not all – direct objects. The analysis in Chapter 2 therefore commends itself, and hence I do not propose to introduce a Patient case.

2. Objects of prepositions

Objects of prepositions appear to pose fewer difficulties for a semantic characterization than direct objects. This is because the meaning of the preposition usually indicates the relation of the noun phrase to the main verb.

Most prepositions have a locative meaning. Of the sixty or so prepositions listed by Quirk, Greenbaum, Leech, and Svartvik (1972, Section 6.4), about 80 percent are locative prepositions. We will therefore tentatively include in our framework a Locative case. I have not worked out a full treatment, but tentatively would include in it the notions Source and Goal, and capture the distinction between these two by dimensions (such as: movement from vs. movement to); see Quirk *et al.* (1985, Sections 9.15–9.31) for a classification which might be formulated in terms of dimensions. Without going into further detail we note that the Locative case is normally linked to a prepositional phrase, the preposition being determined by the feature composition of the noun phrase. Exceptions to this rule will be dealt with in Section 4.

Another case linked to the object of preposition is the C-case, the linking rules of which have been discussed in Chapter 3, Section 4.

Many objects of prepositions, however, are not to be classified by any one of these cases. As Quirk *et al.* (1972: 320) put it: "Fields of prepositional meaning are notoriously difficult to classify." The problem is the same as with the direct object. Many instances are clearly metaphorical extensions of objects of locative preposition. Thus, the temporal *to* in (10)b is a metaphorical extension of the locative *to* of sentences like (10)a.

(10) a. She drove the car from London to Edinburgh.
     b. She drove the car from Sunday to Tuesday.

Likewise, the locative *at* can be extended to a temporal *at*, as in (11)a–b. But this is not always so. Take (11)c–g; even though a case can be made for these being metaphorical extensions of the locative meaning, they are no longer transparently so, and the question of the origin of these non-locative usages should not be confused with that of their case assignment.

(11) a. Jack and Jill met at the theater.
     b. Jack and Jill met at night.
     c. Jill excels at languages.
     d. Jill marvels at Jack's courage.
     e. Jack is driving at 100 miles per hour.
     f. Jack shot the burglar at first sight.
     g. Jack and Jill are playing at hide-and-seek.

Another example is the preposition *for*. Besides temporal meanings, as in (12)a, we find what Quirk *et al.* (1985, Section 9.46) call "intended recipient, goal, or target" in (12)b–c; "cause – purpose" (which they view as a dimension, a continuum; see Section 6.35) in (12)d–e. But there are also other notions expressed by this preposition as can be seen in (12)f–j.

(12) a. She remained there for five days.
     b. She provided for her children.
     c. She fights for the underprivileged.
     d. She did not go near the precipice for fear of falling.
     e. She is making plans for the next vacation.
     f. She asked us for a favor.
     g. She bought a dress for £100.
     h. She mistook a garden hose for a snake.
     i. She knows this for a fact.
     j. She is very smart for a five-year-old.

Other prepositions are similarly variegated in respect to the notions they express. *By* takes the A-case as well as the Locative as its object – see (13)a–b. It may also have a temporal meaning – (13)c – and (13)d–f show that it may have other meanings as well (see also Chapter 2, Section 5.2).

(13) a. The radio was invented by Marconi.
     b. The house stands by the river.
     c. He will have arrived by two o'clock.
     d. She pulled him by the ears.
     e. He spilled the soup by accident.
     f. They judged him by his looks.

Besides the locative and temporal meanings of *after*, we have:

(14) a. She asked after her father.
     b. She thirsts after revenge.

In Chapter 3, Section 4, we saw that the C-case is linked, among others, to the *with*-phrase, but that there are *with*-phrases that do not express the C-case. Other prepositions appear to behave similarly. We can describe the main semantic properties of the object for most prepositions, but there remain many non-central instances that express other notions, among them such as are not captured by any case. As observed previously (Section 1.2), not every noun phrase has a case assigned to it.

3. Linking of core arguments

In the first section we arrived at a negative conclusion concerning the possibility of characterizing the direct object in terms of cases or features. This does not mean that no semantic–syntactic regularities can be stated for direct objects. The present section discusses such regularities.

3.1 Core arguments expressed by direct objects

The concept of core argument was introduced in Chapter 2, Section 3.2. A core argument is part of the mental definition of a verb. It pertains to the participant that is inherently implicated in the event or state expressed by the verb; that is, for the event or state to occur it is necessary that there be such a participant. The direct objects in (1), for example, are core arguments. It is totally inconceivable that an act of demolishing could occur without something being demolished; accordingly, the lexical entry of the verb *demolish* has as one of its core arguments a noun phrase referring to the structure that gets broken down. Similarly, the lexical entry for *paint* has as its core argument a noun phrase referring to something that gets paint spread on it, and that for *embarrass* has as its core argument the Experiencer who is affected.

The thesis I propose is that direct objects typically express core arguments. This takes care of affected objects, as those in (1); effected objects ("factitives"), as those in (2); Locations, Stimuli, Recipients, and Instruments, as in (3). Those direct objects that express notions which are difficult to assign to any one of the generally accepted case categories, like those in (7) and phrasal predicates, e.g., (8), which do not have verbs with independent meanings, also have direct objects that stand for core arguments. There are only a few exceptions to the rule that a direct object stands for a core argument, and these will be discussed further on.

A caveat is in order here. That a noun phrase is a direct object standing for a core argument does not preclude ellipsis. Although the lexical entry of *build* specifies as a core argument the structure that is built, *he is building* is quite acceptable. Such ellipses are very common.

In each of the sentences in (15), the second noun phrase is a direct object by our definition (although some would not regard them as such; see Quirk *et al.*, 1972, Section 7.19, note b). These, too, express core arguments: the mental definition of *weigh* involves a certain weight, that of *run*, a certain distance, and so on.

(15) a. He weighs 130 pounds.
     b. He ran a mile.
     c. He grew a lot last year.
     d. The book cost £15.

Cognate objects – see (16) – are direct objects by our definition, but they do not represent core arguments. The verb *sleep* does not require a direct object and its lexical entry does not specify any core argument besides that of the "sleeper." However, when a sentence with *sleep* as main verb has a cognate object, as in (16), the latter is inextricably tied to the process denoted by the verb *sleep*: one can sleep a sound sleep, a quiet sleep, an unhealthy sleep or whatever, but one cannot sleep no sleep at all. In this sense, then, cognate objects are similar to other direct objects.

(16) a. He slept a sound sleep.
     b. He dreamt a disturbing dream.

The characterization of direct objects in terms of core arguments preserves the insight of Jespersen (1961: 229), for whom the object "is intimately connected with the verb of a sentence."

3.2 A linking rule for core arguments

While most direct objects are core arguments, the reverse is not true: not all core arguments are direct objects. First, most sentence subjects are core arguments. Further, some of the objects of prepositions in (11)–(12) are also core arguments.

We can state the following linking rule: A core argument is linked to a syntactic construction in accordance with the case assigned to the noun phrase expressing it on the basis of its feature composition; if none of the cases is assigned to it, it becomes the direct object. Thus, if the noun phrase expressing a core argument is in the A-case, it may become subject or be included in a *by*-phrase (Chapter 2, Section 5); if it is C-case, it may be expressed by, e.g., *with, by means of* or *use . . . to* (Chapter 3, Section 4); if it is in the Locative, it is expressed as an object of the appropriate preposition (above, Section 2); and if no case can be assigned to it, it will be the direct object by default.

When a verb has more than one core argument that is not assigned to a case, there will be the following possibilities:

(i) One of the core arguments is expressed as direct object, and the other is left unexpressed (recall that a core argument may be elided):

(17) a. The pupil answered the teacher.
     b. The pupil answered the question.

(ii) One of the core arguments becomes direct object, while the other becomes object of preposition. Examples are (4) and (5), and also:

(18) a. He begged the governor for mercy.
     b. He begged a favor of the governor.

(19) a. She blamed the secretary for the delay.
     b. She blamed the delay on the secretary.

(iii) Both core arguments become direct object (in our sense, i.e., objects without prepositions). An example is the verb *envy*. Both the person envied and what he or she is envied for are expressed as direct objects.

(20) I envy Mary the promotion.

3.3 Double-object constructions

In the foregoing we have seen that when there are two core arguments that are not assigned any other case, they may both be realized as direct objects. These double-object constructions have been much discussed in the literature (see Hudson, 1992, for a review). Examples are (20), above, and (21) (the verbs *call* and *make* have subentries that permit their uses in (21)f–g).

(21) a. We wished John success.
     b. The guard denied us access to the private rooms.
     c. They forgave me the insult.
     d. The policeman fined the driver £5.
     e. The student asked the teacher a question.
     f. He called his brother a coward.
     g. The president made him Chief-of-Staff.
     h. The new car cost us a fortune.
     i. The policeman asked the driver two questions.

Other verbs that enter into double-object constructions are listed in Quirk *et al.* (1985, Sections 16.46 and 16.55–57).[4]

In some double-object constructions only one of the objects expresses a core argument (Hudson, 1992: 260):

(22) a. Jack peeled me an orange.
     b. Jill sang me a song.
     c. Jean found us a hotel.
     d. John built them an igloo.
     e. Jane bought her a villa.
     f. Judy cooked her some potatoes.

The first of the objects in each sentence – which many linguists call the indirect object – denotes the Recipient, or the intended Recipient (Quirk *et al.*, 1985, Section 9.46). It does not express a core argument. We may speculate that the double-object construction was deployed originally to express the notion of Recipient, as in (23), where the latter is a core argument, and through a kind of routinization process it was subsequently extended to sentences that do not express this notion, as in (22).

> (23) They gave the boy an apple.

The double-object construction is reserved for a relatively small number of verbs. A problem that has recently been investigated by various writers is the eligibility of verbs to the direct object construction. Solutions have been proposed by Pinker (1989) and Schlesinger (1977: 211–15), among others.

3.4 Some exceptions

The regularities discussed in the foregoing have some exceptions:

(i) Some direct objects do not express core arguments. First, there are verbs that may take two objects without prepositions, as in (22). Further, there are a few verbs that require a single direct object that does not express a core argument:[5]

> (24) protest his innocence
>   nod approval

(ii) Conversely, there are a few verbs whose core arguments are realized as objects of prepositions. These include:

> (25) marvel at   [= (11)d]   belong to
>   excel at   [= (11)c]   aspire to
>   provide for [= (12)b]   wonder about
>   mistake for [= (12)h]   arrive in/at
>   long for   desist from

(iii) A considerable number of verbs can take either a direct object or an object of preposition. For example,

> (26) flee the country – flee from the country

The object of *flee* in (26) is Locative, which according to our linking rule (Section 3.2) should be the object of a preposition. What has to be explained, then, is why *flee* can also take a direct object. This problem will be addressed presently.

4. Deletion of prepositions

Our linking rule states that noun phrases in the Locative have a preposition. Some verbs seem to be an exception in that they require a direct object in the Locative case (see Quirk *et al.*, 1985, Section 9.31); for instance:

(27) reach the airport
      leave the airport
      approach the airport
      surround the airport
      walk the streets

In verbs like *reach* and *leave*, the preposition is part of the meaning of the verb, whereas in others, like *walk*, this is not the case (one may walk on the bridge, under it, etc.). But in *walk the streets* the preposition *in* can be easily recovered, and there appears to be a rule to the effect that for certain verbs, when the preposition is recoverable from the context it may be deleted. One should not, of course, expect a sharp boundary line between verbs the meaning of which is conflated with that of the preposition, to use Talmy's (1985b) term, and those where the preposition may be recoverable.

There are verbs that may have the Locative noun phrase either as direct object or as object of a preposition. Besides (26), we have, among others:

(28) ride a horse   ride on a horse
      cross the square   cross over the square
      turn the corner   turn round the corner
      pass the statue   pass by the statue
      walk the streets   walk in the streets

The prepositions in the right-hand column of (28) can be recovered fairly easily. Knowledge of the world leads us to construe *ride a horse* as "ride on a horse." The notion expressed by *over* is incorporated in the verb *cross* (cf. Quirk *et al.*, 1985, Section 9.31), and hence *cross the square* can be construed only as "cross over the square." *Turn the corner* can mean only "turn round the corner." Passing something (when it is more similar in size to a statue than to a saltcellar) can mean only passing by it.

The right-hand column of (28) also shows that for some verbs the deletion rule is not obligatory; the speaker has the option to use either the direct object or an object with a preposition. That English offers both alternatives is not surprising, considering that recoverability is not an all-or-nothing affair. The speaker has the option of using either the shorter direct object construction, or else, if it serves to make his meaning clearer or more easily accessible, the prepositional object. The choice between the two alternatives has pragmatic determinants.

The pragmatic factors leading to deletion of locative prepositions are presumably not language-specific. Languages may differ, though, in the

Table 8.1. *Verbs taking direct objects in eight languages*

	Russian	Italian	Hebrew	Spanish	Hungarian	German	French	English
walk	x	x	x	x	x	x	x	d
pass	x	x	x	x	d	x	x	d
turn	x	d	x	x	x	x	d	d
mount	x	x	x	d	x	x	d	d
reach	x	x	x	x	d	d	d	d
jump	x	x	x	d	d	d	x	d
penetrate	x	x	d	d	x	d	d	d
swim	d	x	d	x	d	d	x	d
climb	x	d	x	d	d	d	d	d
cross	d	d	d	d	x	d	d	d
leave	d	d	d	d	d	d	d	d
surround	d	d	d	d	d	d	d	d

Note:
d = direct object

weight given to these factors. Thus, languages other than English often permit direct objects in locative phrases like (28), but not all languages: while German seems to be very much like English in this respect, Hebrew appears to prefer prepositional objects in many instances where English has direct ones.

In a small crosslinguistic study, the eight languages listed in Table 8.1 were compared in respect to the availability of direct object constructions for Locatives. In the table, "d" stands for direct object and "x" for a prepositional one. When a language has two translation equivalents for an English verb, one taking a direct object and one a prepositional one, this is entered as d. The variability found between languages may in part be due to factors specific to each language (the degree to which the language tends to incorporate prepositions into the verb, like German and Hungarian, etc.). But the table shows that this is not the whole story; for instance, although French does not incorporate prepositions, it has no fewer direct object constructions for the verbs dealt with in the table than German, and many more than Hungarian.

What is striking in Table 8.1 is the patterning of the data. The verbs form a quasi-scale, or implicational hierarchy. This is indicated by the line dividing the "d"s and "x"s in the table. The existence of such a scale suggests that selection of the direct object is largely determined by a uni-dimensional factor, to which each language assigns a different weight. Presumably, this factor is the recoverability of the preposition; that is, the verbs in Table 8.1 are ordered according to the degree to which the locative preposition is recoverable, and the languages in the sample differ in respect to the degree of recoverability they require to permit omission of the preposition (that is, to license the direct object construction). But a study comprising more languages, more verbs, and more detailed analyses is obviously required before anything more definite can be said on this issue.

In the following section we will see that for some verbs there may be additional determinants of the choice between a direct object and an object of a preposition.

5. Features of verb phrases

In Chapter 2 we introduced features for the analysis of agentive noun phrases, and in Chapters 3 and 6 features pertaining to other cases were proposed. These are all features of the noun phrase. In this section it will be shown that the semantic characterization of the direct object requires a different type of feature, namely one that pertains to the verb phrase that comprises a noun phrase.

5.1 Completion

For some verbs there is a difference in meaning between the direct object construction and one with an object of a preposition. Thus, the verbs *swim* and *climb* may take either direct objects, as in (29), or objects of prepositions, as in (30).

(29) a. swim the Channel
     b. climb Mount Everest

(30) a. swim in the Channel
     b. climb up Mount Everest

The direct object construction in (29) implies that the activity has been successfully brought to its completion (Quirk *et al.*, 1985, Section 9.31); *swim the Channel* means that the Channel has been successfully crossed, and *climb Mount Everest* implies that the top of the mountain has been reached. The prepositional object constructions in (30) do not have this implication: *swim in the Channel* can also be said of a leisurely swim close to the shore, and *climb up Mount Everest* of an abortive attempt to scale it (Moravcsik, 1978: 256). The same distinction applies to (26). One who *fled the country* has actually succeeded in leaving it, whereas one who *fled from the country* might have been caught before leaving it.[6]

This property which distinguishes some direct objects from prepositional objects, will be called here **Completion** (a notion very similar to Vendler's Accomplishment). Note that this feature pertains to *swim the Channel* and *climb Mount Everest* in (29), and not to *the Channel* or *Mount Everest*; in other words, it pertains to the verb phrase as a whole.

Completion is also a determinant in the locative alternation. It has often been pointed out that sentences like (31)a and (32)a require "wholistic" interpretations. Thus, (31)a says that the wagon ended up being fully loaded, whereas (31)b is neutral on this point; and (32)a – but not (32)b – implies that the whole wall was covered with paint.[7]

(31) a. They loaded the wagon with hay.
     b. They loaded the hay on the wagon.

(32) a. Susan sprayed the wall with paint.
     b. Susan sprayed the paint on the wall.

The verbs in (33) may take direct objects when Completion is involved; otherwise oblique noun phrases are required, as in the right-hand column.

(33) shot the fox   shot at the fox
      grasp the rope   grasp at the rope
      kick the table   kick at the table
      push the table   push (away) at the table

The object of the preposition in (33) is a sort of Locative (Quirk *et al.*, 1985, Section 9.46: "intended goal or target"). The left-hand phrases with the direct object involve Completion. When you have *shot* the fox, it is necessarily hit; when you have *shot at* it, you may have missed; and similarly for the other two verbs. Pushing away at something means that one does not quite succeed at the job. Several other verbs can appear with or without prepositions: *stab (at)*, *catch (at)*, *clutch (at)*, and *strike (at)*.

The examples given so far are of Locatives. According to our linking rule, these should have prepositional objects, but Completion serves here to license the direct object alternative. By contrast, in (34) the preposition indicates the *lack* of Completion. Knowing of somebody implies less complete knowledge than knowing somebody.

(34) know the boy – know of the boy

5.2 Feat

Use of the direct object for the verbs *swim* and *climb* is subject to an additional condition. With these verbs, the direct object tends to be chosen when the activity leads to a somewhat unusual achievement. Only when the activity presents some difficulty do we use the verb with a direct object. Compare the sentences in the following pairs:

(35) a.   Sheila swam the lake.
     b.   ??Sheila swam the pond.

(36) a.   Jack climbed Mount Everest.
     b.   *Jack climbed the bed.

We will call this property **Feat**. When the activity does not have the property

Feat, the locative noun phrase will appear in a prepositional object, even though the activity has the property Completion:

(37) a. Sheila swam in the pond.
b. Jack climbed into/onto the bed.

Feat in conjunction with Completion may license the direct object. In (38)a, *jump* takes a direct object because the verb phrase describes a Feat, whereas no Feat is involved in (38)b, and the direct object construction is unacceptable.

(38) a. Jill jumped the fence.
b. *Jill jumped the stool/the gutter.
c. Jill jumped over the stool/the gutter.

When both the direct object construction and the prepositional object construction are acceptable, as in (39), there will be a different nuance of meaning. Riding a horse, (39)a, may be viewed as something of a Feat, not merely "sitting on top of it, but 'controlling,' 'mastering' it" (Givón, 1984b: 99).

(39) a. Jane rode a horse.
b. Jane rode on a horse.

The core argument of *play* is a piece of music, and not the place where it is played. However, when one intends to express the notion of Feat, as in (40)a, the place becomes the direct object. When there is no such Feat, as in (40)b, the direct object construction is odd in spite of the presence of Completion (this example is due to And Rosta, personal communication, 1992):

(40) a. John is a promising young violinist; he has already played the Albert Hall.
b. ??John has already played the market place.

When the activity has a strongly accentuated characteristic of Completion, however, the direct object construction may be acceptable even in the absence of Feat. Out of context, the sentences in (41) will be exceedingly odd, because of the absence of Feat, but when the notion of Completion is focused on, they might be appropriate (Richard Hudson, personal communication, 1992). Thus, after making a bet that I will jump every gutter in the neighborhood, I may say (41)a – compare this to (38)b – and after betting that I will climb on every seat in a lecture hall I may say (41)b.

(41) a. I have already jumped this gutter.
b. I have already climbed this seat.

For verbs that permit two alternative constructions, direct object and prepositional object, Completion and Feat may decide which of the two alternatives is appropriate. But these features of the verb phrase do not license deletion of the object for all verbs. This is shown in (42) for Completion and in (43) for Feat; the prepositions here are mandatory before the noun phrases.

(42) a. She dismounted from her horse.
     b. He did away with his opponents.
     c. They escaped from the drizzle.

(43) a. Michelangelo exceeded in productivity.
     b. Cassandra peered into the future.
     c. Hercules succeeded in the seven tasks.

The features Completion and Feat do not explain all alternations of direct object and object of preposition; see, for instance, the verbs in (28) and the following pairs:

(44) ponder   ponder over
     forget   forget about
     improve   improve on
     check   check on
     permit   permit of
     approve   approve of
     confess   confess to
     believe   believe in
     meet   meet with

The lexical entries of some verbs, then, specify that the verb is sensitive to the features Completion and Feat; that is, the lexical entry contains the information that when the verb phrase has one of these features, deletion of the preposition is permitted. The lexical entries of the verbs in (42)–(43) and in (44) do not contain such a specification.

5.3   A semantic saturation effect

Why should Completion and Feat be associated with the direct object? I propose the following three-step explanation:

(i) Both Completion and Feat are intimately related to affectedness. Other things being equal, a participant will be more affected when the action has been successfully completed; and the more the object is affected, the greater and the more spectacular will the achievement be, in other words, the more of a Feat will it be (compare breaking a piece of wood with one's hands to smashing it with one's hands).[8]

(ii) Affectedness is the notion most frequently expressed by direct objects (as mentioned in Section 1.3, many, perhaps most, direct objects are Patients).

(iii) Due to (ii), there is an effect in the reverse direction: participants that are relatively more affected will tend to be expressed by direct objects.

In short, that Completion and Feat are associated with the direct object is presumably due to a semantic saturation effect. This explanation is in line with Gropen, Pinker, Hollander, and Goldberg's (1991) account of the locative alternation – (31)–(32) in Section 5.1 – in terms of affectedness of the direct object.

Note that here semantic saturation does not just impose constraints on the use of a construction, but (as in Chapter 7, Section 5.2) actually licenses the use of a construction.

6. Conclusions

The notions expressed by direct objects are so variegated that they have foiled our attempts to find a set of features that characterize at least the most typical members of this category. The objective – fruitfully pursued in our treatment of the subject – of describing syntactic categories as semantically relatively homogeneous thus has had to be abandoned as far as the direct object is concerned. The direct object is not a purely formal category, though. It has been shown that what most direct objects have in common is that they express core arguments. A linking rule for core arguments has been formulated.

A new type of feature, that of a verb phrase as a whole, has been introduced. The verb-phrase features Completion and Feat have been used in an account of many of the alternations between constructions having direct objects and prepositional objects.

9   Verb classes and Agents

> They've a temper, some of them – particularly verbs: they're the
> proudest – adjectives you can do anything with, but not verbs ...
> Humpty Dumpty.

This chapter discusses the internal structure of the verb class. In previous
chapters various distinctions were made between verbs. These are reviewed
in Section 1, and I then examine in Section 2 a proposal for an additional
subdivision of the verb class. Some linguistic effects of this classification are
examined in the next two sections, and its relation to features of the Agent is
discussed in Section 5. In Section 6 it is shown that the proposed
classification of verbs reflects the graded structure of the Agent category, and
Section 7 deals with the question of the extent to which naive speakers are
aware of these distinctions between verbs.

1. Subdivisions of verbs

The lexical entry of a verb specifies what are its core arguments (Chapter 2,
Section 3.2). Intransitive verbs have only one core argument, which becomes
the sentence subject, whereas transitive verbs have (at least) two. Some verbs
can be used both transitively and intransitively; as for instance the verb *hang*
(Chapter 2, Section 3.3.2). The verb class, then, can be subdivided according
to the number of core arguments verbs enter into.

The lexical entry of a verb also specifies the features of each of its core
arguments, and this permits an additional, and finer, subdivision, which
determines, among other things, the possibility of using the passive voice; see
Chapter 2, Section 5.2.

Another distinction, introduced in Chapter 5, is that between States and
Events. This subdivision, too, has linguistic consequences. It determines
whether the sentence subject is Agent or Attributee (Chapter 6, Section 1.1).
Verbs in Event predicates may take the progressive form and the imperative,
whereas there are restrictions on the use of these forms for stative verbs
(Quirk, Greenbaum, Leech, and Svartvik, 1972, Sections 2.6 and 2.24).

Events are distinguished from States in respect to activity, among other
things. It has been proposed that verbs whose subjects are Agents have an
underlying element *do* (Ross, 1972a), which manifests itself in constructions
like those in the following sentences:

(1) a. What I did was go there myself.
   b. I went there myself, and John did so, too.
   c. Waxing the floors I have always hated to do.
   d. Solving this puzzle is impossible to do.

These constructions are usually unacceptable with State predicates; but the situation here is far from simple, as Cruse (1973) has shown. The reason is, partly, that activity is a matter of degree, as shown in Chapter 1, Section 5.

The studies reported in this chapter furnish further evidence for the gradedness of the notion of activity, as reflected in the acceptability of constructions with *do*. In the following section we present a proposal for a further subdivision of verbs, which is related to the acceptability of various *do*-constructions.

2. A proposal for a subdivision

The proposal for a classification of verbs that will be discussed in this chapter is based on Quirk *et al.* (1972, Section 3.41). These authors distinguish seven classes of verbs (the parenthesized examples are among those they give):

(i) Activity verbs (*abandon, write, work*)

(ii) Momentary verbs (*jump, kick, knock*)

(iii) Transitional Event verbs (*arrive, die, fall*)

(iv) Process verbs (*deteriorate, grow, mature*)

(v) Verbs of Inert Perception and Cognition (*impress, please, think*)

(vi) Relational verbs (*depend on, deserve, need*)

(vii) Verbs of Bodily Sensation (*feel, hurt, itch* in their intransitive use)

The sequence in which these classes have been listed here differs from that of Quirk *et al.* in order to draw attention to a property that distinguishes between them. Note that the classes higher in the list are such that the subject of these verbs may be said to engage in an activity, and the lower down you move in the list, the less activity can be ascribed to the subject. Quirk *et al.* call the last two classes "stative" verbs and all the others "dynamic," but degree of activity varies also within the "dynamic" group: evidently there is more activity in classes (i) and (ii) than in (iii) and (iv).

In our system, verbs of the lower-activity classes are clearly State verbs, and their subjects will therefore be Attributees, whereas the high-activity verbs will tend to appear in Event predicates, and their subjects will be Agents. Further, as pointed out in the previous section, activity is held to be associated with an underlying element *do*, and as Quirk *et al.* (1972, Section 10.55) show, this has an interesting linguistic effect: the foregoing seven classes differ in respect to substitutability by various proforms with *do*, such as those for which examples are given in (2). Consider (2)b–g as rejoinders to the utterance in (2)a:

(2) a. John cut down two trees.
    b. Yes, he did.
    c. So did Bob.
    d. So he did.
    e. I know he did so.
    f. I wonder why he did that.
    g. I wonder why he did it.

All of these replies sound suitable for the verb collocation *cut down*, but things are different for certain other types of verb. Consider, for instance,

(3) Old men sat in the park.

The reply *Yes, they did* is perfectly normal, but *Yes, they did so* is questionable, and *I wonder why they did it* even more so.

According to Quirk *et al.*, Activity verbs and Momentary verbs take all the pro-forms in (2); for Transitional Event verbs and Process verbs, (2)g is unacceptable (*John arrived today*, **I wish I knew why he did it*); Verbs of Inert Perception and Cognition and Relational verbs rule out not only (2)g, but also (2)f (*John loves music*, **I wonder why he does that*); and Verbs of Bodily Sensation prohibit even (2)e. The seven verb classes are thus arranged in a sequence of what one might call decreasing "tolerance" for pro-forms with *do*, and the pro-forms exemplified in (2) – in a sequence of decreasing "tolerability."[1] These classes thus form a sort of "squish" (Ross, 1972b; except that the Rossian squish spans more than one syntactic category, while Quirk *et al.*'s squish is intra-categorial).

In the following, studies will be reported of linguistic effects of the distinctions between the various classes in Quirk *et al.*'s system. However, first a modification of their classification is introduced. It is proposed that three of their categories ought to be further subdivided as follows:

(i) *Activity verbs* Intuitively, it seems that this class is a mixed bag. Among the examples given by Quirk *et al.* there are some verbs, such as *work* and *abandon*, that do not appear to refer to any specific situation, whereas others, like *drink*, *slice*, and *write*, may evoke a relatively specific image. I shall therefore distinguish between two classes of Activity verbs, which will be called **specific** and **diffuse**. It is realized that these concepts in fact form a gradient. In the studies we conducted we included what seemed reasonably clear exemplars of the two poles of this continuum.

(ii) *Transitional Event verbs* There is a distinction between verbs typically referring to intentional actions, like *arrive* and *leave*, and those referring to typically unintentional ones, like *fall* and *die*. This, again, is a continuum, and in our studies we used examples that are as far as possible clear cases of what we will call **Transitional-Intentional** and **Transitional-non-Intentional** verbs.

(iii) *Verbs of Inert Perception and Cognition* A distinction has to be made between verbs the subjects of which are the Stimulus of the mental experience and those the subjects of which are the Experiencer; see Chapter 7. The former include, e.g., *satisfy* and *astonish*, and the latter, *adore* and *believe*.

We thus add three classes to Quirk *et al.*'s seven. Further, it is proposed to add to the foregoing ten classes a category from Quirk, Greenbaum, Leech and Svartvik (1985, Section 4.28): Stance. This class includes the verbs *sit*, *lie*, and *stand*.

To summarize, instead of Quirk *et al.*'s seven classes, I propose to distinguish between the following eleven:

(i) Activity-specific (*write, throw, slice*)

(ii) Activity-diffuse (*abandon, work, learn*)

(iii) Momentary (*jump, kick, knock*)

(iv) Transitional-Intentional (*arrive, stop over, leave*)

(v) Transitional-non-Intentional (*die, fall, lose*)

(vi) Process (*deteriorate, grow, mature*)

(vii) Stance (*sit, lie, stand*)

(viii) Mental-Stimulus (*impress, please, surprise*)

(ix) Mental-Experiencer (*think, hear, suppose*)

(x) Relational verbs (*depend on, deserve, need*)

(xi) Bodily Sensation (*feel, hurt, itch* in their intransitive use)

The studies reported below examine the linguistic effects of this classification and show that the modifications introduced into Quirk *et al.*'s list are justified.

3. Substitutability by pro-forms

The purpose of this study – which was conducted in cooperation with Laura Canetti[2] – was to investigate the extent to which verbs from various classes can be substituted for by pro-forms like those in (2).

Quirk *et al.* (1972) did not find any difference in substitutability by pro-forms between some of the verb classes they had previously identified on independent grounds, e.g., between Activity verbs and Momentary verbs. Since they used their intuitions and an analysis of a large body of data made available through the Survey of English Usage (at University College

London), they naturally limited themselves to dichotomous judgments (grammatical/ungrammatical). Presumably these carve up an underlying continuum of acceptability (see Lakoff, 1974). In our study we used judgments of acceptability on a scale from "totally acceptable" to "totally unacceptable." It was expected that these would yield a more fine-grained picture of substitution possibilities for various types of verbs.

3.1 Procedures

The study comprised ten of the eleven classes described in Section 2. The category of Bodily Sensation verbs has only a very limited number of members and was not included. For each of the ten classes we selected three verbs, which were each embedded in a sentence. The three sentences constructed for each verb class were of a very similar structure, as can be seen in Table 9.1, but in the second list, the Transitional–Non-intentional sentence had to have a slightly different structure. As far as feasible, the verbs were selected randomly from Quirk *et al.*'s (1972) examples, but the possibility of embedding in similar sentence structures had to be taken into account in choosing the particular examples. Three rating forms were prepared – one for each of the three lists. Each of these had two versions, differing in the sequence in which the sentences were presented, which was randomly determined.

For each sentence there was a list of "replies" – see (2), above – and respondents were instructed to rate each of these replies for its acceptability in spoken English on a scale from 1 – totally unacceptable, to 5 – totally acceptable. Six different "replies" were used:

(a) Yes, he did.

(b) Yes, so he did.

(c) Yes, he did so.

(d) Yes, he did that.

(e) Yes, he did it.

(f) And Bill did the same.

Of these, (a)–(e) were modeled on the pro-forms discussed in Quirk *et al.* (1972; Section 10.55), and (f) – mentioned by them in Section 10.55, note c – was added in order to find out where it would be located in the squish we expected to find. The "replies," like the sentences in Table 9.1, were in the past tense; it was easier to construct natural-sounding sentences in the past than in the present tense. The sequence of "replies" was determined randomly, four different randomizations being used for the ten sentences in any given form.

Sixty native speakers of American English volunteered to participate in

Table 9.1. *Sentences used in acceptability study*

Verb class	
	First list
Momentary	H. jumped on the table.
Activity-specific	H. threw a letter on the table.
Activity-diffuse	H. abandoned his cottage a year ago.
Stance	H. stood close to the lady in the blue dress.
Mental-Stimulus	H. pleased her with a beautiful gift.
Transit.-Int.	H. stopped over in Chicago on December 20th.
Transit.-non-Int.	H. fell yesterday while he was skating in the park.
Process	H. matured a lot in the last years.
Mental-Exper.	H. supposed that you were waiting for him.
Relational	H. deserved the promotion in the office.
	Second list
Momentary	H. knocked on the table.
Activity-specific	H. wrote a letter on the table.
Activity-diffuse	H. worked in his cottage a year ago.
Stance	H. sat close to the lady in the blue dress.
Mental-Stimulus	H. impressed her with a beautiful gift.
Transit.-Int.	H. left Chicago on December 20th.
Transit.-non-Int.	H. lost his watch while he was skating in the park.
Process	H. grew a lot in the last years.
Mental-Exper.	H. thought that you were waiting for him.
Relational	H. depended on the promotion in the office.
	Third list
Momentary	H. tapped on the table.
Activity-specific	H. sliced bread on the table.
Activity-diffuse	H. learned drawing in the cottage a year ago.
Stance	H. lay close to the soldier in the tattered uniform.
Mental-Stimulus	H. surprised her with a beautiful gift.
Transit.-Int.	H. arrived in Chicago on December 20th.
Transit.-non-Int.	H. died yesterday, while he was skating in the park.
Process	H. deteriorated a lot in the last years.
Mental-Exper.	H. heard that you were waiting for him.
Relational	H. needed the promotion in the office.

Note:
H. = Henry

the study. Each of the three rating forms was responded to by twenty respondents, and each of the two versions of a given rating form was presented to half of the twenty respondents.

3.2 Results

The mean ratings of acceptability (collapsed over the two versions of each list) for each sentence are presented in Tables 9.2–9.4. The row means are given in the column on the right.

The pro-forms in Table 9.2 are arranged in decreasing order of mean

Table 9.2. *Mean acceptability ratings – first list*

	did	did same	so did	did that	did so	did it	Mean
Momentary	4.90	4.30	3.50	3.90	3.25	2.95	3.80
Activity-specific	4.90	4.30	3.45	3.90	3.10	3.15	3.80
Activity-diffuse	4.85	4.15	3.50	3.75	3.35	2.95	3.76
Stance	4.95	4.40	3.50	3.90	3.15	2.55	3.74
Mental-Stimulus	4.90	3.95	3.90	3.75	3.25	2.15	3.65
Transit.-Int.	4.90	4.35	3.75	3.60	3.10	2.05	3.63
Transit.-non-Int.	4.95	4.10	3.70	3.50	2.90	2.25	3.57
Process	4.80	4.10	4.10	2.80	2.95	1.45	3.37
Mental-Exper.	4.80	3.30	4.00	1.80	2.35	1.40	2.94
Relational	4.95	1.75	4.10	1.15	2.05	1.50	2.58
Mean	4.89	3.87	3.75	3.21	2.95	2.24	

Notes:
1 totally unacceptable
5 totally acceptable

Table 9.3. *Mean acceptability ratings – second list*

	did	did same	so did	did that	did so	did it	Mean
Momentary	4.75	4.15	3.95	4.15	3.20	3.40	3.93
Activity-specific	4.60	4.05	3.80	3.80	3.40	2.95	3.77
Activity-diffuse	4.65	4.10	4.15	3.95	2.85	2.30	3.67
Stance	4.70	3.75	3.85	3.95	3.00	2.60	3.64
Mental-Stimulus	4.65	3.65	3.85	3.25	3.00	2.65	3.51
Transit.-Int.	4.45	3.90	4.10	3.90	3.15	2.60	3.68
Transit.-non-Int.	4.60	3.45	4.00	3.85	3.05	2.45	3.57
Process	4.75	3.55	3.90	3.10	2.65	2.35	3.38
Mental-Exper.	4.70	2.80	4.20	2.20	2.10	2.10	3.02
Relational	4.70	3.80	3.85	3.45	2.50	2.15	3.41
Mean	4.66	3.72	3.97	3.56	2.89	2.56	

Notes:
1 totally unacceptable
5 totally acceptable

acceptability ratings. In every row – that is, for each of the verb classes – there tended to be a gradient: with few exceptions, the mean ratings decrease as we move from left to right in each row. The pro-form *did* had the highest mean acceptability score; *did the same* had a lower score; and so on, up to *did it*, which had the lowest one (see also the column means). Quirk *et al.* (1985, Section 12.24, note) observe that *do it* requires a predication that conveys volition.

Verb classes in Table 9.2 are arranged in decreasing order of "tolerance" to the pro-forms. The sequence of verb classes in Table 9.2 is according to the size of row means (i.e., the right-hand column), and for the two upper

Table 9.4. *Mean acceptability ratings – third list*

	did	did same	so did	did that	did so	did it	Mean
Momentary	4.95	4.75	3.60	4.10	2.70	2.80	3.82
Activity-specific	5.00	4.40	3.15	3.70	2.55	3.00	3.63
Activity-diffuse	4.70	4.60	4.00	3.70	2.75	1.90	3.61
Stance	5.00	4.80	3.35	3.60	2.90	2.20	3.64
Mental-Stimulus	4.65	4.65	3.60	3.55	2.35	2.10	3.48
Transit.-Int.	4.70	4.10	3.65	2.85	2.60	1.95	3.31
Transit.-non-Int.	4.70	4.10	3.75	2.65	2.10	1.55	3.14
Process	5.00	4.05	4.00	2.60	2.35	1.45	3.24
Mental-Exper.	4.55	2.55	3.80	1.70	1.80	1.40	2.63
Relational	4.95	1.35	3.85	1.10	1.80	1.25	2.38
Mean	4.82	3.94	3.68	2.96	2.39	1.96	

Notes:
1 totally unacceptable
5 totally acceptable

rows of Table 9.2, according to the row means of Tables 9.3 and 9.4. In Tables 9.3 and 9.4 verb classes appear in the same sequence as in Table 9.2.

Comparison of the three tables shows that closely parallel results were obtained for the three verb lists. Spearman rank-order correlations between the sequence of verb classes in Table 9.2 and that in Table 9.3 was 0.86 ($p < 0.0005$), between those in Tables 9.2 and 9.4, 0.94 ($p < 0.0005$), and between Tables 9.3 and 9.4, 0.78 ($p < 0.005$).

The slight discrepancies between the three lists in the order accorded to the verb classes by the ratings (unless they are the result of noise factors) may be due to factors pertaining to the specific verbs. Thus, conceivably, the sentence with the Relational verb in the second list, *depend on*, which was rated higher than the Process verb and the Mental-Experiencer verb (Table 9.3), was construed by some respondents as "behave in a way showing dependence on."

The means over pro-forms, then, assign a rather consistent order to verb classes. Henceforward I will refer to this empirically obtained sequence of verb classes as the **hierarchy** of classes. In later sections it will be shown that other syntactic constructions reveal a similar hierarchy, and that the latter may be partially explained in terms of agentive features.

The ratings of the six different pro-forms are much less consistent than the means. Still, Kendall's Coefficients of Concordance for the various pro-forms were significant, with $W = 0.619$ ($p < 0.01$) for the first, $W = 0.427$ ($p < 0.025$) for the second, and $W = 0.4078$ ($p < 0.05$) for the third list.

It may be objected that in view of the divergent results obtained for the different pro-forms there is little justification for basing a hierarchy on the mean ratings. Thus, the ratings of verb classes on *so did* in Table 9.2 suggest a completely different sequence from the means. Perhaps, then, one may speak only of the hierarchy of a given pro-form. However, the ratings of individual pro-forms show little stability across the three lists. Thus, ratings of *so did* in Table 9.3 imply a sequence differing from that in Table 9.2, and those in Table 9.4 present a still different picture. These divergences are presumably due to lack of reliability of measurement, and to obtain a more stable measure it was decided to use the means over pro-forms.

The fact that our results were replicated for three different lists of verbs bears out the classification proposed by Quirk *et al.* (1972) as adapted in Section 2, above. Our findings are based on ratings rather than on dichotomous judgments, and they show that, not surprisingly, there are continuous categories underlying Quirk *et al.*'s binary squish. Comparing our graded acceptability ratings to Quirk *et al.*'s dichotomous classification into grammatical and ungrammatical substitutions, we find that mean ratings above about 2.70 correspond to substitutions that Quirk *et al.* consider grammatical, and those below 2.60 to those they reject as ungrammatical, with some fuzziness between these two values.

Perusal of the results supports our decision to diverge from Quirk *et al.*'s classification by subdividing several of their verb classes:

1. The findings justify the subdivision of their class of Verbs of Perception and Cognition into Mental-Stimulus and Mental-Experiencer verbs. Mental-Stimulus verbs showed much more tolerance to pro-forms than Mental-Experiencer verbs in each of the three lists.

2. The subdivision of Activity verbs into "specific" and "diffuse" verbs was also reflected in the data; the former had higher tolerance to substitution, as shown by the slightly larger means of ratings in each of the three lists.

3. The distinction made between intentional and non-intentional Transitional Event verbs is corroborated by the higher mean ratings of the former in each of the three lists.

The findings of the present study, then, are in accord with Quirk *et al.*'s observations. Substitutability of verbs by *do* and related pro-forms differs for various verb classes, and the latter form a kind of squish.

3.3 A replication study

While every effort was made to include in each list ten sentences of similar structure, some structural differences were inevitable; for instance, some of the verbs were transitive and others intransitive. It was also found to be impossible to hold the lexical composition of the sentences constant. It might be argued therefore that the respondents' ratings could have been affected by the specific sentences in which the various verbs were embedded, rather than by the verbs themselves. To check on this possibility, a replication of the rating study was performed for the verbs of the first list. The replication differed from the study described above in that only the beginning of the sentence was presented to the respondent, e.g., *Henry threw* ..., or *Henry abandoned* ....

Instructions stressed that "only the beginning of each sentence [was] typed out" and asked the respondent to think of a full sentence and then indicate to what extent the reply was acceptable. The rating forms for this replication study were in the same versions and randomizations as those of the previous study. Twenty native speakers of American English volunteered to participate in the study.

In the replication study the mean acceptability ratings ranked the sentence fragments very similarly to the sentences in Table 9.2; the Spearman rank-order correlation was 0.92 (p < 0.005). This shows that the results obtained were not due to contamination by the structure or content of the specific sentences.

3.4 Findings on pro-forms

As shown in Tables 9.2–9.4, acceptability ratings occasionally revealed differences in "tolerability" of pro-forms that were not picked up by Quirk *et al.* (1972). Thus, Quirk *et al.* do not report any differences between *did* and *so did*, whereas our acceptability judgments turned out to be more sensitive: *did* received consistently higher ratings than *so did*.

Did is an auxiliary verb, but it may also function as a regular verb with the meaning of performing an action (cf. *make*). Apparently, the latter meaning is predominant in *so did*, *did that*, *did so*, and *did it*, which is why these pro-forms are appropriate only for verbs involving activity, i.e. those high in the hierarchy.

As mentioned, the sequence of pro-forms (columns) in Tables 9.2–9.4 was determined according to their relative "tolerability" in Table 9.2 (for most verb classes). Note, however, that this relative "tolerability" changes with the place of the verb class in the tolerance hierarchy. There are some trends in the data that require an explanation:

1. While *did same* rated higher than *so did* for verb classes high in the hierarchy, the reverse was true for those low in the hierarchy; *so did* received higher ratings than *did same* in the lower rows of all three tables, and the same reversal was observed in the replication study.

2. There was a trend – though not a stable one – of a reversal of the *did that* and *did so* ratings. In Tables 9.2 and 9.4, *did so* received higher scores than *did that* for the verb classes low in the hierarchy. Quirk *et al.* also state that *do so*, but not *do that*, is acceptable in reply to Relational verbs and Verbs of Inert Perception and Cognition (the category subdivided by us into Mental-Stimulus and Mental-Experiencer). Since these

authors dichotomized substitutions into those that are and those that are not acceptable, they did not capture the fact that *did so* receives lower scores than *did that* on all verb classes except those at the lower end of the "tolerability" continuum. Intuitively, *did that* connotes a more concrete event than *did so*, and this may be part of the reason why for more concrete verbs – i.e., those higher in the hierarchy – *did that* was preferred.[3] In the replication study, *did so* was rated higher than *did that* for all verbs, except *throw*, which is in the Activity-specific class.

In the replication study, reversals were observed for additional verb classes. Some additional reversals in Tables 9.2–9.4 did not appear in the replication study and thus do not seem to be reliable effects.

4. Pseudo-cleft sentences

In the studies reported in the preceding section, the hierarchy of verb classes was reflected by the substitutability of verbs belonging to these classes by various phrases containing *do*. Now, in English, *do* is used both as an auxiliary verb and a full verb. In many other languages – Hebrew, for instance – the translation equivalent of *do* is not used in negations and questions; in short, it is not an auxiliary. But in Hebrew, too, *do* can substitute for a verb in pseudo-cleft sentences; for instance:

> *Ma sheHenry asa ze shehu kafats al hashulxan*
> What Henry did that-is that-he jumped on the-table

It was of interest therefore to investigate how the various verb classes in a language like Hebrew behave in respect to substitution by a full verb like *do*.

4.1 Procedures

For each of the ten verb classes in Table 9.1, three Hebrew verbs were selected. As far as possible, these were translation equivalents of English verbs used in the English study in Section 3; but where no unambiguous Hebrew translation equivalents could be found, another Hebrew verb was selected. The English verb *throw* was replaced by the Hebrew translation equivalent of *draw* (pictures); *abandon* by *retire*; and *deteriorate* and *mature* by *grow fat* and *grow lean*, respectively. Further, the three Relational verbs had to be replaced by the translation equivalents of *win* (a prize), *serve as* (= act as), and *be fit for*.

For each verb a pseudo-cleft sentence was constructed (e.g., *What Yossi did was to* [verb] . . .; "Yossi" is a common Hebrew first name, like "John" in English). For verbs of the First list (Table 9.1) this was, as far as possible, a translation of the English sentences used in the English study (the difference between the languages, however, dictated some changes in the interest of

Table 9.5. *Mean acceptability*
of verbs in pseudo-cleft
sentences

Momentary	3.77
Activity-specific	3.79
Activity-diffuse	2.94
Stance	3.17
Mental-Stimulus	3.26
Transit.-Int.	2.58
Transit.-non-Int.	1.12
Process	1.41
Mental-Exper.	1.09
Relational	1.96

Notes:
1 quite unacceptable
7 acceptable

clarity). Other verbs were embedded in sentences similar to those used for verbs in the same class. A rating form was prepared containing thirty sentences – one for each of the thirty verbs (three verbs for each class). The sequence of sentences was randomized. Respondents were thirty native speakers of Hebrew, to whom the rating forms were administered individually.

Instructions required the respondent to rate the acceptability of each sentence on a seven-point scale. Pseudo-cleft sentences with *do* may sound somewhat awkward in Hebrew, even when used with verbs high in activity, and to ensure that our respondents would not rate all these sentences as unacceptable, the instructions included an example of a sentence with this structure embedded in a short paragraph, where it sounded quite appropriate.

4.2 Results

Mean ratings of the verbs in each of the ten verb classes (averaged over the three lists of verbs) are given in Table 9.5, where the sequence of verb classes is the same as that in Tables 9.2–9.4. As expected, sentences with verbs high in the hierarchy obtained in the previous study were generally rated as more acceptable in the pseudo-cleft form than those low in the hierarchy; the Spearman rank-order correlation between acceptability ratings of pseudo-cleft sentences and the ratings obtained in the English acceptability study was 0.85. This confirms the hierarchy obtained in the study on substitutability by pro-forms.

In this study, too, our modification of Quirk *et al.*'s classification (Section 2) was vindicated: Activity-specific verbs scored higher than Activity-diffuse

Table 9.6. *Features of the subjects of verbs belonging to ten classes*

1. Momentary	CAUSE	CONTROL	CHANGE
2. Activity-specific	CAUSE	CONTROL	CHANGE
3. Activity-diffuse	CAUSE	CONTROL	CHANGE
4. Stance	CAUSE	CONTROL	—
5. Mental-Stimulus	CAUSE	CONTROL	—
6. Transitional-Intentional	CAUSE	CONTROL	CHANGE
7. Transitional-non-Intentional	—	—	CHANGE
8. Process	—	—	CHANGE
9. Mental-Experiencer	—	CONTROL	—
10. Relational	—	—	—

verbs, Mental-Stimulus verbs higher than Mental-Experiencer verbs, and Transitional-Intentional verbs higher than Transitional-non-Intentional verbs.

Inter-judge reliabilities were computed for the ten verbs of each list separately. Kendall's W was 0.169 (p < 0.01) for the first list, 0.427 (p < 0.01) for the second list, and 0.408 (p < 0.05) for the third list. A comparison of the three lists of verbs showed that the ten verb classes were ordered similarly. Pearson correlations were 0.751 between the first and second list and 0.736 between the first and third list; these were statistically significant at the 0.01 level. The correlation between the second list and the third, however, was only 0.311, and was not significant.

5. Accounting for the hierarchy

The rationale for the system of cases and features presented in this book is that it enables us to make perspicuous statements of linguistic regularities. Our findings on substitutability by pro-forms and on acceptability of pseudo-cleft sentences have revealed a hierarchy of verb classes. The question now arises of whether it is possible to account for this hierarchy in terms of the cases and features considered in the preceding chapters. Unless this is feasible, it will have to be concluded that there is a need for additional constructs to state these regularities.

In regard to the hierarchy of verb classes it should be kept in mind that there were some discrepancies between the sequences of classes obtained in the various studies reported in the preceding sections (and even between the results for the three lists of verbs in one study: see Tables 9.2–9.4). That the correlations between these sequences were high permits us to assume that they all reflect the "real" hierarchy underlying them, but we do not know exactly how this hierarchy is structured. In speaking of "the" hierarchy we will refer to the sequence of classes in Table 9.2, on the assumption that it is a reasonably good approximation of the "real" hierarchy.

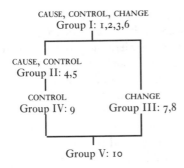

Figure 9.1. The partial order of verb classes. Arabic numerals refer to the classes in Table 9.6.

5.1 Agentive features and the hierarchy

As pointed out above (Section 2), one of the properties distinguishing between the various verb classes is degree of activity. Activity is of course typical of Agents, and Table 9.6 shows the agentive features of the subjects of the verbs in the various classes. The verb classes appear in the same order as that in Tables 9.2–9.4.

On CONTROL in the subjects of Mental-Experiencer verbs, see Chapter 7, Section 4.1.

The verb classes in Table 9.6 can be seen to fall into several groups, according to the features of the verbs' subjects:

Group I: the subjects have all three agentive features.
Group II: the subjects have only CAUSE and CONTROL.
Group III: the subjects have only CHANGE.
Group IV: the subjects have only CONTROL.
Group V: the subjects have no agentive feature.

Quirk et al.'s class Verbs of Bodily Sensation, which was not included in our empirical studies, belongs in Group V.

In respect to agentive features, these groups form a partial order, as seen in Figure 9.1, where the partial order is indicated by vertical lines. For example, Group IV has only part of the features of Group II and no other features besides, and accordingly, Group II precedes Group IV in the partial order. This leads to a prediction regarding the sequence of these groups in the hierarchy: verb classes in Group II should precede those in Group IV in the hierarchy. Table 9.2 shows that this is indeed the case: both Stance verbs and Mental-Stimulus verbs precede Mental-Experiencer verbs.

But the order is only partial: no vertical line connects Group II with Group III, for instance, because the features of the latter are not a proper subset of the former. The partial order therefore makes no prediction about the relative positions of Groups II and III in the hierarchy.

The only deviation from position in the hierarchy predicted by the partial order of agentive features is due to class 6, Transitional-Intentional. In terms of agentive features, this class belongs to Group I and should therefore precede classes 4 and 5, which belong to Group II. Respondents' acceptability judgments should therefore put this class higher than classes 4 and 5, together with the other Group-I classes (1, 2, and 3). This was indeed the sequence of classes for the verbs of the second list (Table 9.3), but not for those in the first and third lists (Tables 9.2 and 9.4). The data on judgments of pseudo-cleft sentences (Table 9.5) also accord with the placing of Transitional-Intentional verbs with other Group-I classes and higher in the hierarchy than Group-II classes.

It appears, then, that the findings on substitutability by pro-forms and on acceptability of pseudo-cleft sentences can be partially accounted for by differences in feature composition of the subject noun-phrases, as shown in Table 9.6. There are finer distinctions, however, that are not captured by the feature composition, namely, the distinctions between verb classes within a given group. For instance, feature composition cannot account for the relative position of Activity-specific and Activity-diffuse in the empirically obtained hierarchy, since both these classes have all three agentive features. Similarly, it cannot account for the fact that Stance verbs rank higher than Mental-Stimulus verbs, although verbs of both classes have CAUSE and CONTROL.

To explain the latter results, one might introduce additional features or dimensions; for instance, one might stipulate that the feature CAUSE has the dimension momentary, and the subjects of all Momentary verbs will accordingly have the feature CAUSE +momentary. This would be an unparsimonious solution, however, and should be adopted only if there is no other way of dealing with this issue.

A different approach is examined in the following, but first, a methodological comment is in order. It will presumably not be feasible to formulate linking rules that predict the two-dimensional gradients in Tables 9.2–9.4 with great precision, because the acceptability judgments on which they are based are influenced by a variety of verb-specific factors. But it should be possible to reveal some general tendencies that accord with composition of features and their relative strength.

5.2 Strength of features and the hierarchy

Conceivably, the distinctions not captured by the features in Table 9.6 might be explained by the relative strength (Chapter 2, Section 2.1) of the features involved. Thus, subjects of the class of Activity-specific verbs would have agentive features of greater strength than those of the class of Activity-diffuse verbs; and subjects of Stance verbs, although they have the same features as those of Mental–Stimulus verbs, would differ from the latter in respect to the strength of one or more agentive features. That Activity-specific verbs can more readily be substituted for by pro-forms and that they are more acceptable in pseudo-cleft constructions may be due to this difference in strength of features; and similarly for the differences obtained between Stance and Mental–Stimulus verbs. The study to be described in the following is relevant to this proposal.

5.3 A study of feature strength

In this study, which was conducted in collaboration with Laura Canetti and Smadar Sapir, respondents were presented with sentences deployed in our acceptability study (Table 9.1) and asked to what extent they exhibited certain notions.

5.3.1 The notions rated

Respondents in our study rated the degree to which the sentences of Table 9.1 expressed each of three notions: Control, Responsibility, and Intention. Intuitively, these notions are closely related to the feature CONTROL, and their ratings thus may be assumed to indicate the strength of the feature CONTROL in the subjects of these sentences.[4] CAUSE is of course closely related to CONTROL, but it is not clear to me how separate measures for these two features might be obtained.

Measuring the strength of CHANGE in noun phrases presents a problem. It will not do to ask a respondent to what extent an entity referred to in a sentence expresses the notion Change, because such a question does not indicate which of the various types of change that an entity may undergo is relevant, or how they should be weighed against each other. Thus, writing involves motion of the hand and fingers, which is a kind of change, and growing involves a different kind of change, but it would be difficult to explain to respondents how the strengths of these different kinds of change might be compared.

To obtain at least some indication of the strength of CHANGE in the subjects of the various sentences, it was decided (following a suggestion made by Smadar Sapir) to ask respondents about Vividness. An event is vivid to the extent that it evokes imagery, and other things being equal, the greater the change involved in an event, the more vivid it is. The notion of Vividness was explained to respondents by an example: an athlete lighting the Olympic flame. Note that while the notions Control, Responsibility, and Intention pertain to the sentence subject, Vividness pertains to the event described in the sentence as a whole.

Recall that in our classification we introduced a distinction between Activity-specific and Activity-diffuse verbs on the basis of the amount of imagery aroused by the verb. This distinction, then, is also partly based on Vividness.

5.3.2 Procedures

The material for this study consisted of thirty sentences, one for each verb used in the acceptability study (Table 9.1). The sentences in the three lists given in Table 9.1 were abbreviated so that they each contained only the subject, verb, and object. For instance, the sentence *Henry left Chicago on December 20th* was abbreviated to *Henry left Chicago*. It was felt that the additional material in the sentence might affect respondents' judgments, and here we were interested only in the effect of the verb.

For each of the four notions – Control, Responsibility, Intention, and Vividness – a rating form was constructed; we will call these Form C, Form R, Form I, and Form V, respectively.

The sequence of sentences within a form was determined randomly, with the constraint that between any two verbs assigned to the same class there had to be at least two verbs from different classes. Two randomizations were used for Form C, with each of the two given to about half the respondents; and the same was true for Forms R, I, and V.

Rating forms were administered individually to 160 native English speakers. Each respondent was presented with only one of the four forms, so that each form was responded to by forty respondents. The data of two of the respondents to Form C and of one to Form V had to be discarded. Each rating form required ratings on a scale from 1 (low on the rated notion) to 7 (high).

The notions of Control, Responsibility, Intention, and Vividness were explained by means of simple examples. Instructions for Form C gave the example of a gangster waiting at the corner for a small storekeeper on his way home and clubbing him on the head; the gangster is accorded high Control. In Form R the example was of somebody walking on a sidewalk being hit by a truck; the victim is accorded low Responsibility. Instructions for Form I asked respondents to state "to what extent the event described in the sentence typically occurs intentionally," and the example of a high degree of Intention was of somebody writing an exam. For Form V, the example of an athlete lighting the Olympic flame was given as an illustration of the concept of Vividness.

5.3.3 Results: intercorrelations between the notions

The notions Control, Responsibility, and Intention were introduced into this study because it was conjectured that they are closely related to each other and to CONTROL. In fact, high intercorrelations were obtained for those notions: the correlation between Control and Responsibility was 0.91, that between Control and Intention 0.82, and that between Responsibility and Intention 0.86; all these are statistically significant at the 0.001 level. Our

Table 9.7. *Mean ratings in Forms C, R, I, and V*

	Control	Responsibility	Intention	Vividness
1. Momentary	6.324	6.208	5.650	4.854
2. Activity-specific	6.570	6.358	6.508	4.786
3. Activity-diffuse	5.088	5.167	5.658	3.444
4. Stance	5.781	5.417	4.658	4.341
5. Mental-Stimulus	5.167	4.792	4.542	3.786
6. Transit.-Int.	5.193	5.167	5.508	3.247
7. Transit.-non-Int.	2.938	3.600	1.892	4.410
8. Process	2.937	3.908	2.567	2.478
9. Mental-Exper.	3.816	3.917	2.992	2.273
10. Relational	3.561	4.717	3.908	2.410

Notes:
1 = low on the notion
7 = high on the notion

three rating forms thus measure closely related notions. These three notions had much lower correlations with Vividness: Control 0.59 (p < 0.001), Responsibility 0.48 (p < 0.01), and Intention 0.39 (p < 0.02).

5.3.4 Results: strength of features
The mean ratings (over three sentences for each verb class) are presented in Table 9.7.

As remarked previously, there are verb classes that do not differ in feature composition. The results of the present study enable us to answer the question of whether the relative position of these classes in the hierarchy in Tables 9.2–9.4 may be predicted from the relative strength of features.

Verb classes belonging to Group I have all three agentive features, and their position in the hierarchy thus cannot be predicted from their feature composition; see Section 5.1, Figure 9.1. Inspection of Table 9.7 shows that the relative position of three classes within this group – Activity-specific, Activity-diffuse, and Transitional-Intentional – is predicted by the strength of CONTROL as measured by ratings of Intention and of Responsibility (with a tie for Activity-diffuse and Transitional-Intentional; ratings of Control, however, do not accord with the relative position of Activity-diffuse and Transitional-Intentional). Likewise, ratings on Vividness predict the position of these classes in the hierarchy. For the remaining class in Group I, Momentary verbs, however, only Vividness makes the correct prediction. The position of Momentary verbs in the hierarchy, then, seems to be due to its greater strength of CHANGE, rather than of CONTROL. (The above is true only of the hierarchy in Tables 9.2–9.4; acceptability ratings of pseudo–cleft sentences [Table 9.5] assign a different order to these four classes, which I do not know how to account for.)

The two verb classes of Group II – Stance and Mental-Stimulus – have the features CAUSE and CONTROL (but not CHANGE). Table 9.7 shows that their relative position in the hierarchy is predicted by each one of the notions rated.

The two classes in Group III have only the feature CHANGE. Intuitively, strength of CHANGE is greater in Transitional-non-Intentional than in Process verbs, and in fact the former were scored higher than the latter on Vividness, which has been introduced as a somewhat indirect measure of CHANGE. Process scored higher than Transitional-non-Intentional on Responsibility and Intention, and scored almost the same on Control, and these notions are presumably unrelated to CHANGE.

Another interesting comparison is that between Mental-Experiencer, on the one hand, and Transitional-non-Intentional and Process, on the other. The subjects of the former have CONTROL, whereas those of the latter have CHANGE; see Figure 9.1 (Section 5.1). Mental-Experiencer rates higher than the other two on the three notions related to CONTROL, but lower on Vividness, which is presumably related to CHANGE. This is not surprising, because mental experiences usually do not have a conspicuous visible expression. The greater strength of CHANGE seems, in this case, to have determined position in the hierarchy. A discordant note is introduced by acceptability ratings of pseudo-cleft sentences, however, because here Mental-Experiencer verbs ranked higher than Transitional-non-Intentional and Process verbs.

Examination of the data for individual sentences revealed that the relatively high mean ratings of Relational verbs on Control and Responsibility were largely due to ratings of the Relational verb *deserve*. Possibly, respondents construed *Henry deserved a promotion* as denoting an activity – doing something to deserve a promotion – rather than a State.

The distinctions introduced into Quirk *et al.*'s classification (Section 2, above) were reflected in the ratings of the present study, just as they were in the acceptability ratings reported in Section 3. All verbs belonging to the Activity-specific class were rated higher than all Activity-diffuse verbs on each of the four notions – Control, Responsibility, Intention, and Vividness. All Mental-Stimulus verbs were rated higher than all Mental-Experiencer verbs on each of the four notions. Transitional-Intentional verbs were all rated higher on Control, Responsibility, and Intention than Transitional-non-Intentional verbs; but the reverse was the case for Vividness ratings.

5.3.5 *Correlations with acceptability ratings*
In the foregoing we have seen that strength of features accounts for the positions of some of the classes in the hierarchy. This raises the question of whether the explanations of some aspects of the hierarchy in terms of feature composition are really needed; perhaps strength of individual features can account for the whole hierarchy.

To answer this question we computed Pearson product-moment correlations (for the thirty sentences) between mean ratings on Control and mean ratings of acceptability of pro-forms (the right-hand columns of Tables 9.2–9.4); and likewise for Responsibility, Intention, and Vividness. The correlation of Vividness with acceptability was 0.63, and those of the notions related to CONTROL – Control, Responsibility, and Intention – were 0.61, 0.55, and 0.53, respectively. All these correlations are statistically significant at the 0.01 level and beyond. The highest multiple correlation with mean acceptability of pro-forms was that for Control, Responsibility, and Vividness: $R^2 = 0.695$. The adjusted R^2 is 0.424, which means that only about 42 percent of the variance in acceptability is accounted for by the strength of features tapped by the notions rated. While these correlations are moderately high, they do not eliminate, in my opinion, the need to resort to feature composition as a partial explanation.

Turning to the acceptability ratings of pseudo-cleft sentences (Section 4), we find somewhat higher correlations with the notions in the present study. Because the Hebrew pseudo-cleft sentences were not all exact translations of the English sentences in the present study, it was thought advisable to compute the correlations on the mean ratings (over three sentences) obtained for each verb class (presented in Table 9.7) rather than for the thirty individual sentences. Instead of Pearson correlations, Spearman rank-order correlations were computed for the mean ratings of the ten verb classes. Mean ratings of acceptability of pseudo-cleft sentences correlated highly with Control, 0.85, Responsibility, 0.89, and Intention, 0.82. Unlike ratings of substitutability by pro-forms, which correlated highest with Vividness, the correlation of acceptability of pseudo-cleft sentences with Vividness was much lower than with the other three notions: 0.71.

5.3.6 Conclusion

The feature composition of verbs (Table 9.6) and the strength of these features (Table 9.7) go a long way toward explaining the position of verb classes in the hierarchy obtained in our acceptability studies. The results of these studies therefore do not indicate that additional features or dimensions are needed to accommodate the findings.

6. The agency gradient

So far we have looked at the implications of the data for the classification of verbs. There is a different angle from which our findings can be viewed: our verb hierarchy reflects a gradient of agency.

6.1 The verb class hierarchy and agency

The idea that the Agent has a graded structure has been recognized by several linguists (see Lyons, 1977: 483–84; Lakoff, 1987). Dowty (1991) views the agent as a cluster concept, that is, a concept defined not by necessary and sufficient features but rather by the presence of characteristic features. Here it is suggested that membership in the Agent category is determined by feature composition.

In the previous sections we saw that the more agentive features a subject has and the greater the strength of these features, the higher in the hierarchy the verb tends to be. The subjects of the verbs high in the hierarchy have all three agentive features, and this suggests that they are prototypical Agents, and those lower in the hierarchy have fewer agentive features or lesser strength of features and are therefore more peripheral members of the A-case. The subjects of Relational verbs have no agentive feature and are, of course, not Agents at all.

In line with this interpretation it was found that verbs that have more prototypical Agents as subjects are more tolerant of pro-forms with *do* (Section 3) and enter more readily into pseudo-cleft constructions, which also involve *do* (*what X did* . . .; see Section 4). As a main verb (though not as an auxiliary verb), *do* suggests activity, a concept that is closely related to agency.

As an additional test of the supposition that the hierarchy of verb classes in Table 9.6 corresponds to a gradient of agency, a study was conducted, deploying sentences fitting one of the two frames in (4):

(4) Henry . . . on purpose.
     They asked Henry to . . .

The subjects of such sentences are usually taken to be "real" Agents (see, for example, Jackendoff, 1972: 29f.). Saying that something was done on purpose implies that it was done intentionally, that the doer has responsibility and control, and these notions are characteristic of agency. Likewise, only activities that are under one's control – that one can engage in intentionally and for which one is responsible – fit into the *ask . . . to* frame. On our analysis, prototypical Agents possess a high degree of the features CAUSE and CONTROL.

6.2 A study of sentence completion

A straightforward way of assessing the appropriateness of verbs to the sentence frames in (4) would have been to obtain ratings of acceptability for sentences like *Henry bored her on purpose*, *Henry wrote to her on purpose*, and so on. Such ratings run into a problem, however. Respondents may construe special contexts in which the verbs in question might be acceptable (cf. van Dijk, 1977). To circumvent this, we adopted a different method: measuring the latency of completing sentence frames. Respondents were asked to complete the sentence frames in (4) with the addition of verbs from our ten classes. For example:

(5) On-Purpose frame:
　　Henry bored her ... on purpose.
　Ask-To frame:
　　They asked Henry to bore her ...

This study was conducted in cooperation with Liat Ozer, and we are indebted to Ram Frost for help in planning the study.

6.2.1 The hypothesis

The study was based on the assumption that sentence frames like those in (5) will take less time to complete when the subject of the verb is a more prototypical Agent than when it is a peripheral member of the Agent category. In other words, the greater the strength of CONTROL and CAUSE in the subject of a verb, the less time it would take the respondent to find a plausible completion for these sentence frames. In view of the correspondence between the verb class hierarchy and degree of agency, this leads to the hypothesis that the latencies of sentence completion would correlate with the position of verb classes in the hierarchy.

6.2.2 Materials

The thirty verbs included in the previous study of acceptability of pro-forms (Table 9.1) were used in the present one. To ensure greater stability of the results we added a fourth verb for each verb class. The verbs added were (in the sequence of the classes in Table 9.1): *kick, drink, beg, live, bore, enter, faint, turn, hate,* and *resemble*. The verbs *bore* and *turn* admit of more than one construal and they were disambiguated by adding another word: *bore her, turn red*. Some of the thirty verbs taken over from the first two studies – *stop over, leave town, grow up* – had to be disambiguated similarly.

　Each of the verbs was embedded in a truncated sentence, using one of the two frames in (5).

　Two rating forms were prepared. The first form contained twenty On-Purpose frames with twenty of the forty verbs and twenty Ask-To frames with the remaining twenty verbs. In the second form, those verbs that were embedded in On-Purpose frames in the first form appeared in Ask-To frames, and vice versa. Assignment of verbs to one of the two frames and sequence of verbs in the form were randomized, and the sequence was the same for the two forms.

6.2.3 Procedures

Forty respondents participated in this study – twenty for each of the above forms. They were all native speakers of English.

　The respondent was seated in front of the computer screen and asked to read each sentence frame and complete it in an acceptable and plausible way. He or she was to think first of an appropriate response and then to say out loud the words completing the sentence frame. Two examples were given of how a frame might be completed, one of an Ask-To frame and one of an On-Purpose frame. Four practice frames were then presented in order to verify that instructions were understood. After that the respondent was encouraged to ask any questions he or she might have.

The respondent's vocal reaction to a frame activated a voice key, so that latency of response could be measured. The first sentence frame appeared on the screen, and as soon as the respondent started to talk, it disappeared from it. After an interval of 2 seconds (including a warning signal – an asterisk in the center of the screen – of 0.5 second's duration), the second sentence frame appeared; and so on for the remaining sentence frames. After responding to half of the form (twenty frames), the respondent rested for a very short period.

If the respondent did not start reacting to a given frame for 5 seconds, it disappeared from the screen. This occurred with only 4.6 percent of the presented frames, and these trials were not included in the analysis.

6.2.4 The analysis

All respondents' responses were tape-recorded, and the experimenter kept notes in the course of the experiment. Occasionally, the voice key was triggered by irrelevant noise (coughs, etc.) or latency was not recorded due to some technical difficulty; these cases amounted to 3.9 percent of all trials and were dropped from the analysis.

The protocols were also checked for cases where a response showed that the verb was not understood in the intended sense. Such responses were deleted from the analysis, because they involved readings of the verb that would have put it into another one of our verb classes. Examples of such misunderstandings are the following:

1. *Please* as a request; e.g., a respondent presented with *They asked Henry to please* ... completed this with *shut the door*.[5]

2. *Deteriorate* was construed as transitive by eight (out of forty) respondents, and their responses to this verb were not included in the analysis.

3. Misreadings of a word. For instance, one of our respondents, who was presented with *Henry resembled* ... *on purpose*, gave the response *the broken toy*; apparently he had misread *resembled* as *reassembled*.

The number of deleted responses in all these categories totalled 102, which is about 6.38 percent of all responses.

Table 9.8. *Mean latencies of sentence completion in seconds*

	on purpose	ask to
Momentary	1.75	1.80
Activity-specific	1.80	1.73
Activity-diffuse	2.19	2.01
Stance	2.05	1.87
Mental-Stimulus	2.37	2.37
Transit.-Int.	2.41	2.06
Transit.-non-Int.	2.45	2.58
Process	3.41	3.04
Mental-Exper.	2.89	2.77
Relational	2.85	2.85

6.2.5 Results

Mean reaction times for each verb class (i.e., summing over the four verbs instantiating the class) were computed for Ask-To frames and for On-Purpose frames separately. These are given in Table 9.8.

The verb classes in the table are arranged according to our verb class hierarchy. Latencies closely correspond to the ratings obtained in the study on acceptability of pro-forms (Tables 9.2–9.4, Section 3). Spearman rank-order correlations with acceptability ratings were 0.94 for On-Purpose sentences and 0.93 for Ask-To sentences. The correlations with acceptability of pseudo-cleft sentences (Section 4) were somewhat lower: 0.91 for On-Purpose and 0.82 for Ask-To, possibly because the study on Hebrew pseudo-cleft constructions included some sentences with verbs that were not exact translation equivalents of the verbs in the present sentence production study.

These correlations were obtained for the mean results for each verb class. A further analysis was carried out for those thirty individual verbs in the present study that were taken over from the previous studies (Section 6.2.2). Pearson product-moment correlations of their mean latencies (summed over respondents) with ratings of acceptability of pro-forms (Section 3) and with the ratings of notions (Section 5.3) were all significant at the 0.01 level and are given in Table 9.9.

Correlations with the notions Control, Responsibility, and Intention were expected to be high, since it is these that are presumably tapped by On-Purpose and Ask-To frames; but interestingly, correlations for Vividness were not any lower.

The results cannot have been due to a simple frequency effect. According to the Francis and Kučera (1982) count, there are sixteen verbs among the 100 most frequently used English words: *be, have, do, say, make, go, take, come, see, know, give, get, find, use, think,* and *seem.* These do not belong to the Momentary and Activity categories. Furthermore, latencies for the forty

Table 9.9. *Pearson correlations between latencies and ratings*

	on purpose	ask to
Acceptability of Pro-forms	0.50	0.63
Notions		
Control	0.70	0.57
Responsibility	0.67	0.44
Intention	0.50	0.47
Vividness	0.60	0.52

verbs did not correlate significantly with the frequencies in Francis and Kučera: 0.01 for On-Purpose frames and 0.15 for Ask-To frames.

In both the On-Purpose and the Ask-To frames, mean latencies for Activity-specific verbs were shorter than those for Activity-diffuse verbs, latencies for Transitional-Intentional were shorter than those for Transitional-non-Intentional, and those for Mental-Stimulus verbs were shorter than those for Mental-Experiencer verbs. This, again, justifies our modification of Quirk *et al.*'s (1972) classification.

7. The psychological reality of verb classes

The ten verb classes identified in Section 2 were shown to have linguistic effects and affect the latencies of completing sentence frames that include the phrases *on purpose* and *ask to*. In Section 5 it was shown that these could be largely accounted for in terms of features and their strength. This makes it doubtful whether these verb classes are needed as additional constructs. Some light may be thrown on this issue by finding out whether speakers of English are in any way aware of our classification of verbs. When given sentences with verbs from various classes, would they perceive those with verbs of the same class as somehow belonging together?

In the study reported here, naive respondents were asked to sort verbs belonging to our ten classes. It seems rather unlikely that respondents would be affected by the relative degrees of strength of features. Therefore, if they respect the class divisions in the sorting task, this gives some credence to the claim that our classification is psychologically real (it would of course not be evidence for people actually being always aware of the class a verb belongs to). A negative result, however, would be quite inconclusive, because all it might show is that the class distinctions are not sufficiently salient to affect sorting; it would not prove that they do not function in other ways.

7.1 Procedures

The thirty Hebrew verbs used in the study on pseudo-cleft sentences (Section 4.1) were used in the present study. Each of the ten verb classes was represented by three verbs.

There are many aspects of verbs that can be focused on in sorting, and hence any set of verbs can be sorted in many ways. It would therefore not have been appropriate for our purpose to ask respondents to sort verbs into as many categories as they wished, without constraining in some way the possibilities of sorting. Instead, it was decided to structure the task somewhat by presenting the respondent with two verbs from a given class and to ask him or her to choose a third verb that belongs to the same class. The two verbs would serve as exemplars, delimiting the class for the respondents and setting them off in the right direction.

Three parallel forms were prepared, differing in the verbs that were presented as exemplars of a class. Thus, one of the forms included *tap* and *knock* as examples of the class of Momentary verbs, another form included *tap* and *jump*, and the third form, *knock* and *jump*. Because some of the thirty verbs in the study have more than one meaning, all verbs were embedded in a phrase; e.g., for the verb *impress* respondents were presented with the phrase *impress (the teacher)*.

Instructions to respondents were as follows:

> There are about ten types of verbs differing in the kind of activity they describe. In the following, you will find examples of these types, and you are asked to sort the verbs in the appended list into these types. There are verbs with two meanings. To make sure these are understood in the way intended, we have added for each verb in parentheses a few words.

An example was then given. The order in which verb classes were presented to the respondents and the verbs given as exemplars in each form were randomly determined.

Each form was responded to by twelve native speakers of Hebrew.

7.2 Results

Table 9.10 shows how respondents' sortings compare with our ten verb classes. There were 360 responses (ten categories sorted by thirty-six respondents), and 257 of the responses – that is 71.4 percent – were sorted in accordance with our classification into ten verb classes. It should be noted, however, that the sortings of the ten sentences were not completely independent of each other: after nine of the ten responses were sorted, the tenth would be assigned the free place automatically (which is why no respondent is listed in Table 9.10 as having got nine sortings correct).

Table 9.10. *Number of correct sortings*

Number correct (out of 10)		Number of respondents
10		11
9		0
8		9
7		4
6		1
5		3
4		2
3		6
	Total	36

The confusion matrix in Table 9.11 shows how well each of the verb classes was identified. Because a few respondents did not supply a response to all of the ten categories (eight responses in all), and one respondent gave two verbs each to two of the categories, the row columns are not identical and neither are the column totals.

The classes most easily identified are Stance, Mental-Stimulus, and Process. At the other end we have Activity-diffuse and Transitional-non-Intentional, with only sixteen correct identifications each (out of a possible thirty-six). The two classes belonging to Group II, Stance and Mental Stimulus (see Figure 9.1 in Section 5.1), were never confused with each other, nor were those belonging to Group III, Transitional-non-Intentional and Process. As stated previously, it is unlikely that respondents held classes apart on the basis of differential feature strength, and that these class distinctions were respected in sorting suggests that they have psychological reality. The classes in Group I (1, 2, 3, and 6), by contrast, were often confused with each other.

It will be remembered that in the original classification by Quirk *et al.* (1972) no distinction was made between Activity-diffuse and Activity-specific and between Transitional-Intentional and Transitional-non-Intentional. These distinctions do not account for the lack of correspondence between respondents' sortings and our Activity-diffuse and Transitional-non-Intentional verb. When the examples were from the Activity-specific category, there were eleven "incorrect" responses, only three of which were of the Activity-diffuse category. When the examples pertained to the Activity-diffuse category, there were eighteen "incorrect" responses, only three of which pertained to the Activity-specific category. Likewise, confusions between Transitional-non-Intentional and Transitional-Intentional accounted for only a small proportion of the confusions due to these two categories.

The other distinction we made was between Mental-Stimulus and Mental-Experiencer. Mental-Stimulus was – with Process – the best

Table 9.11. *Confusion matrix for sorting verbs into categories*

Examples from category	Response category									
	1	2	3	4	5	6	7	8	9	10
1. Momentary	26	3	1			2	1		2	1
2. Activity-specific	3	23	3	1		1	1			2
3. Activity-diffuse	2	3	16	2			3		4	4
4. Stance		1	1	31			4			
5. Mental-Stimulus			1		34	1				
6. Transit.-Int.		1	3	1	1	27	3		1	
7. Transit.-non-Int.	3	1	5	1		2	16		1	5
8. Process					1			35		
9. Mental-Exper.		1	3			2	1		26	1
10. Relational		2	3		1	1	4		2	23

identified category, and it was not confused even once with Mental-Experiencer.

It should be noted that the matrix in Table 9.11 is not symmetrical; that is, if a was confused with b, this did not imply that b was confused with a. Adjacency of two categories in the hierarchy did not seem to affect confusions: errors did not tend to cluster around the diagonal.

Analysis of the three forms revealed that there was little consistency between them in regard to the pattern of confusions. To the extent that this is not due to noise factors, it is probably an effect of verb-specific factors on sorting.

7.3 Subjects' explanations

The fact that a respondent sorted verbs in accordance with the classes defined by us does not show of course that his conception of the class meshes with ours. To find out what criteria were deployed in sorting, three of the respondents were asked (after completion of the task) to state for each of the categories sorted what the verbs had in common. Here are some of their definitions that seemed to indicate that the categories the respondent had in mind correspond at least roughly with our verb classes:

> Stance: Body position
> Mental-Stimulus: Creating feeling in others
> Transitional-Intentional: Relation between person and a place
> Process: Changes in body

In many cases, however, it is hard to tell what criterion a respondent was operating with. In some instances the definition was definitely too restrictive. This might mean that the respondent had a more narrow category in mind; but alternatively, it might just be the influence of the particular examples we had provided for the verb class, and the respondent may have operated in fact with the intended category. Here are examples:

Stance: Physical, of body
Transitional-Intentional: Relating to motion
Process: Not necessarily intentional
Mental-Experiencer: Information sources relating non-physical
Relational: Correspondence between person and demands

In other instances the respondent apparently had a different category in mind, his definition being patently "incorrect" (by the standards of our classification). Interestingly, such a definition need not prevent correct sorting. Thus, the respondents providing the following definitions supplied the correct missing verb:

Momentary: Producing a noise
Activity-specific: Activity with the hands

This shows that "correct" responses should not be counted as compelling evidence for the psychological reality of a verb class.

Finally, some of the definitions supplied by the respondents show that for some verb classes the two examples provided may be construed as examples of a category different from the one we had in mind. Respondents gave an "incorrect" definition and, in line with it, supplied an "incorrect" verb. Here are examples of these definitions and the English translation equivalents of the three Hebrew verbs sorted as belonging together by the respondent. (The labels of the verb classes are according to the two verbs provided in the rating form.)

Momentary: Directed at physical object – *tap, knock, draw*
Activity-specific: Related to physical object – *write, slice, fall*
Transitional-non-Intentional: Passive – *lose, die, be fit for*
Transitional-non-Intentional: Independent of person – *lose, die, be fit for*
Transitional-non-Intentional: Loss – *lose, die, retire*
Relational: Lack of awareness – *win (prize), act as, surprise*

At the beginning of this section the question was posed whether naive speakers are in some sense aware of the class distinctions. An answer to this question would have implications for the theoretical status of our verb classes in the grammar. While the sorting data did lend some support for the psychological reality of our verb classes, the qualitative data presented here seem to suggest that it is too early to draw any definite conclusion.

8. Conclusions

Verbs can be subdivided into ten classes, which can be shown to differ in respect to the degree of agency of their subjects. The more agentive features a subject has and the greater the strength of these features, the closer it comes to a prototypical Agent. Verb class, or position in the Agent gradient, are linguistically relevant: sentences with verbs high in the hierarchy of verb classes – namely, those whose subjects are more prototypical Agents – tend to have more acceptable pro-forms with *do* than those with verbs lower in the hierarchy (and subjects that are more peripheral members in the Agent category). A similar relationship holds for position in the hierarchy and acceptability of pseudo-cleft constructions. Verbs high in the hierarchy have also been shown to lend themselves more easily to inclusion in sentences with *on purpose* or *ask to*; these phrases are associated with agency.

10   Retrospect and prospects

... it's puzzling work, talking is.
Mr. Tulliver in George Eliot's *The Mill on the Floss*

In this concluding chapter I summarize some of the main themes, the threads that run through the book, as it were; then I briefly discuss the question of where we go from here, suggesting some of the issues that will have to be investigated next.

1. The traditional view

The approach to cases – semantic roles, thematic relations, or whatever one chooses to call them – advocated in this book presents a challenge to the customary approach, which views cases as directly reflecting the categories in human cognition (Chapter 1, Section 1). But cognitive psychology does not tell us which categories function in cognition, and linguists have proceeded with what Cruse (1973: 11) has called "cheerful intuitivism" in positing case categories. Cognitive relations realized in language are legion (Chapter 8, Section 1.2), and the problem is therefore which of these should be accepted into the fold and which should be excluded, or else subsumed under a wider category. In the absence of a principled way of defining cases, there emerged a complete lack of agreement as to the number of cases required and their definitions (Chapter 2, Section 1). Some writers (e.g., Dowty, 1991) feel that the approach of providing a list of cases has now reached an impasse.

Viewing cases as cognitive categories led to another problem. Syntactic categories do not correspond in any simple fashion to cases. Theorists have proposed selection hierarchies in terms of which linguistic regularities could be stated. However, as I have shown repeatedly, such hierarchies fail to do the job. Unsolved problems with subject selection hierarchies are discussed in Chapter 2, Section 1; see also Chapter 4, Section 1, on instrumental subjects, and Chapter 7, Section 1, on Experiencer subjects. Nor does an object selection hierarchy serve its purpose (Chapter 8, Section 1.2).

These problems are endemic to a view of cases as direct mappings from cognitive space into syntactic structures. The proposal made in this book presents an attempt at a solution.

2. The present approach

The essence of my proposed solution to the problems outlined in the foregoing is a three-level system in which cases mediate between cognitive space and syntactic structure. Cases are not viewed as cognitive categories *tout court*, but as linguistic constructs that subserve the statement of grammatical regularities. They belong to the semantic, not to the cognitive level (although this distinction between terms, semantic and cognitive, is not made use of in the book). Because they are linguistic rather than cognitive constructs, cases are language-specific (Chapter 2, Section 2).

A case category is introduced into the system only if it satisfies the Principle of Linguistic Relevance, which states that only those constructs are to be admitted that figure in syntactic rules (Chapter 1, Section 6.3). Thus, no sufficient grounds were found for including in our system a Patient case (Chapter 8, Section 1.3) or an Experiencer case (Chapter 7, Section 2).

The Principle of Linguistic Relevance entails that, unlike the procedure in traditional treatments, not every noun phrase in a sentence is assigned a case. True, every noun phrase stands in some sort of relation to some other part of the sentence – usually the verb – but these are cognitive relations (Chapter 1, Section 1) and not necessarily semantic ones. In many instances, nothing would be gained by subsuming such a cognitive notion under some case category, because this would not further the objective of stating linguistic regularities (Chapter 2, Section 6; Chapter 3, Section 3.2; Chapter 8, Section 1.2).

When two sentences describe identical situations, it has been customary to assign the same case to the corresponding noun phrases; in fact, such synonymity has been used as a heuristic for assigning cases. The view of cases as linguistic rather than cognitive categories implies that there is no such rule. Thus, it has been shown in Chapter 4, Section 1, that *a knife* is in a different case in *the cake was cut with a knife* and in *the knife cut the cake*.

A noun phrase may be assigned to more than one case, for example, to the C-case and to the A-case (Chapter 3, Section 3.3) or to the Attributee and the A-case (Chapter 6, Section 2).

Cases are decomposed into features, which are cognitive primitives (or near-primitives – we return to this question in the next section). The Agent, or A-case, is defined by the features CAUSE, CONTROL, and CHANGE, the presence of any one of which in a noun phrase may suffice for assigning it to the A-case; the C-case is defined by the features ACCOMP, INSTR, and MANN; and the Attributee case is an exception in so far as it is defined by a single feature. Features of the verb phrase are discussed in Chapter 8, Section 5.

A feature may have second-order features, or dimensions: CAUSE has the dimensions activity and affecting, and ACCOMP may be + distributive or − distributive. Features and their dimensions are rooted in cognition, but their assignment to noun phrases is determined in part also by the lexical entry of the predicate verb (Chapter 2, Section 3.3.1): when a feature is included in the entry, it will be contracted by a noun phrase. One of the issues treated in this book concerns the extent to which features and dimensions are represented in the lexical entry. In Chapter 3, Section 2.1, this question is discussed in regard to C-case features; in Chapter 3, Section 2.3, in regard to the distributive dimension; and in Chapter 8, Section 5.3, in regard to verb phrase features.

Features may be present in noun phrases to varying degrees, and we therefore speak of the strength of a feature in a noun phrase (Chapter 2, Section 2.1; see also Chapter 7, Section 5, on strength of CONTROL in the Experiencer noun phrase). Feature strength is not represented in the lexical entry (Chapter 2, Section 3.3.1).

Features and their dimensions and cases are linked to syntactic categories. Linking rules may take into account the number of features, their strength, and their relative weights (Chapter 2, Section 5). Feature strength affects, *inter alia*, subject selection (Chapter 2, Section 4.1), choice of preposition in C-case noun phrases (Chapter 3, Section 5), and the admissibility of having an instrument in subject position (Chapter 4, Section 3). Furthermore, a definition of the degree of membership in a case category is possible in terms of number and strength of features in a given noun phrase, as has been shown for the A-case (Chapter 9, Sections 5.1–5.2). Our linking rules enable us to account for linguistic regularities, among them some that are not accounted for by the subject selection hierarchy.

One of the recurring themes in this book is the interplay of categories in cognitive space with linguistic constructs. Features, we have noted, originate in cognitive space, but their assignment is governed by a linguistic factor: the lexical entry of the verb. Linking is thus not determined exclusively by the situation or event referred to, but largely by the speaker's choice of a verb from among those made available by the language. Further, linking is wholly dependent on what is made explicit by the sentence, and not on what knowledge of the world permits us to infer from it (Chapter 2, Section 3.1).

Syntactic categories are selected by cases and features according to linking rules; but they affect, in their turn, feature assignment. Due to semantic saturation, a noun phrase may be assigned properties that are typical of the syntactic function it fulfills. Thus, once a noun phrase with the features CAUSE or CHANGE is assigned to the A-case and becomes the subject of the sentence, it will acquire the feature CONTROL through semantic saturation. This process accounts for certain syntactic constraints, such as the deliberation and the mediation constraints on the subjectivization of instrument phrases (Chapter 4, Section 2; see also Chapter 6, Section 4.3). Furthermore, it predicts that the subjects of mental verbs are endowed with a measure of CONTROL (Chapter 7, Section 5.2) and accounts for differences in the meaning between direct object and prepositional object constructions of some verbs (Chapter 8, Section 5.3).

One of our working hypotheses was that syntactic categories are semantically more homogeneous than had been previously recognized. This has turned out to be only partially true: while the subject has been shown to express, in the vast majority of instances, one of two cases, the direct object may express a very wide variety of notions, and it cannot even be said to typically express any given case.

3. Prospects

It will have been evident at every juncture that, as the formula goes, "further research is needed . . . ." Let me just outline in what directions the present approach needs to be extended.

Only three cases have been dealt with at length in this book: the A-case, the C-case, and the Attributee; the Locative has been discussed briefly in Chapter 8, Section 2. The question of which additional cases have to be posited in the grammar awaits investigation. Presumably, their number will be smaller than in previous theories, because – as shown by our A-case and C-case – definition of cases in terms of features permits much more comprehensive categories than those in most traditional case grammars, and because we do not make the usual assumption that every noun phrase has a case.

Cases are viewed as linguistic constructs. The features in terms of which they are defined, by contrast, are rooted in cognitive space. But are they necessarily universal?

There is an indefinitely large set of cognitive notions. Features like CAUSE, ACCOMP, and ATTRIBUTEE are based on a subset of these notions, but each language may select its own subset. Thus, in some languages, the notion of animateness may be a feature, in others there may be a gender feature; and while the notion of cause is universal, there is no a priori reason why it has to figure as a feature in the grammar of all languages, as it does in English. Furthermore, a given feature may be differently delimited in two languages; for instance, what is regarded as INSTR in one language is not necessarily regarded so in all others having this feature. This is an empirical question calling for detailed analysis of languages other than English, a task that has not even been begun in this book.

It is possible that some of the features identified in the preceding chapters are not primitives but ought to be broken down into components. CAUSE may possibly be analyzed in terms of more primitive concepts of force dynamics (Talmy, 1985a). The question of further decomposition has been raised also in regard to the feature INSTR (Chapter 3, Section 2.2). The issue of the "ultimate" constituents cannot be settled on a priori grounds, but has to be decided on the basis of an analysis as to which concepts permit the statement of linguistic regularities.

Cases are, by definition, relations between the predicate and its arguments.

There are other semantic relations in sentences that have not been explored in this book; for instance the relation between a noun and its modifying adjective or between the nouns in a genitive construction (*John* and *ball* in *John's ball*); see Chapter 2, Section 3.1. It remains to be seen whether the approach developed here may be fruitfully applied to other relations.

Only simple sentences have been dealt with in this book. It is evidently important to investigate how the approach developed here can be extended to the relations between clauses in a sentence.

Finally, I would like to point out two fields of inquiry that are closely related to grammatical analysis and have been dealt with only perfunctorily in the preceding chapters. Language processing is one such field, and in Chapter 2, Section 5.3, some sketchy remarks have been made about possible implications of my approach to a production model.

The other field of inquiry that has a bearing on linguistic analysis is language acquisition. In fact, many of the ideas propounded in this book were first formed in the course of my work on a theory of the child's early acquisition of syntax. The linguistic work presented here has convinced me that my previous proposals in this area (e.g., Schlesinger, 1982, 1988) need to be modified. A few remarks on how the analyses proposed here may mesh with a theory of language learning have been made in Chapter 2, Section 8, but clearly, much remains to be done to fill in the details.

Notes

1 Cognitive space

1 The research reported in Sections 2 and 3 was carried out in part while I was a Fellow of the Institute for Advanced Studies, The Hebrew University, Jerusalem. Partial support of this study by the Center for Human Development at The Hebrew University is also gratefully acknowledged. I am indebted to Moshe Anisfeld, Martin Braine, Edit Doron, Philip Johnson-Laird, Harlan Lane, Robert Lees, Yonata Levy, Anita Mittwoch, and Benny Shanon for valuable discussions and comments. Comments to a previous paper by Dwight Bolinger and Sidney Greenbaum were also helpful in clarifying the ideas in the present report. Collection of data was made possible through cooperation of, among others, Shoshana Blum-Kulka, E. Levenston, and A. A. Mendilow.

2 After the study had been carried out it was pointed out to us by Sidney Greenbaum (personal communication, 1981) that ... *with the bones* is ambiguous: it might mean that they were cooked together (with bones giving some taste to the meat) or else that there was meat on the bones.

3 I am indebted to Yael Shweid for collecting and analyzing the data.

4 That speakers of English learn to distinguish between the three words does not mean that they do so through the use of previously existing concepts (as some theorists have it), but only that they have concepts of the dimensions along which the distinctions are made.

5 Thus, despite elaborate instructions, people understood different things by our definitions of some case-like notions (see Section 4.1).

6 For a previous treatment of the distinction between semantics and cognition, see Schlesinger (1979).

7 In a study on the acquisition of motion verbs in Korean, Bowerman and Choi (1991) found that children are influenced by the semantic organization of their language from early on. This does not fit in with the view of language as a system into which a universal cognitive organization is mapped.

8 This would be an alternative to the more usual practice of reserving the Agent for non-ergative languages and introducing other cases for ergative ones.

2 Agent and subject

1 This is not to say that these notions are not further analyzable; see, for instance, Talmy's (1985a) analysis of the notion of cause. But at certain ages and for certain purposes they function as primitives.

2 That instruments are close to Agents is shown also by the fact that they may be formed by the same suffix: − *ant*. Among the examples given by Marchand (1969: 251–52) for Agents are *participant*, *applicant*, and *informant*, and among his examples for "impersonal agents" (i.e., instruments): *deodorant*, *disinfectant*, and *lubricant*.

3 Sentence (25)a might describe a true state of affairs without anyone ever having slept in the room. Therefore *two* in (25)a is not accorded CAUSE or CONTROL, as it is in "Two (people) have slept in this room." It may also be argued that *sleep* in the latter sentence and *sleeps* in (25)a belong to different subentries; cf. Section 3.3.2.

4 In Section 2.4 we mentioned Lakoff's thesis that the subject has primary responsibility. A sentence similar to (28)a is discussed by Lakoff (1977: 249): "The police arrested John, but John was primarily responsible."

Lakoff claims that "the first clause suggests that the police were primarily responsible and the *but* signals that that suggestion is being cancelled," and that this is why this sentence is not a counter-example to his thesis. Note, however, that the sentence will still be grammatical when *but* is replaced with *and* (which hardly can be said to do much signalling of this sort). Similarly, one can say: "The police arrested John, and it was John's fault." Lakoff's explanation thus does not hold water. According to my treatment of (28), there is no problem in the first place: John is not assigned CAUSE, because his responsibility, if any, can only be inferred from contingent information and is not inherent in the statement made by the sentence.

5 It is also impossible for an activity to occur except at a certain time and a certain place. Time and place, however, are not core arguments. Because they are invariably present, we do not think of them primarily in comprehending a verb; they remain "background" roles rather than being part of our mental definition of a verb.

6 Siewierska (1991: 47–49) suggests that in sentences like (30)b the feature CONTROL is "cancelled." But note that by the same token *not* would cancel agentive features of a negative sentence like (35)b.

7 As a consequence, the Agent category has a graded structure, as will be shown in detail in Chapter 9. There are typical Agents at the center of the category and non-typical ones at the periphery.

That the Agent is a cluster concept has also been stated (in these and other terms) by Cruse (1973), DeLancey (1984), Givón (1984b: 107–108), and Dowty, 1991.

8 The verbs *walk*, *run*, *exercise*, *parade*, and *jump* are like *march* in that (i) they can be used both causatively and intransitively, and (ii) when they are used causatively, the sentence implies that the entity referred to by the object engages in an activity denoted by the verb in its intransitive use. Compare (37), which implies an activity of the soldiers (*The soldiers marched*), unlike sentences with causative *open* and *break*, which do not imply an activity; see (16) (*He opened the door* implies *The door opened*, which is not an activity). The subjects of the former verbs have greater strength of CAUSE and CONTROL than their objects; cf.

> He walked her home.
> She ran two rats in the maze.
> They are exercising the dog.
> I jumped the horse over the fence.

This may be why these verbs do not take inanimate subjects:

*The downpour marched the soldiers to the tents.

(See Levin and Rappaport Hovav, 1992: 94, for a discussion of this example in a different theoretical framework.)

9 One would also expect the positive values of a dimension to take precedence over negative ones:

CAUSE $+$ act $>$ CAUSE $-$ act
CAUSE $+$ aff $>$ CAUSE $-$ aff.

But so far I have found no instances of two noun phrases in one sentence differing in their value on these dimensions only.

10 Schmalstieg (1988: 247) observes that in Lithuanian "The Instrumental of manner can easily be interpreted as an instrumental of cause." His Lithuanian examples translate: *With pain and annoyance her forehead became red* and *Almost with hunger already we are dying.*

   The oblique noun phrases in (42) cause the event only in a very feeble way – they are CAUSE $-$ act. But if we were to stipulate that CHANGE takes precedence over CAUSE $-$ act, no solution to our problem would have been obtained, in view of the subjects of sentences like (43) and (8).

11 An alternative would be to stipulate that the A-case is not assigned to an adjunct. But adjunct is a syntactic construct, and our objective in defining cases is to state the rules linking linguistic constructs to case categories. The above stipulation makes no contribution to this: it leaves open the question of why the noun phrase with CAUSE is expressed as an adjunct rather than as the subject.

   The choice of a verb – e.g., the choice of *kill* rather than *die* – commits the speaker to assigning the A-case to one specific noun phrase; but the Core Argument Principle does not deal with the question of why *kill* is chosen in the first place. Here pragmatic factors, among others, come into play.

   In Navaho, sentences like (43) are unacceptable (Witherspoon, 1977). In that language, a noun phrase can be surface subject only if it is assigned CONTROL to a greater extent than other noun phrases. Likewise, in the Babylonian Talmud, the surface subject in an Aramaic sentence is construed as having CONTROL (Schlesinger, 1982: 298).

12 Note that it is the lexical entry of the verb that determines which noun phrases are included as core arguments. In (36), the same verb is used in the same way in both sentences, and the problem posed by this example – see Section 4.1 – is therefore not solved by the Core Argument Principle. The rule pertaining to the relative strength of features has therefore to be resorted to for the explanation of (36). For (39), however, the Core Argument Principle provides an additional reason for not assigning the A-case to the oblique noun phrase.

13 There are obvious similarities between the present approach and that of Van Valin and Foley (1980). Their actor macro-role is somewhat like the A-case, but unlike the latter, a macro-role subsumes other case-like categories.

14 Cleft and pseudo-cleft sentences will not be dealt with here. The *get*-passive may require the feature CAUSE in the noun phrase that becomes the surface subject; cf. Dixon (1991: 302). An additional linking rule is introduced in Chapter 4, Section 5.1.

15 This is not so in all languages; see Keenan (1985: 250).

16 Keenan (1985: 249–50) remarks that (45) is much better than the same sentence without the agent phrase; see Chapter 6, Section 4.2 for an explanation of this fact.

17 Sentences (48)i–j are examples of what Levin and Rappaport Hovav (1992) call "verbs of emission." Some of these (e.g., *flash* and *squirt*) have arguments with the feature CHANGE, and others (e.g., *roar* and *whistle*) have arguments with CAUSE and CONTROL. The arguments of these verbs (unlike those in (48)a–k) are therefore in the A-case, according to the present proposal, rather than underlying objects, as Levin and Rappaport Hovav suggest.

18 It was not thought advisable to ask for ratings of CAUSE, because there is reason to believe that the label "cause" evokes a notion that differs from CAUSE as defined in the present system (Section 2.2.1), having to do more with a distant cause rather than with the more immediate one.

3 The Comitative

1 To be more precise, it is what is referred to by the argument that is assisted by or is associated with what is referred to by the other one; but for convenience we eschew here this cumbersome manner of formulation.

2 The label "natural force" or "force" is often used for certain non-animate agents, as in (11), and some authors (e.g., Nilsen, 1973) regard this as a sub-case of Instrument: "The wind dried the clothes." According to our definition, "force" is not INSTR; it does not assist an entity referred to by another argument. *The wind* has CAUSE (and is in the A-case); recall that animateness is not relevant for the assignment of CAUSE (Chapter 2, Section 2.2.1).

3 In Chapter 2, Section 2.2.1, it was stipulated that only the immediate cause merits assignment of the feature CAUSE. This does not apply to sentences in which an agent is said to engage in an activity with an instrument, e.g., to *Jack* in (6). In a sense, an instrument causes the result of the activity more immediately than the agent, but of course it is only through the activity of the latter that the instrument is a cause.

4 The converse does not hold. If Linda and Burt have been eating at different times, and the coffee and the milk have been served separately, (16)a'–b' are true while (16)a–b are not.

5 The verbs *fight* and *wrestle* take noun phrases expressing the notion of Opposition as objects (see Chapter 1, Section 4.1 on this notion). But there seems to be no need to introduce such a concept into our system, since its expression does not differ from that of other noun phrases with ACCOMP.

6 As noted by Wierzbicka (1980: 131), Instrument and Accompaniment are related "because both indicate physical closeness of two entities involved in one event" (but see note 10, below). Walmsley (1971) regards Instrument and Comitative as "sub-parts" of the same case. Lakoff and Johnson (1980: 135) argue that "our conceptual system is structured by the metaphor AN INSTRUMENT IS A COMPANION." In fact, many languages have the same marker for these two cases (Nilsen, 1973: 72–73). The close connection between Instrument, Accompaniment, and Manner is also attested to by the fact that they all may serve as answers to questions of *how* (Nilsen, 1973: 28).

7 Nilsen (1973: 72–75) cites seventeen languages that have the same marker for

Manner and Instrumental, and ten for Manner and "Comitative," which is our ACCOMP. He also considers the possibility of Manner and Instrumental being the same case; Nilsen (1973: 76).

8 The Fillmorian principle that each noun phrase may be assigned to one case only could be abided by if we were to introduce a case-selection hierarchy giving the A-case priority over the C-case. Thus, in (3)b, below, *Linda* would be A-case (due to CAUSE), and this would prevent her being C-case as well. But I see no reason to adopt the one-noun-phrase-for-a-case principle for the present system. There are several other theorists who do not subscribe to it, among them Huddleston (1970); Culicover and Wilkins (1986); and Jackendoff (1990: 59–61). Chomsky (1986: 97) also gives an example of two theta roles for one noun phrase.

9 In the following sentence, *the sun* is in the C-case, because, besides being temporal, it also has ACCOMP + distr: "He rose with the sun." The sun also rises.

10 It should be clear that ACCOMP is to be distinguished from physical proximity, although the two tend to co-occur. In *Len corresponds with his uncle* (= (18)c) there is typically no proximity (Len's uncle might live overseas), but there is ACCOMP: both are engaged (intermittently) in the same activity. On the other hand, there can be proximity without ACCOMP. Thus, in *Rome stands on the Tiber* the two noun phrases do not stand jointly.

11 There are instances where the noun phrase in the *with*-phrase has, objectively speaking, more CONTROL than that in the subject; e.g., "Two assistants arrived with the president." But this information is not explicit in the sentence; it can only be inferred. Therefore both noun phrases are A-case, the subject being selected on the basis of pragmatic considerations.

12 These studies were conducted before the approach in the present chapter had been developed. In retrospect, some changes would have been advisable in order to provide empirical tests of additional claims made in this chapter.

13 In the rating form for "interchange" paraphrases, the indefinite articles in sentences 3, 4, 6, 8, 9, and 10, and *his* in sentence 2, were replaced by definite articles, because it was felt that the sentences sounded better that way. This change was made for both the source sentence and the "interchange" paraphrase.

In the source sentence the prepositional phrase was placed at the end of the sentence. In the *together* paraphrase and the "interchange" paraphrase it was placed immediately after the subject (see Table 3.3). This was done because otherwise the sentence might have been somewhat ambiguous: *the smuggler with the officer* might also be construed as the smuggler accompanied by the officer, and this ambiguity might lead to respondents judging the two sentences as not being good paraphrases of each other.

14 The data of the acceptability study in Section 5.2 were collected by Nasser On, and Jorge Vulej helped with the statistical analyses.

4   Non-comitative instruments

1 Noun phrases having CAUSE – act behave in a manner that seems, at the moment, not to be quite predictable. While (a), below, is acceptable, (b) is definitely not; (c) is acceptable as a personification, and (d) is fine only because *covered* describes a state, unlike in (e), where *covered* describes an event.

(a) This liquid will soften your washing.

(b) *Airmail summoned him.

(c) Kind words persuaded him.

(d) Varnish covered the wood.

(e) We covered the wood with varnish.

2 Although the *bricks* in (2)b′ do not have CAUSE, they do have CHANGE, which is an agentive feature. But *the house* has CHANGE (though of a different kind) to a greater degree than the *bricks*, and there is thus no sufficient ground for assigning the latter to the A-case.

3 In (3)b, *the knife* has CAUSE, but this feature is outweighed by the two features CAUSE and CONTROL that have to be assigned to *Jack*. Hence only *Jack* and not *the knife* is in the A-case in (3)b. See Chapter 3, Section 3.3.

4 Subjectivization is possible for noun phrases with ACCOMP + distr, as in (5)a, but not for those having ACCOMP − distr (on the dimension distributive see Chapter 3, Section 2.3), as in:

(a) Lisa shopped last Wednesday with the baby.

(b) *The baby shopped last Wednesday.

Noun phrases with MANN cannot be subjectivized unless they are also INSTR – see (f) – in which case they may have CAUSE (which is a feature that goes with some noun phrases having INSTR):

(c) His father came into the room with a smile.

(d) *A smile came into the room.

But

(e) You ought to persuade him with kind words.

(f) Kind words ought to persuade him.

5 According to Lakoff's (1977) account of the same phenomenon, however, the fact that the noun phrase bears some sort of responsibility is the reason that it becomes the subject, and not vice versa.

6 There are crosslinguistic differences in respect to the possibility of assigning instruments to the A-case and to putting them in subject position. In Ozark English, subjectivization of the instrument sounds awkward in most instances (Forster, 1979). In Dutch, inanimate instruments cannot be subjectivized, except in children's stories and the like (Van Voorst, 1992). In colloquial Japanese, the subject of a transitive verb can only be a higher animal; even *A typhoon broke this window* is unacceptable, although the typhoon is not used as an instrument by some other agent (Kuno, 1973: 31). In Hara, subjectivization of the instrument is permitted only when there is no human involvement, e.g., when a gun goes off spontaneously it can be expressed as subject (DeLancey, 1984: 187). It appears, then, that there are differences between languages in the extent to which semantic saturation operates and in the readiness of different languages to extend the feature CONTROL to inanimates.

7 However, as Professor Greenbaum (personal communication, 1993) points out,

gun behaves differently from *bow*, perhaps because it is a more complex mechanism (see below, Section 3.1.1); cf.

(a) The gun killed him.

(b) The gun hurt him.

8 Several constraints are located in lexical entries. For some verbs the lexical entry specifies that the argument having CAUSE also has CONTROL. Compare the verbs *murder* and *kill*, *beat* and *hit* (Schlesinger, 1989):

(a)   The bullet killed the president.

(b) *The bullet murdered the president.

(c)   The stick hit the horse.

(d) *The stick beat the horse.

9 Sentence (23) is adapted from Quirk, Greenbaum, Leech, and Svartvik (1972: Section 6.41, note a). Their explanation of its acceptability is refuted in Schlesinger (1989).

10 Interestingly, (21)c and (22)c sound much better when *his* is substituted for *a* (Anat Ninio, personal communication, 1993). Perhaps the possessive pronoun enhances the aspect of togetherness: *the prisoner and his lawyer* are felt to be more closely allied in the event – and thus have more ACCOMP – than *the prisoner and a lawyer*.

5 Predicates

1 Here I disregard the distinctions between different kinds of arguments (argument and satellite, complement and adjunct).

2 Quirk *et al.* (1985, Section 3.71) point out that a *by*-phrase is obligatory for some passives, because without it the sentence would be informationally vacuous; e.g.,

> The music was followed by a short interval.
> *The music was followed.
> The rebels were actuated by religious motives.
> *The rebels were motivated.

3 The difference is not simply one between verbs that require an object and those that don't. *Give* requires an object, but unless it is used as an "empty" verb (as in *give a smile*), it does carry some information. Although *Sophie gives* is ungrammatical it conveys some meaning, and the predicate in *Sophie gave me a book* is not phrasal.

6 The Attributee

1 It will be noted that the concept of Attributee is closely related to that of topic. There is of course more to topicalization than the phenomena discussed in this chapter under the heading of Attributees, and it seems to me that treating attribution as a case category is more fruitful than regarding it as a pragmatic phenomenon.

2 As for (2)b, there is no need as far as I can see for a separate Possessor case. The possessive construction *John's cat* does not involve an argument–predicate relation and so does not concern us here.

3 To the four aspectual categories identified by Vendler–Dowty – State, Activity, Achievement, and Accomplishment – one might add the category Inchoate, which is that of an Event resulting in a State of the Agent of the Event, as in (15). Activity and Achievement are distinguished by the dimension "affected": The subject of Activity is CAUSE − aff, whereas that of Achievement is CAUSE + aff.

4 These subentries – like those for their active counterparts – also contain an argument with agentive features (for the one who washes, inserts, etc.). This is a core argument, but can be elided, as in (19), below.

   Verbs in passive sentences that do not have corresponding active forms, like (18), may have only the passive subentry, whereas verbs that do not passivize, like *deserve* and *lack* – see (28) in Section 4.2, below – will have only the active type of subentry.

   Homonyms will not be registered in subentries of the same verb, but rather in different entries.

5 Surface subjects of passive sentences have usually been analyzed as Patient or Theme, like the objects of the corresponding active sentences. In the present framework there is no place for these two cases; see Chapter 8.

6 Sentences (24)a–b are from Bolinger (1977b: 70–71). Sentences (26)b–c are due to Quirk, Greenbaum, Leech, and Svartvik (1972, Section 12.7) and (26)d to Bolinger (1977a: 10).

7 Quirk *et al.* (1972, Section 12.7) observe that sentences like (26) sound much better with abstract subjects; thus (a)–(b) are better than (26)b–c:

   (a) The expected result was arrived at.

   (b) The problem was carefully gone into.

   There was no result before it was arrived at, and the problem may be said to be in a new state after having been considered carefully (cf. Bolinger, 1977b: 68). These are therefore "good" Attributees.

8 (34)a–b' and (35)b' are quoted or adapted from Antonopoulou (1991) and (34)c–c' from Palmer (1974: 86).

9 Richard Hudson (personal communication, 1992) has pointed out to me that the following is acceptable: "This bookcase holds 140 books; 70 are held (contained) by the upper shelf and 70 by the lower shelf."

   However, such constructions will occur only in very special contexts. It seems that here, too, routinization of the passive form (Section 4.2) has licensed some deviations from the Second Constraint on Passivization.

7 Mental verbs

1 Van Voorst (1992) fails to take into account the distinction between, e.g., (1)a and (1)b (= (6)a), and thus arrives at the conclusion that all mental verbs, including E-verbs, describe Achievements. And Rosta (personal communication, 1992) has pointed out to me that there is an Achievement component in S-verbs, but not in E-verbs. Thus, one can say (a), but not (b):

(a) It took Stella five minutes to fascinate Erna.

(b) *It took Ed five minutes to respect Stan.

Siewierska (1991: 51, quoting an unpublished study) remarks that in (c) the time phrase refers to the preparatory phase leading up to the state of affairs; cf. (d).

(c) It took him five minutes to notice the picture.

(d) It took him all of thirty seconds to sneeze.

2 In Shigatse Tibetan "verbs of perception can take either an ergative or a dative-marked perceiver according to the degree of control exercised" (DeLancey, 1990: 314).

The only construction, to my knowledge, in which a perceptual E-verb can describe a State involves modals. Thus, the following sentence is ambiguous, being either a comment on good eye-sight (i.e., a State) or an entomological comment on a currently occurring Event: "I can see a fly on the window pane across the road." (But see Chapter 5, Section 3.2, on predicates with modal verbs.)

3 When the Stimulus is expressed by a subordinate phrase it will also have the feature CAUSE, e.g., "He is angry because of the letter." However, the noun phrase *the letter* is not a core argument, and hence will not be assigned the A-case; see Chapter 2, Section 4.4.

4 Pesetsky (1990: 34) assigns to the Stimulus in S-sentences the role Cause, and to that in E-sentences one of the roles Target or Subject Matter. But it becomes clear from his treatment (36) that the latter two presuppose the feature CAUSE. Brown and Fish (1983) found that the Stimulus is accorded responsibility and conceived of as cause in E-sentences as well as in S-sentences. The notion of cause that is tapped in their study (and in the various studies replicating their finding) is presumably that of indirect cause and thus differs from our CAUSE, which pertains to direct causation; see Chapter 2, Section 2.2.1. Thus, a jaywalker may be responsible for getting run over by a car, but the driver of the car is the cause of the accident; see Schlesinger (1992).

5 The *should-not* test does not assign CONTROL to the subject of *hear*: (*You shouldn't hear/see the noise outside*). However, among the earliest recorded senses of *hear* is "listen to" (cf. *Hear me!*), the subject of which clearly does have CONTROL. Likewise, "look at" was – and to some extent still is – one of the senses of *see* (cf. *See here!*). Another verb that sounds odd with *should not* is *like*.

When *persuade* is used with an E-verb, it refers to an Event (resulting in someone else being in a State; see Chapter 6, Section 3). *She persuaded him to like gypsy music* means that she made him come to like it. (Incidentally, this sentence confirms that one has some CONTROL over one's emotions.)

6 I am indebted to Laura Canetti, who analyzed the data with great skill and care.

7 An additional experiment with sentences like (a) and (b), below, in which the Stimulus was inanimate, is reported in Schlesinger (1992).

(a) The storm impressed Erna.

(b) Erna feared the storm.

The findings were:

(i) The inanimate Stimulus had significantly more CONTROL in S-sentences (a) than in E-sentences (b).

(ii) In an S-sentence, the inanimate Stimulus had about as much CONTROL as the animate Experiencer; i.e., the storm as much as Erna in (a).

(iii) The animate Experiencer had significantly more CONTROL in E-sentences than in S-sentences; this replicates the results of the experiment reported in the preceding.

When the inanimate Stimulus is expressed as sentence subject, it may have CONTROL due to semantic saturation (Chapter 4, Section 2.1.3); but it is curious that it should be judged to have any CONTROL when it is expressed as object. Possibly, respondents take this term in a much broader sense than the one given to it by our definition in Chapter 2, Section 2.2.1, conflating somehow the notions of CONTROL and CAUSE.

8 Talmy (1985b: 101) makes a similar proposal, going even further: "subjecthood, perhaps because of its frequent association with agency, may tend to confer upon any semantic category expressed in it some initiatory or instigative characteristics. ... with Experiencer as subject, the mental Event may be felt to arise autonomously and to direct itself outward toward a selected object." So far I have found no evidence for the subject having any "initiatory or instigative" characteristics over and above CONTROL.

The finding reported in Chapter 2, Section 7, that people perceive the subjects of converse verbs as having more CONTROL than their objects, may also be due to semantic saturation. This explanation does not necessarily contradict the one given in the discussion of that study: Conceivably, semantic saturation reinforces the effect of differential degrees of CONTROL associated with the verbs initially.

9 But often an E-sentence may be formed from an S-verb by adding a preposition – *puzzle over*, *grieve over*, *delight in* – or with an adjective related to an S-verb – *be content with*, *be furious about* (cf. *infuriate*), *be angry at* (cf. *anger*).

10 Manney also reports that in Modern Greek verbs of perception are almost exclusively active. In this respect Modern Greek differs from English, where verbs of perception are E-verbs.

One might argue that this dearth of complementaries is due to language being economical; it does not provide us with two verbs where one will do. The introduction of *frighten* is a rare luxury English has indulged in, considering that *be feared by* might do just as well:

(a) Ervin fears Stanley.

(b) Stanley is feared by Ervin.

(c) Stanley frightens Ervin.

But note that the messages conveyed by (b) and (c) are not identical: (b) describes a State, (c) an Event.

11 I am indebted to Professor Jane Brigg for information on the Eskimo dialect of S. Baffin Island.

12 In English we have the hyperbolic expressions *I am boiling* and *I am starving* (to which Rita Watson has drawn my attention).

13 In German there are some verbs that can be used as E-verbs as well as in the

accusative: *ich friere/mich friert, ich hungere/mich hungert*. Cf. the English *I think* and the archaic *methinks*, and also *I hunger for....*

14 In Latin this is also frequent: *Habeo timorem/invidiam/odium* (I have fear, jealousy, hate; Nikiforidou, 1991).

8 Objects

1 Copular verbs (see Quirk, Greenbaum, Leech, and Svartvik, 1985, Sections 16.21–22) include *be, become, turn* (as in *turn traitor*); the subject complements in sentences with these verbs are not direct objects on this definition. Double-object constructions will be dealt with in Section 3.3.

A discussion of the direct object, similar to the present one but within a somewhat different theorical framework, is to be found in my chapter "On the semantics of the object" in B. Aarts and C. Meyer (eds.), *The verb in contemporary English: theory and description*. Cambridge University Press (in press).

2 It is possible, though, to characterize the direct object negatively as not having the feature CAUSE (and probably also not CONTROL). As shown in Chapter 7, Section 3, when the direct object of a mental verb is the Stimulus (e.g., *He admires her*) it does not have the feature CAUSE.

3 Apparent counter-examples are:

> He left the acid in the wooden bowl.
> He directed the laser beam at the delicate tissue.

A change of state is undergone by *the wooden bowl* and *the delicate tissue*, which are objects of prepositions and not direct objects. However, the inference of a change of state is due to our knowledge of the world; the sentences do not say so explicitly. As stated in Chapter 2, Section 2.2.1, feature assignment is determined only by information that is explicit in the sentence and not by inferred information.

4 Only one of the objects in (21) is usually regarded as direct object (see Hudson, 1992; Quirk *et al.*, 1985, Sections 16.46 and 16.55–57), but according to our definition at the beginning of this chapter, both the objects in each sentence of (21) are direct objects.

Double objects are also found in other languages, e.g. Hebrew. Double accusatives in Old Lithuanian are quoted by Schmalstieg (1988: 237, 250).

5 According to the definition given at the beginning of this chapter, some noun phrase adverbials would be direct objects, and these also do not express core arguments (Sidney Greenbaum, personal communication, 1993). For instance:

> Our grandson visits us every week.
> Bella cooks French-style.
> They parted good friends.

6 Similar differences in meaning between objects with and without prepositions are found in several other languages (Moravcsik, 1978: 256–61).

7 The same alternation exists in other languages; see Moravcsik (1978: 256–57) on Hungarian, Wunderlich (1987) and Booij (1992) on German, and Schmalstieg (1988: 245) on Lithuanian.

8 While there are many activities where this relationship does not hold, it is instantiated often enough to establish an association in our minds between affectedness and the notion of Feat.

9 Verb classes and Agents

1 When a verb admits of a number of pro-forms – that is, when *do so*, *do that*, or *do it* are acceptable – the choice between them is determined by various considerations; see Crymes (1968: 57–75) and Quirk, Greenbaum, Leech, and Svartvik (1985; Sections 12.23–27).

2 We are indebted to Gershon Ben-Shachar, Samuel Shye, and Estella Melamed for advice on data analysis, to Alon Halter for help in the early stages of this study, to Rina Steierman for help with the experiments, and to Tamar Galai for literature research. A preliminary study has been reported in a Working Paper by I. M. Schlesinger and L. Canetti, entitled "Do verbs form a 'squish'? Yes they do.," The Goldie Rotman Center for Cognitive Science in Education, The Hebrew University, Jerusalem, 1988.

3 In this connection, Crymes' (1968: 57–75) observation is pertinent: for "suffusive" verbs (roughly, those that are not activity verbs) that are non-mental, *do that* (and *do this*) are applicable only in generic predicates.

4 Recall that notions pertain to the cognitive space, whereas the features that are based on them are theoretical constructs pertaining to the linguistic level. Only notions, and not features, are therefore directly accessible to people's judgments.

5 This interpretation was so common that it was decided to omit all responses to this verb in the Ask-To frame. (No similar problem occurred for the On-Purpose frame, since there verbs were in the past form: *pleased*.)

References

Allerton, D. J. (1982) *Valency and the English verb*. London: Academic Press.

Anderson, J. (1971) *The grammar of case: towards a localistic theory*. Cambridge University Press.

Anisfeld, M. and Klenbort, I. (1973) On the function of structural paraphrase: the view from passive voice. *Psychological Bulletin*, 79, 973–79.

Antonopoulou, E. (1991) *Agent defocusing mechanisms in spoken English: a cognitive explanation of impersonalization*. Athens: Atanasopsylos–Papadames.

Atkinson-Hardy, J. and Braine, M. D. S. (1981) Categories that bridge between meaning and syntax in five-year olds. In W. Deutsch (ed.), *The child's construction of language*, pp. 201–23. London: Academic Press.

Barcia, R. (1948) *Sinonimos castellanos*. Buenos Aires: Editorial Sopena Argentina.

Bolinger, D. (1977a) *Meaning and form*. London: Longman.

(1977b) Transitivity and spatiality. In A. Makkai, V. Becker Makkai, and L. Hailman (eds.), *Linguistics at the crossroads*, pp. 57–78. Lake Buff, IL: Jupiter Press.

Booij, G. (1992) Morphology, semantics and argument structure. In I. M. Roca (ed.), *Thematic structure: Its role in grammar*, pp. 47–64. Berlin: Foris.

Bowerman, M. and Choi, S. (1991) Learning to express motion events in English and Korean: the influence of language-specific lexicalization patterns. *Cognition*, 41, 83–121.

Braine, M. D. S. and Wells, R. S. (1978) Case-like categories in children: the actor and some related categories. *Cognitive Psychology*, 10, 100–122.

Broadwell, G. A. (1988) Multiple θ-role assignment in Choctaw. In W. Wilkins (ed.), *Syntax and semantics*, vol. XXI, *Thematic relations*, pp. 113–29. San Diego: Academic Press.

Brown, R. (1973) *A first language: the early stages*. Cambridge, MA: Harvard University Press.

Brown, R. and Fish, D. (1983) The psychological causality implicit in language. *Cognition*, 14, 237–73.

Carlson, G. N. and Tannenhaus, Michael K. (1988) Thematic roles and language comprehension. In W. Wilkins (ed.), *Syntax and semantics*, vol. XXI, *Thematic relations*, pp. 263–89. San Diego: Academic Press.

Chafe, W. (1970) *Meaning and the structure of language*. University of Chicago Press.

Chomsky, N. (1982) The generative enterprise. A discussion with Riny Huybregts and Henk van Riemsdijk. Dordrecht-Holland: Foris Publications.

(1986) *Knowledge of language*. New York: Praeger.

Cruse, D. A. (1973) Some thoughts on agentivity. *Journal of Linguistics*, 9, 11–23.

Crymes, R. (1968) *Some systems of substitution correlations in modern American English*. The Hague: Mouton.

Culicover, P. W. and Wilkins, W. (1986) Control, PRO, and the projection principle. *Language*, 62, 120–53.

DeLancey, S. (1982) Aspect, transitivity, and viewpoint. In P. J. Hopper (ed.), *Tense and aspect: between semantics and pragmatics*. Amsterdam: John Benjamins.

(1984) Notes on agentivity and causation. *Studies in Language*, 8, 181–213.

(1990) Ergativity and the cognitive event structure in Lhasa Tibetan. *Cognitive Linguistics*, 1, 289–321.

de Villiers, J. (1979) The process of rule learning in child speech: a new look. In K. E. Nelson (ed.), *Child language*, vol. II, pp. 1–44.

Dixon, R. M. W. (1991) *A new approach to English grammar*. Oxford: Clarendon.

Dowty, D. (1979) *Word meaning and Montague grammar: the semantics of verbs and times in generative semantics and in Montague's PTQ*. Dordrecht: Reidel.

(1982) Grammatical relations and Montague grammar. In P. Jacobson and G. K. Pullum (eds.), *The nature of syntactic representation*, pp. 79–130. Dordrecht: Reidel.

(1988) Thematic proto-roles, subject selection, and lexical semantic defaults. 1987 LSA Colloquium paper.

(1991) Thematic proto-roles and argument selection. *Language*, 67, 547–619.

Epstein, L. (1988) The "irreversibility" of Spanish experience verbs. Unpublished paper, Department of Psychology, The Hebrew University.

Ertel, S. (1977) Where do the subjects of sentences come from? In S. Rosenberg (ed.), *Sentence production: developments in research and theory*, pp. 141–67. Hillsdale, NJ: Lawrence Erlbaum Associates.

Fillmore, C. J. (1968) The case for case. In E. Bach and R. T. Harms (eds.), *Universals in linguistic theory*, pp. 1–91. New York: Holt, Rinehart, and Winston.

(1971) Types of lexical information. In D. Steinberg and L. Jakobovits (eds.), *Semantics*, pp. 370–93. Cambridge University Press.

(1977) The case for case reopened. In P. Cole and J. M. Sadock (eds.), *Syntax and semantics*, vol. VIII, *Grammatical relations*, pp. 59–81. New York: Academic Press.

Forster, J. F. (1979) Agents, accessories and owners: the cultural base and the rise of ergative structures with particular reference to Ozark english. In F. Plank (ed.), *Ergativity: towards a theory of grammatical relations*, pp. 489–510. London: Academic Press.

Francis, W. B. and Kučera, H. (1982) *Frequency analysis of English usage: lexicon and grammar*. Boston: Houghton-Mifflin.

Givón, T. (1984a) *Syntax: a functional-typological introduction*, vol. 1. Amsterdam: John Benjamins.

(1984b) Direct object and dative shifting: semantic and pragmatic case. In F. Plank (ed.), *Objects: toward a theory of grammatical relations*, pp. 151–82. London: Academic Press.

Greenbaum, S. (1973) Informant elicitation of data on syntactic variation. *Lingua*, 31, 83–84.

Grimes, J. E. (1978) *The thread of discourse.* The Hague: Mouton.

Grimshaw, J. (1990) *Argument structure.* Cambridge, MA: MIT Press.

Gropen, J., Pinker, S., Hollander, M., and Goldberg, R. (1991) Syntax and semantics in the acquisition of locative verbs. *Journal of Child Language*, 18, 115–51.

Guberman, A. (1992) The development of the verb category in the Hebrew child language. Ph.D. dissertation, The Hebrew University, Jerusalem.

Hill, L. A. (1968) *Prepositions and adverbial particles.* London: Oxford University Press.

Huddleston, R. D. (1970) Some remarks on case grammar. *Linguistic Inquiry*, 1, 501–11.

Hudson, R. (1992) Raising in syntax, semantics and cognition. In I. M. Roca (ed.), *Thematic structure: its role in grammar*, pp. 175–98. Berlin: Foris.

Jackendoff, R. (1972) *Semantic interpretation in generative grammar.* Cambridge, MA: MIT Press.

(1983) *Semantics and cognition.* Cambridge, MA: MIT Press.

(1990) *Semantic structures.* Cambridge, MA: MIT Press.

Jakobson, R. (1936) Beitrag zur allgemeinen Kasuslehre: Gesamtbedeutungen des russischen Kasus. Reprinted in R. Jakobson (1971), *Selected writings*, vol. II, *Word and language*, pp. 23–72. The Hague: Mouton.

James, W. (1892/1962) *Psychology: Briefer course.* New York: Collier Press.

Jespersen, O. (1933) *Essentials of English grammar.* London: Allen & Unwin.

(1961) *A modern grammar of English on historical principles*, Part III, *Syntax*. London: Allen & Unwin.

Johnson, S. (1755) *Dictionary.* Excerpts reprinted in E. L. McAdam Jr. and George Milne (1963) *Johnson's Dictionary: a modern selection.* New York: Pantheon.

Kasof, J. and Lee, J. Y. (1993) Implicit causality as implicit salience. *Journal of Personality and Social Psychology*, 65, 877–92.

Katz, J. (1972) *Semantic theory.* New York: Harper and Row.

Keenan, E. L. (1976) Towards a universal definition of "subject." In C. Li (ed.), *Subject and topic*, pp. 303–35. New York: Academic Press.

(1985) Passive in the world's languages. In T. Shopen (ed.), *Language typology and syntactic description*, vol. I, *Clause structure*, pp. 243–81. Cambridge University Press.

Kuno, S. (1973) *The structure of the Japanese language.* Cambridge, MA: MIT Press.

Lakoff, G. (1974) Fuzzy grammar and the competence/performance terminology game. *Papers from the fifth regional meeting of the Chicago Linguistic Society*, pp. 52–59. University of Chicago Press.

(1977) Linguistic Gestalts. *Papers from the thirteenth regional meeting of the Chicago Linguistic Society.* University of Chicago Press.

(1987) *Women, fire, and dangerous things: what categories reveal about the mind.* University of Chicago Press.

Lakoff, G. and Johnson, M. (1980) *Metaphors we live by.* University of Chicago Press.

Lee, J. Y. and Kasof, Joseph (1992) Interpersonal verbs and interpersonal experiences. *Journal of Social Psychology*, 132, 731–40.

Leslie, A. M. and Keeble, S. (1987) Do six-month old infants perceive causality? *Cognition*, 25, 265–88.

Levin, B. and Rappaport Hovav, M. (1992) The lexical semantics of verbs of motion: the perspective from unaccusativity. In I. M. Roca (ed.), *Thematic structure: Its role in grammar*, pp. 247–69) Berlin: Foris.

Lyons, J. (1977) *Semantics*, vol. II. Cambridge University Press.

Manney, L. (1990) Mental experience verbs in Modern Greek: a cognitive explanation for active versus middle verb. *Proceedings of the sixteenth annual meeting of the Berkeley Linguistics Society*. pp. 229–40. Berkeley, CA: Berkeley Linguistics Society.

Maratsos, M., Kuczaj, S. A., and Fox, D. M. C., and Chalkley, M. A. (1979) Some empirical studies in the acquisition of transformational relations: passives, negatives, and the past tense. In W. A. Collins (ed.), *Children's language: the Minnesota Symposium on child psychology*, vol. XII, pp. 1–47. Hillsdale, NJ: Lawrence Erlbaum Associates.

Marchand, H. (1969) *The categories and types of present-day English word formation: a synchronic-diachronic approach*. Second edition. Muenchen: C. H. Beck.

Moravcsik, E. A. (1978) On the case marking of objects. In J. H. Greenberg (ed.), *Universals of human language*, vol. IV, *Syntax*, pp. 249–91. Stanford, CA: Stanford University Press.

Mourelatos, A. P. D. (1981) Events, processes, and states. In P. J. Tedeschi and A. Zaenen (eds.), *Syntax and semantics*, vol. XIV, *Tense and aspect*, pp. 191–213. New York: Academic Press.

Nikiforidou, K. (1991) The meanings of the genitive. *Cognitive Linguistics*, 2, 149–205.

Nilsen, D. L. F. (1973) *The instrumental case in English*. The Hague: Mouton.

Osgood, C. E. (1971) Where do sentences come from? In D. D. Steinberg and L. A. Jakobovits (eds.), *Semantics: an interdisciplinary reader in Philosophy, Linguistics, and Psychology*, pp. 497–530. Cambridge University Press.

Osgood, C. E. and Bock, K. (1977) Salience and sentencing: some production principles. In S. Rosenberg (ed.), *Sentence production: developments in research and theory*, pp. 89–140. Hillsdale, NJ: Lawrence Erlbaum Associates.

Palmer, F. R. (1974) *The English verb*. Second edn. London: Longman.

Pesetsky, D. (1990) Experiencer predicates and universal alignment principles. Unpublished manuscript, MIT.

Pinker, Steven (1989) *Learnability and cognition: the acquisition of argument structure*. Cambridge, MA: MIT Press.

Quine, W. V. (1973) *The roots of reference*. La Salle, IL: Open Court.

Quirk, R., Greenbaum, S., Leech, G., and Svartvik, J. (1972) *A grammar of contemporary English*. London: Longman.

    (1985) *A comprehensive grammar of the English language*. London: Longman.

Quirk, R. and Svartvik, J. (1966) *Investigating linguistic acceptability*. The Hague: Mouton.

Rappaport, M. and Levin, B. (1988) What to do with θ-roles. In W. Wilkins (ed.), *Syntax and semantics*, vol. XXI, *Thematic relations*, pp. 7–37. San Diego: Academic Press.

Ravin, Y. (1990) *Lexical semantics without thematic roles*. Oxford: Clarendon.

Rice, S. (1987) Towards a transitive prototype: evidence from some atypical English passives. *Proceedings of the thirteenth annual meeting of the Berkeley Linguistics Society*, pp. 422–34. Berkeley, CA: Berkeley Linguistics Society.

Ross, J. (1972a). Act. In D. Davidson and G. Harman (eds.), *Semantics of natural language*, pp. 70–127. Dordrecht: Reidel.

(1972b) The category squish: Endstation Hauptwort. *Papers from the eighth regional meeting of the Chicago Linguistic Society*. University of Chicago Press.

Sapir, E. (1921) *Language: an introduction to the study of speech*. New York: Harcourt, Brace, and World.

Schlesinger, I. M. (1977) *Production and comprehension of utterances*. Hillsdale, NJ: Lawrence Erlbaum Associates.

(1979) Cognitive structures and semantic deep structures: the case of the Instrumental. *Journal of Linguistics*, 15, 307–24.

(1982) *Steps to language: toward a theory of language acquisition*. New York: Lawrence Erlbaum Associates.

(1988) The origin of relational categories. In Y. Levy, I. M. Schlesinger, and M. D. S. Braine (eds.), *Categories and strategies in language acquisition theory*, pp. 121–78. Hillsdale, NJ: Lawrence Erlbaum Associates.

(1989) Instruments as agents: on the nature of semantic relations. *Journal of Linguistics*, 25, 189–210.

(1992) The experiencer as an agent. *Journal of Memory and Language*, 31, 315–32.

Schlesinger, I. M. and Canetti, L. (1988) Do verbs form a squish? Yes, they do. Working Paper, The Goldie Rotman Center for Cognitive Science in Education, The Hebrew University, Jerusalem.

Schmalstieg, W. R. (1988) *A Lithuanian historical syntax*. Columbus, OH: Slavica.

Siewierska, A. (1984) *The Passive: a comparative linguistic analysis*. London: Croom Helm.

(1988) The passive in Slavic. In M. Shibatani (ed.), *Passive and voice*, pp. 243–90. Amsterdam: John Benjamins.

(1991) *Functional grammar*. London: Routledge.

Simmons, R. S. (1973) Semantic networks: computation and use for underlying English sentences. In R. C. Shank and K. M. Colby (eds.), *Computer models of thought and language*, pp. 63–113. San Francisco: Freeman.

Slobin, D. I. (1992) Introduction. In D. I. Slobin (ed.), *The crosslinguistic study of language acquisition*, vol. III, pp. 1–13. Hillsdale, NJ: Lawrence Erlbaum Associates.

Spencer, N. J. (1973) Differences between linguists and nonlinguists in intuitions of grammaticality-acceptability. *Journal of Psycholinguistic Research*, 2, 83–98.

Starosta, S. (1988) *The case for lexicase*. London: Pinter.

Svartvik, J. (1966) *On voice in the English verb*. The Hague: Mouton.

Talmy, L. (1985a) Force dynamics in language and thought. Parasession on causatives and transitivity. *Papers from the twenty-first regional meeting of the Chicago Linguistic Society*, pp. 293–337. University of Chicago Press.

(1985b) Lexicalization patterns: semantic structure in lexical forms. In T. Shopen (ed.), *Language typology and syntactic description*, vol. III, *Grammatical categories and the lexicon*, pp. 57–149. Cambridge University Press.

Thalberg, I. (1972) *Enigmas of agency*. London: George Allen & Unwin.

Tversky, A. (1977) Features of similarity. *Psychological Review*, 84, 327–52.

Van Dijk, T. A. (1977) Acceptability in context. In S. Greenbaum (ed.), *Acceptability in language*, pp. 39–63. The Hague: Mouton.

Van Oosten, J. (1977) Subjects and agenthood in English. In W. A. Beach, C. E. Fox, and S. Philosoph (eds.), *Papers from the thirteenth regional meeting of the Chicago Linguistic Society*. University of Chicago Press.

Van Valin, R. and Foley, W. A. (1980) Role and reference grammar. In E. A. Moravcsik and J. R. Wirth (eds.), *Syntax and semantics*, vol. XIII, *Current approaches to syntax*, pp. 329–52. New York: Academic Press.

Van Voorst, J. (1992) The aspectual semantics of psychological verbs. *Linguistics and Philosophy*, 15, 65–92.

Waisman, F. (1962) The resources of language. In M. Black (ed.), *The importance of language*, pp. 107–21. Englewood Cliffs: Prentice-Hall.

Walmsley, J. B. (1971) The English comitative case and the concept of deep structure. *Foundations of Language*, 7, 493–507.

Webster's Ninth New Collegiate Dictionary (1983) Springfield, MA: Merriam.

Whorf, B. L. (1956) *Language, thought and reality*. Cambridge, MA: MIT Press.

Wierzbicka, A. (1980) *The case for surface case*. Ann Arbor: Karoma.

Wilkins, W. (1988) Thematic structure and reflexivization. In W. Wilkins (ed.), *Syntax and semantics*, vol. XXI, *Thematic relations*, pp. 191–215. San Diego: Academic Press.

Witherspoon, G. (1977) *Language and art in the Navaho universe*. Ann Arbor: University of Michigan Press.

Wunderlich, D. (1987) An investigation of lexical composition: the case of German *be*-verbs. *Linguistics*, 25, 283–331.

Ziv, Y. and Sheintuch, G. (1981) Passives of obliques over direct objects. *Lingua*, 54, 1–17.

Subject index

Bold numbers indicate pages on which concepts are introduced or defined.

Author index